T0271007

China's Post-Reform Economy – Achieving Harmony, Sustaining Growth

China has enjoyed heroic growth rates in the last twenty-five years of reform and transition, pulling more people out of poverty more quickly than at any other time in human history. Nonetheless these successes have had costs: today China is faced with increasing environmental difficulties and there is a dangerous level of inequality of income and wealth leading to large numbers of often violent disputes and demonstrations in the countryside.

This book discusses the very latest issues relating to China's remarkable economic growth. It provides comprehensive coverage of these issues, including economic, political-economic, environmental and philosophical questions, presenting material in as non-technical a way as possible. The issues discussed reflect key concerns within China itself at present. These focus not just on how to sustain fast rates of economic growth but also on how to solve the problems resulting from it, problems including widening levels of income equality, new forms of environmental degradation including water shortages, health issues, governance dilemmas, and new problems for the banking, strategic industrial and agricultural sectors.

This book not only encompasses the current socio-economic situation in China, accepting its strengths while highlighting dilemmas, but also provides suggestions for policy. As such, it reflects a growing recognition in China that the attainment of both continued strong economic growth and a greater degree of social harmony are mutually interdependent: one will not be achieved without the other.

Richard Sanders is Director of the China and Transitional Economies Research Centre at the University of Northampton, UK, and past president (2006–07) of the Chinese Economics Association (UK). His main research interest is the political economy of modern China, with particular reference to environmental protection, property rights and organic farming.

Yang Chen is Senior Lecturer in Economics at Northampton Business School, UK, and is the Assistant Director of the China and Transitional Economy Research Centre. Her principal research interests are institutional change and evolutionary economics in transitional countries. Her most important publications examine the change of property rights and ownership in transitional China.

Routledge Studies on the Chinese Economy
Series Editor
Peter Nolan
University of Cambridge

Founding Series Editors
Peter Nolan
University of Cambridge

and

Dong Fureng
Beijing University

The aim of this series is to publish original, high-quality, research-level work by both new and established scholars in the West and the East, on all aspects of the Chinese economy, including studies of business and economic history.

China's Post-Reform Economy – Achieving Harmony, Sustaining Growth

Edited by Richard Sanders and Yang Chen

Routledge
Taylor & Francis Group

LONDON AND NEW YORK

First published 2007
by Routledge
2 Park Square, Milton Park, Abingdon, Oxon OX14 4RN

Simultaneously published in the USA and Canada
by Routledge
711 Third Avenue, New York, NY 10017

*Routledge is an imprint of the Taylor & Francis Group, an informa
business*

© 2007 Editorial selection and matter Richard Sanders and Chen Yang;
individual chapters the contributors

Typeset in Times New Roman by Prepress Projects Ltd, Perth, UK

All rights reserved. No part of this book may be reprinted or reproduced or
utilised in any form or by any electronic, mechanical, or other means, now
known or hereafter invented, including photocopying and recording, or in
any information storage or retrieval system, without permission in writing
from the publishers.

British Library Cataloguing in Publication Data
A catalogue record for this book is available from the British Library

Library of Congress Cataloging in Publication Data
China's post-reform economy – achieving harmony, sustaining growth /
edited by Richard Sanders and Chen Yang.
    p. cm. – (Routledge studies on the Chinese economy)
  Includes bibliographical references and index.
  1. China—Economic conditions—2000- 2. China—Economic
policy—2000- 3. China—Social conditions—2000- I. Sanders,
Richard, 1947– II. Yang, Chen, 1970–
  HC427.95.C4565 2007
  330.951—dc22
                    2007027296

ISBN10: 0-415-43432-7 (hbk)
ISBN10: 0-203-93331-1 (ebk)

ISBN13: 978-0-415-43432-4 (hbk)
ISBN13: 978-0-203-93331-2 (ebk)

Contents

Figures

Tables

Notes on contributors

Björn Alpermann is Lecturer in Modern Chinese Studies at the University of Cologne, Germany. He wrote his PhD thesis on China's cotton industry. His research interests include China's rural politics and economy as well as social stratification in contemporary China.

Yang Chen is Senior Lecturer in Economics at the University of Northampton and Assistant Director of the China Centre there. She completed her PhD at the University of Leicester with a thesis on changing forms of ownership and property rights in transitional China. Her main research interests are the political economy of China's 'new economy', property rights and corporate governance.

Yiu Por Chen is Assistant Professor in the School of Public Service, DePaul University, and a consultant for the Labor Studies Program at the National Bureau of Economic Research, USA. His research investigates labour mobility within and from China, the political economy of development and inequality in China. He received his PhD from Columbia University.

Ian Cook is Professor of Human Geography and Head of the Centre for Pacific Rim Studies at Liverpool John Moores University. His main research interests are China's environment, and ageing and health inequalities in China. He is co-author or co-editor of six books on these subjects.

Charles Goodhart is an Emeritus Professor with the Financial Markets Group of the London School of Economics and a past member of the Monetary Policy Committee of the Bank of England.

Zhongwei Han is a Lecturer in Economics at the Middlesex Business School in London, UK. He is currently writing his PhD thesis on the efficiency of Chinese financial institutions in China using a DEA approach.

John Kidd a member of the Aston Business School, Birmingham, UK. His research focuses on the overlap of technological and human factors in information and communication systems, especially those which have a global reach. He has authored many papers for journals, and has written book chapters across several management disciplines. He has authored, co-authored and co-edited several books within this research area.

Marielle Stumm is a senior researcher at INRETS. Her main research focus is upon electronic communication and logistics; generally on the economic impact of advanced systems for freight transport, and more specifically on new information systems and telecommunications which constitute strategic tools in the intermodal transport sector. Having participated in several European Union projects she is also a visiting professor at the Ecole Nationale des Ponts et Chaussées (ENPC), and at the Université de Versailles-Saint Quentin en Yveline.

Richard Sanders is Reader in Political Economy at the University of Northampton, UK, and is Director of the China Centre there. He lectured at Beijing Foreign Studies University China for two years in the early 1990s before gaining his PhD on Chinese sustainable development. He has published widely in the areas of the Chinese political economy, rural development, environmental protection and property rights in China.

Richard Schiere has a PhD from the CERDI-Institute in France and currently focuses his research on the nexus of vulnerability, inequality and public administration in transitional economies. Before becoming a researcher he worked at the United Nations for five years on governance and development challenges.

Pei Sun is Associate Professor in Industrial Economics at the School of Management, Fudan University, Shanghai, China. He received his PhD in Business and Management Economics from the University of Cambridge, and was a lecturer in Industrial/Managerial Economics at Nottingham University Business School until November 2007. His research interests include corporate governance, business/corporate strategy, and industrial policy in transition and developing countries, especially China.

John Q. Tian received his PhD from Cornell University, USA, and is now Associate Professor of Government at Connecticut College, USA. His research interests include Chinese and East Asian political economy, in which field he has published widely.

Jinmin Wang is a Lecturer in Economics at Zhejiang University, Hangzhou, China. He was a visiting scholar at the London School of Economics in 2003–04 and he is currently a PhD candidate at the University of Northampton, writing a thesis on industrial clusters within China's clothing and textile industries.

Wing Thye Woo is Professor in the Department of Economics, University of California at Davis. He is also Senior Fellow in the Global Economy and Development Program and the Foreign Policy Studies Program at The Brookings Institution, and the Director of the East Asia Program within the Center for Globalization and Sustainable Development at Columbia University. His current research focuses on the economic issues of East Asia (particularly China and Indonesia), international financial architecture, economic growth, and exchange rate economics. He has published over 100 articles in professional economic journals and books on these topics, being ranked number seven of all China scholars in the world specialising in the study of the Chinese economy in a recent article in the *Journal of Asian Economic Literature.*

Shujie Yao is Professor of Economics and Head of the School of Contemporary Chinese Studies at Nottingham University, UK. He is an prominent expert on economic development in China and has published six research monographs and edited books as well as over seventy refereed journal articles in addition to acting as consultant to the Chinese leadership on development of the Chinese economy. He has been ranked number eight of all Chinese scholars in the world specialising in the study of the Chinese economy in a recent article in the *Journal of Asian Economic Literature.*

Xiaosong Zeng, CFA, was a senior analyst covering Chinese banks for a global investment bank. He holds the degree of Master of Science in Accounting and Finance from the London School of Economics and previously studied, in turn, at the graduate school of the People's Bank of China and Wuhan University.

1   Introduction

China's post-reform economy

Richard Sanders

Opening remarks

As Will Hutton[1] argued in an international conference of (mostly) Chinese economists in 2006,[2] 'the next twenty-five years will be a great deal harder for China than the last twenty-five years'.

Once the Third Plenary Session of the Eleventh Party Congress had accepted the reforming ideas of the fully rehabilitated Deng Xiaoping in December 1978, the political economy of China that had been created by and in the image of Communist China's first supreme leader, Mao Zedong, including its unique autarkic, anti-capitalist and anti-market stances and policies, was finally set aside. Indeed, China embarked upon a reform process beginning in the very early 1980s under the slogan 'Reform and Open to the Outside World' (*gaige kaifang*), which set in train such radical shifts in policy that the political economy of China has now become almost unrecognizable from its form twenty-five years ago. Some of the earliest reforms, including the abolition of the commune system in the countryside – where 90 per cent of the population then lived – and its replacement with small-scale, *de facto* privatized family farming between 1980 and 1983 with the introduction of the 'Household Responsibility System', struck deeply at the very fabric of Chinese socio-economic life. As the state began a partial withdrawal from its top-down, autocratic, *direct* management of the economy, markets were reintroduced into the countryside, price controls were partially lifted and local political leaders were encouraged to engage in economic enterprises of all kinds, as were farmers to undertake a wide variety of sideline activities which had been denounced by Mao as 'capitalist tails' (*zebenzhuyi weiba*) during the first twenty-five years of the life of the People's Republic.

Other fundamental economic reforms followed. In particular, China abandoned its isolationist stance in relation to the rest of the world. Embracing traditional Western economic principles associated with Ricardian theories of comparative advantage, China embarked upon the development of international trading relations with all comers, including the Western capitalist nations, so vilified in the days of Mao. Hotels sprang up in Beijing, Shanghai and Guangzhou to cater for the foreign tourists that the government, determined to attract hard currency, became so eager to woo. Loans from international aid agencies including the World Bank began to pour in with official encouragement. And to cap it all (given the Chinese Communist Party's historic detestation of the international concessions which humbled the Chinese in pre-Communist times), Deng Xiaoping's government created four (then five) Special Economic Zones (and subsequently a tranche of 'open cities') to allow *foreign* companies, albeit with Chinese partners in new joint venture operations, special privileges, to include a relaxed regulatory and bureaucratic environment as well as tax holidays, in order to encourage direct foreign investment in China by overseas multinational companies.

As China's autarkic economy opened up through the 1980s, so its planned economy began its transformation to one powerfully influenced by market forces. While China's attitude to the privatization of the often massively loss-making state-owned enterprises (SOEs) remained very cautious, 'soft budget constraints' were strengthened and private companies began to jostle with state- and collectively owned enterprises for shares in China's rapidly growing domestic markets. Two stock exchanges, in Shenzhen and Shanghai, were established in 1989. And thus by the end of the 1980s, at the time when the break-up of the Soviet Union and the collapse of its hold over its European client states created a new class of 'transitional economies', China's transition from plan to market had already achieved spectacular results, with gross domestic product (GDP) per head rising annually at double-digit growth rates. In 1980, Deng Xiaoping had set an optimistic target of quadrupling GDP by the year 2000. Given that this target was achieved by the early 1990s it is hardly surprising that China's paramount leader, after his well-publicized 'Southern Tour of Inspection' in 1992, gave his blessing to the reforms that had occurred up till then, giving the green light to future reforms, reinforcing the reform process in general and *ensuring that it could never be reversed.*

After 1992, the second phase of reform began in earnest. Privatization of the SOEs, particularly the smaller ones, was further encouraged, new forms of enterprise restructuring, including stockholder restructuring, were subsequently initiated, price controls were abandoned and wholly foreign-owned enterprises were permitted to enter China. Thus, by the time China became the 144th member of the World Trade Organization (WTO) in December 2001, China was so far down its path of reform that many observers both within China and without began to query whether the Chinese government's officially termed polity of 'Socialism with Chinese Characteristics' was simply capitalism by any other name.

Whatever the answer to that question, no-one who has taken any interest in international political-economic issues in recent years can be unaware that China's transition has, at the very least in material terms, achieved remarkable results. While per capita GDP growth rates have averaged close on 10 per cent per annum, *for twenty-five years*, average material standards of living have been transformed, pulling more people out of poverty – perhaps 800 million or more – than at any other time in human history. Not everyone has benefited equally. While an elite of dollar billionaires has been created alongside an urban middle class enjoying the accoutrements of affluence previously enjoyed only in the highly developed economies of North America, Europe and Japan, there still remain 80 million or more mostly rural Chinese in the middle and western regions of China whose lives have been largely untouched by the reform process and who continue to live in abject poverty.[3] Nonetheless, it is difficult to gainsay the fact that China's economic achievements from 1980 to date have been spectacularly successful. China is now recognized as a major player in the global economy, with President Hu Jintao accepted as the leader of the ninth member of the G8 group of countries,[4] as China plays an increasingly important and decisive role within the World Trade Organization and becomes an ever more active and significant permanent member of the United Nations Security Council. China is now, in purchasing power parity terms, already the fourth largest economy in the world and is confidently predicted by many to overtake the United States of America as the richest absolute economy well before this current century is fifty years old. China, in any conceivable terms, is a formidable global economic power, a status it has achieved in little more than a generation.

Given China's remarkable success to date, therefore, why do so many commentators agree with Will Hutton that things may well get much more difficult for China in the next twenty-five years than in the past twenty-five years?

China's post-reform economy

China's transition to a market-based economy along the lines of North American and European capitalist economies has some way to go as the reform process, though radical and fundamental in so many respects, continues on its gradualist, pragmatic and experimental path.[5] Even today, there are over 150 super-large state-owned industrial and commercial enterprises and the government still plays a significantly more pivotal and direct role in the social and economic life of the Chinese than is common in Western, market-based economies. Nonetheless, I believe it to be reasonable, at this particular conjuncture, to talk about China's *post-reform economy*, if only in the sense that the Chinese leadership, as personified by President Hu Jintao and Premier Wen Jiabao, has *itself* for the very first time begun to take stock of what has been achieved so far, and, perhaps more poignantly, what has not.

Thus, very recently, and particularly since 2006, new themes and new directions have begun to emerge. As Professor Wing Thye Woo of the Brookings Institution reminds us in Chapter 2, the Chinese leadership – at least in official policy pronouncements and propaganda – has begun to de-emphasize the importance of achieving ever faster economic growth rates[6] (as measured by GDP) by speaking of other goals – equality, honesty, democracy, caring, justice, above all *harmony*, harmony not just of society with nature but within society itself. Hu Jintao and Wen Jiabao can thus be interpreted as realizing that China's 'GDPism' of recent decades, while solving many problems associated with the past, has created new problems, limiting the capacities of *all* Chinese to appropriately enjoy the fruits of economic growth achieved by it so far and thereby providing obstacles for China to create a society *at ease with itself*.

Those problems, political as well as socio-economic, have arisen partly as a result of the sheer speed and scale of growth. Fast growth is clearly a great deal easier from a lower than from a higher base: maintaining growth rates at double-digit levels is clearly impossible indefinitely, certainly without either appropriate adaptation of prior institutions and/or new institutional innovation to deal successfully with rapidly changing socio-economic circumstances. But even if it *were* possible, there are questions whether it would be *desirable* to do so without addressing the problems that have been thrown up by the growth process to date, problems which themselves result from slow or inappropriate institutional adaptation and innovation.

In this introduction, I want to stress perhaps the most critical of issues currently confronting China today and arguably the problem which underlies many of the difficulties for China in, on the one hand, achieving harmony and, on the other, sustaining growth: that of inequality. As I suggested in my opening remarks, the benefits of growth have not been equally enjoyed. This, perhaps, is inevitable in a political economy hell-bent on fast rates of economic growth and encouraged within an institutional context of increasing marketization in which 'to get rich is glorious'.[7] Markets do not pretend to be equal, and liberal economists are frequently contemptuous of those who criticize the market for leading to inequality. This is hardly surprising: after all, according to such economists, markets 'work' to (re)allocate resources optimally as a result of price *differences* which encourage factors of production (including people) to move out of unprofitable, inefficient sectors into more efficient ones. If prices (including incomes) were equal, liberal economists would argue, the market would lose its essential dynamic and rationale. However, even *they* accept that there comes a point where the inequalities created in the course of market-based growth pose difficulties for future growth, particularly at the point where inequality leads to social dislocation and threatens social breakdown, a breakdown that is much more likely to occur where appropriate institutional adaptation and/or innovation has not taken place.

The new themes aired and programmes initiated currently suggest that the country's leaders believe that China has reached just this point on its reform path. It was not difficult to persuade the Chinese in the early 1980s that 'socialism is not poverty'[8] and to mobilize them to escape the poverty that was more-or-less *equally shared* under Mao (at the end of the 1970s, China had, in the estimation of Brugger and Reglar (1994) a Gini coefficient of 0.26,[9] one of the lowest in the world). But it is hardly surprising that problems would arise once the distribution of income had become markedly skewed, as in contemporary China. Thus, China has in the course of its transition in the last twenty-five years transformed itself from one of the most equal societies on the planet to one, as measured by the Gini coefficient, of the most unequal. With the Gini index standing at 0.45 (World Bank, 2004; Wu, 2007), China exhibits income inequality on a greater scale than either the USA or UK; indeed, China's measured income inequality is not far short of the inequalities exhibited by many sub-Saharan African nations, plagued as so many of them are with instability, corruption, political chaos and civil war. And this inequality is clearly that much more politically difficult, indeed dangerous, in a country led by a nominally communist government, committed to the development of *all* the people.

As mentioned earlier, there are, currently, stark gaps in absolute levels of income in China, but it is not absolute income differentials, however grotesque, that threaten socio-economic and political stability but *perceived relative differentials* (Sanders, Chen and Cao, 2007), differentials not only between the incomes of some social groups and other groups but also between their actual incomes and their expectations. Such differentials in income, allied with differentials in power and access to resources, throw up serious problems in the current institutional setting of China, a setting in which the 'iron rice bowl' of the days of Mao has been smashed apart while new institutions – dealing, for example, with new forms of welfare provision or environmental protection or civil rights – have yet to be created. As a result, the Chinese countryside is characterized by recurring protest and conflict (see, for example, Chapter 2) as well as environmental dilemmas (see Chapter 3), a vacuum of effective governance (see Chapter 4), huge streams of outward migration (see Chapter 5), posing all sorts of socio-economic problems for both the migrants themselves and the host communities in which they settle, and increases in vulnerability (see Chapter 6). Inequality is a bad hand-maiden of harmony.

Yet, although China must deal with inequality through appropriate redistributive policies and institutional innovations, it cannot afford to ignore future growth. Without growth, the government will simply be unable to satisfy the growing expectations of the middle classes let alone those of the common people (*laobaixing*) or those effectively marginalized within the growth process (see Zhang, Wu and Sanders, 2007). And therein lies the dilemma: the dual need for China not merely to achieve harmony, but to sustain growth *at the same time*. I believe that, although institutional adaptation and innovation and appropriate policy initiatives are needed to reverse China's growing inequality in China, they must also take place to ensure that China's growth trajectory remains strong. And therein lie the difficulties to which Will Hutton and others have alluded.

The next twenty-five years?

This book thus encompasses many of the problems that confront China in the short to medium term in achieving harmony on the one hand and sustaining growth on the other, providing suggestions for future institutional adaptation, institutional innovation and policy initiatives so to do. It is organized into two parts: Part 1 deals with issues pertaining, in the first instance, to the achievement of harmony; Part 2 focuses on questions associated with sustaining economic growth.

Part 1 begins with Wing Thye Woo's discussions in Chapter 2 on the origins of China's quest for social harmony and on the background to the Chinese government's historic decision, made at the Sixth Plenum of the Sixteenth Congress of the Chinese Communist Party in October 2006, to shift its chief policy orientation from 'economic construction' to the 'establishment of a harmonious society'. He argues that such policy reorientation has come about through the realization by China's new, younger and better educated leadership, led by Hu Jintao and Wen Jiabao, that future 'economic construction' using the models applied in the past twenty-five years will be unsustainable in the next twenty-five and that, unless there are significant policy shifts and institutional innovations to improve the degree of social harmony in China, the leadership of the Communist Party within the Chinese polity will be equally unsustainable. He discusses the possible challenges to China's capacity to deliver sustained economic growth, concentrating upon two key issues: (i) the need to improve the institutions of governance in China and (ii) the need to confront environmental problems, particularly the ever more serious clean water shortages in China. Although posing dilemmas for China, Wing Thye Woo remains cautiously optimistic that China will, indeed, succeed in establishing a harmonious society through creative policy formation and political management which encourages access to education, meritocracy and the emergence of democracy under the rule of law.

In Chapter 3, Ian Cook takes up some of the questions posed by Wing Thye Woo, notably water shortages and other environmental problems, including dust, desertification, water and air pollution. He continues by discussing one of the most serious consequences of a deteriorating natural environment, the deleterious impact on the health of the Chinese. He records that air pollution, for example, is thought to have caused 411,000 premature deaths from respiratory problems and heart disease, with 100 million people living in cities in which the air quality is regarded as 'very dangerous'. He warns of other health issues in China today, including not only new diseases (such as HIV/AIDS, severe acute respiratory syndrome (SARS) and, most recently, avian flu) but also the re-emergence of diseases (such as schistosomiasis and TB) that were once thought to have been eradicated, or at least under control, in a political economy within which health services are becoming increasingly privatized and out of the financial reach of many Chinese. Cook, nonetheless, remains cautiously optimistic that a 'rosy' scenario may well transpire, emphasizing the increasingly clear change of political will within the current leadership and arguing for institutional innovation and adaptation, including increased use of environmental appraisal, further development of a Green GDP index, more honest information provision, more teeth for the State Environmental Protection Administration and more power for local environmental watchdogs to bring about the rosy scenario that he hopes for.

One of the more prominent aspects of the inequalities that have been accentuated in the reform era has been the urban/rural divide, and it is the fate of those in the countryside that are the focus of John Q. Tian's work in Chapter 4. Discussing the increasing levels of unrest in the form of protests and demonstrations in the Chinese countryside, Tian reports that in 2002, for example, there were 37,500 cases of public protests in rural areas, involving more than 12 million people. The seriousness and urgency of the situation, argues Tian, coupled with the expected harmful impacts on Chinese agriculture of WTO membership after 2000, led in the course of events to absolute improvements in the incomes of rural people (even though their relative position worsened, as urban incomes climbed faster) as a result of government policy initiatives and institutional innovation to include tax-for-fee reforms, the partial elimination of agricultural taxes and experiments in village democracy. Nonetheless, Tian is fearful for the future of the country-side. Indeed, he argues that the financial and democratic reforms there have led to potential crises of finance and governance there as a vacuum of power has opened up at local level. Less money is now available for education, health-care and the maintenance of order in rural communities, with fearful implications for disorder and crime. Although Tian applauds new institutional innovations in the country-side, including the initiative to build the 'New Socialist Countryside Movement', he remains fearful that, unless the power vacuum within local government in rural areas is appropriately and immediately addressed, an increasingly disharmonious society in the countryside is the likely result.

Chen Yang continues the focus on the countryside with her study of involution and de-involution in rural China in Chapter 5. She defines involution as 'growth without development', i.e. growth that does not lead to increases in per capita incomes. She argues that, in coastal regions, de-involution (i.e. growth *with* development) has clearly occurred in the countryside in the last two decades, through the processes of industrialization and urbanization, as *litu bu lixiang* farmers have augmented their incomes from the land by working in the increasingly numerous and/or prosperous local township and village enterprises there *while remaining in their local communities*. Despite this development, however, Chen argues that involution is *still* the case in inland areas, indeed that a more *intensified* involution has resulted as a result of limited industrialization there and the emergence of a class of farmers who have become migrant, *litu lixiang*, workers who have left and continue to leave the countryside in search of better paid work, leaving behind them older, weaker and frailer farmers, adding to the vacuum of capacities in the countryside that Tian discusses in the previous chapter. Highlighting what is required in the 'New Countryside Movement' Chen argues, with Tian, that rural institutional innovation is desperately needed in the form not only of the development of economic cooperatives, such as producer, sales and small finance cooperatives to reduce the vulnerability of those left behind, but also of *non-economic* cooperatives, based perhaps on local elderly associations, women's associations and youth trusts, to de-emphasize the raw dynamics of economic growth and help build rural communities that are, above all, *at ease with themselves*, with a moderate level of self-sufficiency.

Part 1 concludes with a technical analysis of changing regional income vulnerability and inequality from 1985 to 2001 by Richard Shiere and Yiu Por Chen in Chapter 6. Using a one-stage Thiel decomposition index, Shiere and Chen distinguish equality not only between the three main regions (eastern seaboard, interior and west) but within regions and between individual provinces. Vulnerability[10] is measured through an asset-based approach, focusing on liquid assets, human capital and health care provision. Their results suggest that vulnerability is affected by the possession of (or lack of) both liquid assets and human capital and that there is both significant inter- and intra-regional variability in vulnerability. Shiere and Chen conclude that, to reduce levels of vulnerability in China, the Chinese government must engage in policy initiatives and institutional innovation to encourage human capital formation in an equitable manner, to increase the accessibility of health care and to reinforce regional policy which prioritizes the interior and western regions.

Part 2, which focuses on key sectors of the economy (including banking, cotton processing, textiles, steel, railways and oil) and possible shifts in policy to maintain and reinforce efficiency within them, thereby contributing to sustaining growth in the years ahead, begins with two chapters analysing the well-known and long-standing problems of China's banking and financial sectors. In Chapter 7, Charles Goodhart and Xiaosong Zeng identify key problems for China's banking sector, including the poor quality of the assets of the state-owned banks, the continued need for taxpayers and depositors to subsidize them, their low loan margins, low capital adequacy ratios and the unreliability of financial data. The *fundamental* problems for the banking system, the authors argue, are associated with the interdependency of the banks and the (often inefficient) state-owned industries and the (often improper) relations between the banks and the government. Goodhart and Zeng argue that an effective capital market needs to be developed in China, the pre-conditions for which include improvements in the information infrastructure, the strengthening of creditors' rights, improvements in managerial incentive structures and the enforcement of an effective system of corporate governance, all in turn dependent upon a strengthened property rights infrastructure.

Shujie Yao and Zhongwei Han continue the focus on difficulties for the banking system in Chapter 8 by analysing the impacts of ownership reform and foreign competition, particularly in the light of China's admission to the WTO, using a data envelopment analysis to measure the relative efficiency of banks and a Malmquist index analysis to study the evolution of productivity changes. Their results are positive in that they find high levels of technical efficiency amongst state banks and that total factor productivity in the sector has risen in recent years, suggesting that Chinese banks have responded well to enterprise reform and foreign competition. At the same time, Yao and Han argue that their research suggests, contrary to often received opinion and, indeed, the views of Goodhart and Chen as expressed in Chapter 7, that China's state banking system is well able to cope with the challenges ahead, although they admit that, for the future, there is a need for the 'Big Four' banks to rid themselves as far as possible of state intervention, at both central and regional levels, to ensure that managers are appointed based on professional qualifications and managerial ability rather than on party seniority and to engage in merger and acquisition activity to exploit any potential economies of scale and scope.

Bjorn Alpermann examines reforms in China's cotton processing sector in Chapter 9, focusing on the institutional environment within which the cotton industry has developed during the reform years, in particular the development of local states and their contribution towards the establishment of a 'regulatory state' for the industry as a whole. Based on an extensive review of the literature and a close examination of two case studies at county level in Shandong and Hubei, Alpermann argues that there has been considerable interplay along the public–private interface with movement towards more market-based arrangements coupled with the development of new instruments of state macro-control, suggesting that new governance structures in the cotton sector are aimed at establishing a managed market in which the state assumes a regulatory as well as developmental role. He concludes that the extraordinary success of the cotton industry since WTO entry in 2001 is partly the result of these *appropriate* institutional responses to change, but that for the future it may well be that best outcomes will be achieved by the state consolidating and strengthening its regulatory capacity while leaving more of the commercial decisions to private businesses.

The Chinese textile industry is also the subject of Wang Jinmin's, Chen Yang's and my research presented in Chapter 10, although here the focus is on the dynamics of industrial clusters in China, with specific reference to the textile and clothing clusters of Zhejiang province that have followed the 'Wenzhou' model of development, a development which has helped China to become, after only five years' membership of the WTO, the largest producer and exporter of textiles and clothing products *in the world*. On the basis of a thorough review of the literature on industrial clusters in both developed and developing countries and of close research of the Ningbo clothing cluster, the authors focus, as Alpermann does in Chapter 9, on the public–private interface, arguing – contrary to much established opinion in China and abroad – that their successes have resulted from a *change* in the role of government, rather than a withdrawal by the state from the management of the industry. Wang, Chen and I argue that, although the state has ceased to provide *direct* management of firms, it has nonetheless created an appropriate institutional framework within which private firms can thrive, providing vital services for their success. The authors' conclusion is that the widely held view of the future development of the textile and clothing sector being predicated on further privatization of and state withdrawal from it results from a misreading of the events of the last twenty-five years.

In Chapter 11, Sun Pei investigates another core economic sector, that of the Chinese steel industry, in its endeavours to 'catch up' consequent upon transition and globalization. Pei describes the heroic growth rates and subsequent importance of China's steel sector within both China and the global economy, examining key institutional initiatives and technological developments along the way. Despite the achievements noted, however, the author identifies serious problems which the industry continues to face, notably an uncompetitive product mix – with failure to sufficiently develop high-value-added products – and persistent industrial fragmentation, weakening its governance structure. He argues, as a consequence, that there is a need for *recentralization* of the fragmented and overlapping administrative system of the steel industry and a rationalization of the system of investment regulation if obstacles to further development of China's steel sector are to be overcome.

In a novel contribution to the book, John Kidd and Marielle Stumm consider the future of railways within the economic development of China in the next decades in Chapter 12. On the basis of an analysis of both economic *and* environmental considerations, Kidd and Stumm make out a strong case for China investing in ultra-high-speed railways and propose the construction of an ultra-high-speed rail track based on the maglev system, already in service between Shanghai International Airport and the Pudong district. The authors, indeed, confront one of Hutton's key arguments in the *Writing on the Wall* (2007), which stresses the sheer logistical difficulties associated with importing and exporting the volumes of goods implied by double-digit growth rates in China in the next twenty-five years. In that China will increasingly trade with European suppliers and markets, there will be increasing commercial pressure to reduce the current forty-five days needed to send a container between Europe and East Asia. Allied with arguments that maglev leaves a lower carbon footprint than other transport systems and is therefore ecologically beneficial, Kidd and Stumm foresee an unanswerable case for its use in China's future transport network.

Part 2 concludes with a consideration of developments by Yang Chen and me in yet another critical industrial sector, that of oil, in Chapter 13. The particular focus of this chapter is the governance structure of the industry and the transition from administrative to regulated monopoly. The authors argue that, although strong industrial and competition policy are not *necessarily* in conflict, it is vital that proper sequencing takes place. It examines the changes wrought over the last twenty years in the industry and, in particular, the formation of a duopolistic structure as 'national champions' have been strengthened. Chen and I argue that there are governance problems inherent in the industry as a result of the fact that the national champions remain as monopolies with enormous regulatory authority and that, if the industry is to continue to thrive in a strong institutional environment, a governing body for the industry, independent of the national champions, should be created with substantial regulatory authority. Chen and I argue that, in order to make industrial policy and competition both *complementary* and *productive for the industry*, 'a long journey of institutional innovation' is called for.

Concluding remarks

Pesident Hu Jintao and Premier Wen Jiabao have launched China on a new strategy which involves creating harmony and sustaining growth at the same time. They do so with a realization that *the fulfilment of each of the objectives is dependent upon the fulfilment of the other*. And they do so, as Wing Thye Woo points out, on the realization that, unless both objectives are fulfilled, the future dominance of the Communist Party in China within the Chinese polity, indeed the very future of the Party at all, is put in doubt.

Will it be possible to fulfil the two goals simultaneously? Will it be possible to create a more humane, equal society within the extant political system dominated by the Chinese Communist Party, a society *at ease with itself?* Some observers think not, notably the Hungarian transitional economist Janos Kornai,[11] who argues that a communist society and a humane society are incompatible. This book is designed to point the Chinese government in directions, through institutional innovation and adaptation and policy initiatives, which may make it possible. But only time will tell. And I expect we will know by the time the next twenty-five years are out.

Notes

1 Will Hutton is Chief Executive of the Work Foundation in the UK and columnist for the *Observer*, where he was editor, and subsequently editor-in-chief, for four years. He published *The Writing on the Wall: China and the West in the 21st Century* in 2007.
2 The annual conference of the Chinese Economic Association (UK), entitled *China in the Age of Globalization,* held at Middlesex University in April, 2006.
3 According to Watts (2004) 85 million Chinese lived on less than a dollar a day, the World Bank poverty threshold, and according to Xinhua (2 July 2004), in 2003 the numbers living on less than 627 yuan – less than two yuan a day – *rose* for the first time since records began, by 800,000, to over 29 million.
4 President Hu Jintao was invited to attend the meetings of the G8 at Gleneagles, Scotland, in 2005.
5 The Chinese government under Deng Xiaoping used the slogan 'crossing the river by feeling the stones' (*mo zhe shitou guo he*) to capture the essentially pragmatic nature of China's reform process, to be contrasted with the 'Shock Therapy' approaches of most other transitional economies to reform, following blueprints for transition determined by outside forces, including the International Monetary Fund.
6 Notwithstanding China's pronouncements in June 2007 concerning its unwillingness to sign any international agreements on limiting carbon emissions which would harm China's economic growth (thus mirroring the USA's position in this regard).
7 This is one of the many slogans associated with the early Deng Xiaoping era which would have been anathema under Mao Zedong.
8 Another slogan identified with the regime of Deng Xiaoping in the early 1980s.
9 The Gini coefficient, accepted by economists as the principal indicator of inequality, varies from 0 (perfect equality) to 1 (perfect inequality).
10 Defined as the risk of events in which a bad outcome could move the household into poverty.
11 Janos Kornai, in a launch of his new book, *By Force of Thought*, at the European Bank of Reconstruction and Development in London in 2007 in front of an audience of prominent international economists and practitioners, argued that 'inhumanity was the *sine qua non* of the communist state.'

References

Brugger, B. and Reglar, S. (1994) *Politics, Economics and Society in Contemporary China,* Houndmills: Macmillan.

Hutton, W. (2007) T*he Writing On the Wall: Why We Must Embrace China as a Partner or Face it as an Enemy*, London: Little, Brown.

Kornai, J. (2006) *By Force of Thought*, Cambridge, MA: MIT Press.

Sanders, R., Chen Yang and Cao Yiying (2007) 'Marginalisation in the Countryside' in H. Zhang, B. Wu and R. Sanders (eds) *Marginalisation in China: Perspectives on Translation and Globalisation*, Aldershot: Ashgate.

Zhang H., Bin W. and Sanders R.(eds) (2007) *Marginalisation in China – Perspectives on Translation and Globalisation*, Aldershot: Ashgate.

Part I
China's Post-reform Economy

Achieving harmony

2 The origins of China's quest for a harmonious society

Failures on the governance and environmental fronts[1]

Wing Thye Woo

October 2006: a turning point in policymaking

It is easy to sing the praises of China's economic performance. An average annual GDP growth rate of 10 percent during the 1978–2006 period has raised GDP per capita almost ninefold over the period. The prevailing expectation in 2006 appeared to be that China would continue to register impressive growth for some time to come. This optimistic outlook is captured in a December 2005 report by Goldman Sachs[2] which predicted that China's GDP would surpass that of the United States in 2040 even after assuming that China's GDP growth rate would slow down steadily from its average annual rate of 10 per cent during the period 1979–2005 to 3.8 per cent between 2030 and 2040.[3]

Since a common dictum of men of practical affairs is "if it ain't broke, don't fix it," it was therefore a surprise when the Sixth Plenum of the Sixteenth Congress of the Communist Party of China (CPC) in October 2006 chose not to follow this route despite the optimistic prognosis from "smart money" (exemplified by Goldman Sachs) that China was on track to even greater prosperity. Instead of repeating what every Plenum had proclaimed since the famous Third Plenum of the Eleventh CPC Congress held in December 1978, that the chief task of the CPC was economic construction, this 2006 Plenum proclaimed instead that the chief task of the CPC was the establishment of a harmonious society by 2020.

The harmonious socialist society enunciated by the 2006 Plenum would exhibit five characteristics: (i) a democratic society under the rule of law, (ii) a society based on equality and justice, (iii) an honest and caring society, (iv) a stable, vigorous, and orderly society, and (v) a society in which humans lived in harmony with nature. The obvious implication from this new party line was that the present major social, economic, and political trends within China might not lead to a harmonious society with the preceding characteristics, or, at least, not lead to this kind of society fast enough.

Among the disharmonious features mentioned in the fifth paragraph of the "resolutions of the CPC Central Committee on major issues regarding the building of a harmonious socialist society" were a serious imbalance in the social and economic development between the urban and rural areas and across China's thirty-one provinces, worsening population and environmental problems, the need for improvements to the system of public management, the inadequate institutionalization of democracy and the rule of law, the inappropriate capacities and work style of some leaders to meet the requirements of the new situation and the new tasks, the continued existence of corruption in some areas, and, finally, problems stemming from the fact that a large proportion of the population finds the national situation with regard to employment, social safety nets, income distribution, education, medical care, housing, occupational safety, and public order to be seriously deficient.

What is revealing is not the existence of these disharmonious features in Chinese society, polity and economy in 2006, but that most of the official descriptions of the envisaged harmonious society downplay the prominence of achieving a prosperous society.[4] Of the nine objectives listed in the Communiqué of the 2006 Plenum, "the objective of building a moderately prosperous society" was not only listed last, it was also qualified with the condition that the prosperity should be shared "all-around." And this qualifier is actually a repetition because the narrowing of income gaps had already been listed as the second objective.

This new emphasis on democratic practice, the rule of law, and income equality represents a turning point that is just as significant as the turning point in 1992 when Deng Xiaoping omitted the word "plan" (which had been ubiquitous since 1949) from the CPC's description of its proposed "socialist market economy with Chinese characteristics." Even the 2005 Plenum had reiterated the Dengist mantra that "economic development is the top priority for the CPC, all efforts should be focused on economic development."[5] This departure in 2006 from past practice can also be seen in that, whereas the 2005 Plenum stressed the centrality of scientific guidance in economic construction, the 2006 Plenum stressed the centrality of "putting people first" in social harmonization.

What is the origin of the CPC's decision to change its primary focus from "economic construction" to "social harmony"? And why include a target date of 2020? I do not believe that this change is merely the consequence of two leaders coming to their final term in office trying to establish their historical legacy by moving out of the shadow of their predecessors. I also do not believe this change to be purely a response to developments that have occurred since the promotion of Hu Jintao to General Secretary of CPC and the designation of Wen Jiabao as the next Prime Minister in late 2002. Instead I believe that this switch in emphasis from "economic construction" to "social harmony" has occurred because the Hu–Wen leadership is well aware that the political legitimacy of CPC rule rests largely on maintaining, first, as before, an economic growth rate that is high enough to keep unemployment low, but, second, a growth pattern that diffuses the additional income widely enough.

Specifically, I believe that the policy change has come about because the younger and better educated CPC leadership led by Hu Jintao and Wen Jiabao recognizes two things: first, that the material conditions and public expectations in China have changed so much since 1978 that, without accelerated institutional reforms and new major policy initiatives on a broad front, further economic construction using the same 1978–2005 policy framework, however successful in the past, is unsustainable for the future; second, that, unless their new policies produced significant improvements in social harmony by 2020, social instability would reduce China's economic growth, making the leadership of CPC in Chinese politics unsustainable. The realization of the above two points is, in my opinion, the most important reason why China has changed its development policy from single-minded pursuit of high GDP growth to building a harmonious society.

The challenges to continued high growth

One way to understand the types of challenges that Hu Jintao and Wen Jiabao face in maintaining the high growth rate and in reducing income inequality is to imagine China as a speeding car. This image is quite an accurate depiction of recent history given how far China has come since 1978. Since past performance is no guarantee of future outcome, this car could still crash and this could happen if the car were to experience any one of the following three classes of failures: (i) hardware failure, (ii) software failure, and (iii) power supply failure.

A *hardware failure* refers to the breakdown of an *economic mechanism*, a development that is analogous to the collapse of the chassis of the car. Possible examples of this class of failure would be a banking crisis that causes a credit crunch that, in turn, dislocates production economy-wide or a budget deficit that spirals beyond the control of the fiscal authorities and generates high inflation and balance of payments difficulties.

A *software failure* refers to a flaw in *governance* that creates frequent widespread social disorders that disrupt production economy-wide and discourage private investment. This situation is similar to a car crash that results from a fight among the people inside the speeding car. Possible examples of such software failures would be the case of a high-growth strategy that creates so much impoverishment, inequality, and corruption that, in turn, severe social unrest is generated, which dislocates economic activities, or the case of rising social expectations clashing with an inadequately responsive state.

A *power supply failure* refers to a situation in which the economy is unable to move forward because it hits either *a natural limit or an externally imposed limit*, a situation that is akin to the car running out of petrol or having its engine switched off by an outsider reaching in and pulling out the ignition key. Possible examples of power supply failures would be an environmental collapse, e.g. climate change, a type of disaster that has happened quite often in history (Diamond, 2005), or a collapse in China's exports because of a trade war.

My perception is that the Chinese leadership is quite confident that it could prevent most hardware failures and that it could respond appropriately to them if they were to occur. The leadership is less confident, however, about its ability to prevent, and react optimally to, software failures and power supply failures. Indeed, the leadership has become aware that the negative trends since the mid-1990s of widening income disparities, worsening corruption, rising social expectations, growing trade imbalances, and a deteriorating natural environment have increased the probability of software and power supply failures.

The thesis here is that this shift in the attention of the Hu–Wen leadership from hardware failures to software failures and power supply failures is the origin of China's quest for a harmonious society. Under the present socio-economic policy regime, the highest probability event in software failure would be social disorder, and the highest probability event in power supply failure would be water shortage. These events need not happen, of course. With the root-and-branch reform of China's society as specified in the Harmonious Society program and with drastic reform of the economic system and of the economic management system, China *can* move to a sustainable mode of economic development. And this fundamental change in the overall policy regime will not only reduce poverty, income inequality, and financial shenanigans, but also enhance macroeconomic stability, strengthen the fiscal basis of the state, raise the efficiency of the financial sector, and lower the tensions in international economic relations.[6]

The need for improved governance to sustain economic growth

The present economic development strategy does not only generate high growth, it also generates high social tensions. At the present stage of economic development, this development strategy has great difficulties in both reducing extreme poverty further and improving income distribution significantly (Woo *et al.*, 2004; Démurger *et al.*, 2002). Furthermore, this mode of economic development also generates immense opportunities for embezzlement of state assets and corruption (Woo, 2001). These features certainly make social harmony hard to sustain.

The elimination of the above negative properties would be helped if the government's actions were monitored more closely by independent mechanisms and if the government were also held more accountable for its performance. I therefore do not think that it is naive to see the Harmonious Society program as a serious attempt at fundamental reform of China's institutions of governance, going well beyond the reform of economic institutions. This assessment is substantiated by the identification of the first component of a harmonious society as "a democratic society under the rule of law." This point was confirmed in a meeting between Premier Wen and the Brookings Board of Trustees in October 2006, in which Premier Wen dwelt at length on how China intends to make greater use of democratic mechanisms (e.g. extending free elections to above the village level) to mediate social conflicts and to improve public administration.

The following report of Premier Wen's words to a group of Chinese citizens in Japan in April 2007 appeared in the *South China Morning Post*:[7]

> During 30 minutes of impromptu remarks, he said the key to pursuing social justice, the mainland's most important task, was to "let people be masters of their houses and make every cadre understand that power is invested in them by the people".
>
> [. . .] Although he did not deviate from the official line and spoke informally on both occasions, Mr. Wen is known for being careful about what he says, whether in prepared remarks or speaking off the cuff. The fact that

he highlighted, in the presence of Hong Kong and overseas journalists, the need for political reform is uncharacteristic and interesting; particularly in the context of the leadership reshuffle looming at the Communist Party's 17th congress later this year.

There have been signs that the leadership under President Hu Jintao is under increasing pressure to undertake drastic political reforms to consolidate the party's grip on power and stamp out widespread corruption.

Although a cynical observer might doubt the sincerity of Premier Wen's words, one cannot doubt that he is at least aware that democracy is one way to solve many of China's problems of governance. More important, the cynic cannot doubt that Premier Wen, like many of his countrymen, must be well acquainted with the history of democratic development in Eastern Europe and in East Asia, particularly in Taiwan and Hong Kong. To understand the reasons behind the Hu–Wen switch to democracy as the new important instrument to introduce external supervision and accountability into governance, it is worth quoting at length from two recent insightful analyses on social unrest in China.

In Albert Keidel's (2006) assessment:

Large-scale public disturbances have been on the rise in China for more than a decade. Media reports describe violence, injuries, and even deaths. . . . Issues include labour grievances, taxation, land confiscation, and pollution. Corruption worsens common injustices and further inflames citizen anger.

[. . .] It is important to emphasize that China's social unrest is not made up of street demonstrations demanding a new government or western-style democracy . . . China's social unrest should be understood as the unavoidable side effects – worsened by local corruption – of successful market reforms and expanded economic and social choice . . . Managing this unrest humanely requires accelerated reform of legal and social institutions with special attention to corruption.

Murray Scot Tanner (2004) reported from his examination of documents prepared by China's police that:

Most available police analyses now blame unrest primarily on approximately the same list of social, economic, and political forces . . . , implicitly relegating enemy instigation [i.e. conspiracy theories] to the role of a secondary catalyst . . . In terms of internal security strategy, this characterization typically, though not always, reduces reliance on coercion . . .

[Many] police see a new social logic taking hold, with disgruntled citizens increasingly convinced that peaceful protest is significantly less dangerous and not only effective but often unavoidable as a means to win concessions. Police sources now routinely quote a popular expression: 'Making a great disturbance produces a great solution. Small disturbances produce small solutions. Without a disturbance, there will be no solution.'

. . . Socioeconomic change may generate these underlying demands and clashes of social interest, but it is usually government failures that cause these contradictions to turn antagonistic and dangerous.

Clearly, the large economic dislocations caused by the reform of the planned economy and the institutional failures in governance[8] are important factors behind the higher frequency of large social disturbances.[9] However, like Tanner, I am of the opinion that there is a third important factor behind the increasing readiness to resort to civil disorder, which is that the richer and more knowledgeable Chinese population now has higher expectations about the performance of the government.[10] The implication of the third factor is that "Beijing may be kidding itself if it believes economic growth alone will bring unrest under control."[11]

The CPC is too astute to kid itself. In its search for new mechanisms to improve its performance on governance, it naturally has to consider democratic institutions as an option because democracy is the well-tested means of governance throughout the developed world. The two basic considerations for the CPC in deciding upon whether democracy should become the new centerpiece in its governance structure are: (i) will democracy, the rule of law, and a stable income distribution constitute an indivisible combination that is necessary to ensure the social stability that will keep the economy on the high-growth path to catch up with the United States (a vision which acts as the bedrock of CPC's legitimacy to rule)? and (ii) will the CPC be both skilful and lucky enough to lead the democratic transition and emerge afterwards as the most important political force? By proposing the Harmonious Society program, the Hu–Wen leadership has replied affirmatively to both questions.

Objectively, this attempt by the CPC to reinvent itself is a difficult and risky undertaking. A functioning democracy requires not just free elections but also a free press that is responsible and a competent judiciary that is independent. So, how would the rank and file of the CPC (who have been used to exercising unchallenged power for fifty years) react to these institutional changes that produce a power-sharing arrangement that is alien and chaotic? Furthermore, a plan of gradual democratization might be initially lauded and endorsed by most segments of society but subsequent changes in social expectations about governmental responsiveness and personal freedom could easily outpace the actual developments as implemented according to the plan.[12] So, would the CPC then be sufficiently pragmatic to accelerate the plan to avoid being run over by events?[13] One possible answer to both these questions is that the CPC would rise to the demands of the occasions and transform itself into a social democratic party. An alternative answer based on the experiences from the Soviet bloc is that CPC would split and social instability would follow.

Although any answer to the two previous questions is necessarily speculative, what is much more definitive is the genesis of the programme to achieve a harmonious society by 2020. The fact that the Hu–Wen leadership, which is well known for its political caution, has embarked on this technically difficult and politically risky project suggests that it has concluded that new far-reaching reforms are less dangerous than partial reforms, and that, given the deep entrenchment of the disharmonious elements (a fact that I will document in the sections that follow), time might not be on its side. The proposition that "without significantly accelerated reforms and major new policy actions, China's rapid growth will unravel before its economy overtakes the U.S." is probably one that the Hu–Wen leadership would agree with.

The need for environmental protection to sustain economic growth

The present mode of economic development has given China the dirtiest air in the world, is polluting more and more of the water resources, and is possibly changing the climate pattern within China. The reality is that CPC's new objective of living in harmony with nature is not optional because the Maoist adage of "man conquering nature" is just as realistic as creating prosperity through central planning. China's fast growth in the last two decades has done substantial damage to the environment. Elizabeth Economy (2004, pp. 18–19) summarized the economic toll as follows:

> China has become home to six of the ten most polluted cities in the world.[14] Acid rain now affects about one-third of China's territory, including approximately one-third of its farmland. More than 75 percent of the water in rivers flowing through China's urban areas is [unsuitable for human contact[15]] . . . deforestation and grassland degradation continue largely unabated[16] . . . The [annual] economic cost of environmental degradation and pollution . . . are the equivalent of 8–12 percent of China's annual gross domestic product.

Water shortage appears to pose the most immediate environmental threat to China's continued high growth.[17] Presently, China uses 67 to 75 per cent of the 800 to 900 billion cubic metres of water available annually, and present trends in water consumption would project the usage rate in 2030 to be 78 to 100 per cent.[18] The present water situation is actually already fairly critical because of the uneven distribution of water and the lower than normal rainfall in the past fifteen years. Right now, "[about] 400 of China's 660 cities face water shortages, with 110 of them severely short."[19]

The extended period of semi-drought in northern China combined with the economic and population growth have caused more and more water to be pumped from the aquifers, leading the water table to drop three to six meters a year.[20] And a study using measurements from satellites (the global positioning system) has established that the part of China north of the 36th parallel has been "sinking at the rate of 2 mm a year."[21] Specifically, "Shanghai, Tianjin, and Taiyuan are the worst hit in China, with each sinking more than two metres (6.6 feet) since the early 1990s."[22]

The overall water situation in northern China is reflected in the fate of the Yellow River, which started drying up every few years from 1972, did so for increasing periods of time over longer distances in the 1990s until 1997, when it dried up for almost the entire year over a stretch of several hundred kilometres.[23]

The utilization rate of Yellow River's water is 60 percent, far exceeding the internationally recommended utilization limit of 40 percent. All the mentioned factors have contributed to lowering the "amount of Yellow River water feeding into the Bohai Sea" from an annual 49.6 billion cubic metres in the 1960s to 14.2 billion cubic metres in the 1990s to the present 4.65 billion cubic metres.[24]

Water shortage and the increasing pollution of what water there is[25] are not the only serious environmental threats to the economy of northern China. The desert is expanding (possibly at an accelerating pace), and man appears to be the chief culprit. The State Forestry Administration reported that 28 percent of the country's land mass was affected by desertification in 1999 and 37 percent was affected by soil erosion. The report identified about 65 per cent of the desert as having been created by "over-cultivation, overgrazing, deforestation and poor irrigation practices."[26] The rate of desertification is 3,900 square miles a year,[27] an annual loss of a land area twice the size of Delaware. One direct upshot is a great increase in the frequency of major sandstorms,[28] a problem that plays "havoc with aviation in northern China for weeks, cripples high-tech manufacturing and worsens respiratory problems as far downstream as Japan, the Korean peninsula and even the western United States."[29] In the assessment of Chen Lai, Vice-Minister of water resources: "It will take nearly half a century for China to control the eroded land and rehabilitate their damaged ecosystems in accordance with China's present erosion-control capabilities."[30]

While northern China has been getting drier and experiencing desertification, nature, as if in compensation (or in mockery), has been blasting southern China with heavier rains, causing heavy floods, which have brought considerable deaths and property damage almost every summer since 1998. The sad possibility is that the northern droughts and southern floods may not be independent events but a combination caused by pollution that originates in China. I will have more to say about this possibility later.

Clearly, without water, growth cannot endure. And in response the government began implementation in 2002 of Mao Zedong's 1952 proposal that three canals should be built to bring water from the south to the north: an eastern coastal canal from Jiangsu to Shandong and Tianjin, a central canal from Hubei to Beijing and Tianjin, and a western route from Tibet to the northwestern provinces, with each canal being over a thousand miles long.[31] Construction of the eastern canal (which builds upon a part of the existing Grand Canal) started in 2002 and the central canal in 2003. Work on the western canal is scheduled to begin in 2010 upon completion of the first stage of the central canal.

The scale of this water transfer project is simply unprecedented anywhere:

> Together, the three channels would pump about 48 billion litres of water a year – enough to fill New York's taps for a quarter century. Only a tenth as much water flows through the next-largest water diversion project, in California.[32]

This massive construction project will not only be technically challenging but also extremely sensitive politically and fraught with environmental risks. The central canal will have to tunnel through the foot of the huge dyke that contains the elevated Yellow River, and the western canal will have to transport water through regions susceptible to freezing. The number of people displaced by the Three Gorges Dam was 1.1 million, and this proposed water transfer scheme is a bigger project than that. The enlargement of the Danjiangkou Dam (in Hubei) alone to enable it to be the source of the central canal will already displace 330,000 people.[33] Moving people involuntarily is certainly potentially explosive politically. The project could also be politically explosive on the international front as well. One plan for the western canal calls for "damming the Brahmaputra river and diverting 200 billion cubic metres of water annually to feed the ageing Yellow river," a scenario that is reportedly "giving sleepless nights to the Indian government . . . [which is concerned that this 'Great Western Water Diverson Project'] could have immense impact on lower riparian states like India and Bangladesh."[34]

The environmental damages caused by this project are most serious for the central and western canals. In the case of the central canal,

> environmental experts [in Wuhan where the Hanjiang River flows into the Yangtze] are worried about . . . [whether the annual extraction of eight billion cubic metres of water could affect] the river's ability to flush out the massive pollution flows released by the thousands of factories and industries along the tributaries . . . The reduced flows could increase the frequency of toxic red algae blooms on the Yangtze near the confluence with the Hanjiang River. There have already been three blooms [by May of that year, 2003].[35]

The western canal has generated a lively controversy. Some scientists are contending that it "would cause more ecological damage than good"[36] because it "could cause dramatic climate changes . . . [and] the changed flow and water temperature would lead to a rapid decline in fish and other aquatic species."[37]

Many opponents of the water transfer project have argued that water conservation could go a long way toward addressing the problem of water shortage because currently a tremendous amount of the water is just wasted, e.g. only 50 percent of China's industrial water is recycled compared with 80 percent in the industrialized countries[38] and China consumes 3,860 cubic meters of water to produce $10,000 of GDP compared with the world average of 965 cubic meters.[39] The most important reason for this inefficient use of water lies in the fact that "China's farmers, factories and householders enjoy some of the cheapest water in the world"[40] even though China's per capita endowment of water is a quarter of the world average.[41]

I now want to raise the unhappy possibility that neither the price mechanism nor the three canals can solve China's water problem and make its growth sustainable unless the present mode of economic development is drastically amended. There is now persuasive evidence that China's voluminous emission of black carbon (particles of incompletely combusted carbon) has contributed significantly to the shift to a climate pattern that produces northern droughts and southern floods of increasing intensity.[42] The biggest source of what has been called the "Asian brown cloud" in the popular media is the burning of coal and bio-fuels in China. If the pollution-induced climate change analysis is valid, it means, first, that China's massive reforestation programme will not succeed in reducing sandstorms in the north because trees cannot survive if the amount of rainfall is declining over time and, second, that the number of south–north canals will have to be increased over time in order to meet the demand for water in northern China, certainly until China reduces its emission of black carbon significantly (presuming no new large emissions from neighboring countries such as India).

The general point is that effective policymaking on the environmental front is a very difficult task because much of the science about the problem is not known. For example, China must no longer select its water strategy and its energy strategy separately. A systems approach in policymaking is necessary because the interaction among the outcomes from the different sectoral policies can generate serious unintended environmental damage. If part of the shift in China's climate is integral to the global climate change, then a sustainable development policy would require a complete rethink of the location of population centres and, at the same time, require new types of enhanced international cooperation on global environmental management.

The uncomfortable reality for China is that, unless ecological balance is restored within the medium term, environmental limits could choke off further economic growth. And the uncomfortable reality for the rest of the world is that the negative consequences of large-scale environmental damage within a geographically large country are seldom confined within that country's borders. The continued march of China's desertification first brought more frequent sandstorms to Beijing and then, beginning in April 2001, sent yellow dust clouds not only across the sea to Japan and Korea but also across the ocean to the United States. China's environmental management is a concern not only for China's welfare but also for global welfare as well.

In discussing the environmental aspects of the water transfer plan, it is important to note that there is now an open controversy in China involving a key government infrastructure project and that this controversy is not limited to members of the technocracy. The very public nature of the controversy and the involvement of more than just scientists, engineers, and economists in it reveal how very far social attitudes have progressed. The important point is that this change in social expectations will require any government in China to live in harmony with nature. However, any government will have great difficulties in doing so even if it wants to because a green growth policy involves a systems approach and scientific understanding of many ecological subsystems while the nature of their interactions remains incomplete.

Final remarks

It might seem surprising to hear that China needs fundamental and comprehensive reform of its social, political, and economic institutions when it has experienced high growth for almost thirty years. Why meddle with success? Why fix it if it is not broken?

There are two parts to the answer. The first part is that it is broken. The reason why growth has stayed so high for so long is because the government has continually changed policies to keep marketizing the economy, deepening integration into the international economy, and, since the mid-1990s, reducing the discrimination against the private sector. In short, policy changes were the reason for keeping past growth high, and they will have to continue if future growth is to remain high.

The second part of the answer is that satisfaction with the status quo depends inversely on the level of expectations, and the expectations of the Chinese people towards their government have risen along with income, and, more importantly, risen along with their growing knowledge of the outside world. A Chinese government that consistently fails to produce results in line with the rise in social expectations runs the increasing risk of being challenged by another faction within the CPC. However, there has been not just rising expectations but also diversification of expectations. In this new situation, the greater use of democratic procedures is a natural way to accommodate the rising social expectations and mediate the emerging differences in social expectations.

In today's China, doing more of the same economic policies will not produce the same salubrious results on every front because the development problems have changed. For example, in the first phase of economic development, the provision of more jobs (through economic deregulation) was enough to lower poverty significantly. At present, many of the people who are still poor require more than just job opportunities, they first need an infusion of assistance (e.g. empowering them with human capital through education and health interventions) in order to be able to take up any job opportunities available. This is why the poverty rate (defined by a poverty line of a daily income of US$1) in China has stayed at about 11 percent since 1998.

Worse yet, it appears that, since 1998, the post-1978 development strategy has not been able to prevent the very poor from getting poorer. Woo *et al.* (2004) found that the average income of the rural poor fell from 72 cents in 1999 to 63 cents in 2002; and a recent World Bank[43] study found that the average income of the poorest 10 percent of China's population fell 2.4 percent in the period 2001–03. As the national average income went up in the period 1998–2003, the implication is that the traditional trickling-down mechanism has morphed into a trickling-up mechanism. Development policymaking has now become even more challenging.

On the sustainable growth front, proper management of the environment has now become critical if China is to continue its industrialization process. Pan Yue, deputy head of the State Environmental Protection Administration, summed up the present situation in China very well when he said:

If we continue on this path of traditional industrial civilization, there is no chance that we will have sustainable development. China's population, resources, environment have already reached the limits of their capacity to cope. Sustainable development and new sources of energy are the only road that we can take.[44]

Development policymaking in China has indeed become even more challenging. So, will China succeed in establishing a harmonious society and completing the overhaul of its economic system? My answer is a very cautious "yes." I am optimistic because both Chinese society and government want the economy to continue its conversion to a modern private market economy, exemplified by the developed world. My considerable caution comes from (i) the new major reforms being technically difficult to implement (e.g. setting up social safety nets), and having few, if any, successful precedents in the world to draw upon (e.g. designing market-compatible environmental regulation), and (ii) the possibility that the many potential losers from these major reforms could successfully organize to resist meaningful implementation of the reforms.

In this new situation, the decisiveness and perseverance in policy actions that have allowed the big successes in the past,[45] although still very important, are less crucial. What is required more is creativity in policy formulation, programme implementation, and political management. But creativity is one thing that is always in short supply. However, given the large number of people in China, it is perhaps justified to be optimistic that enough creative managers will emerge as long as access to education continues to accelerate, meritocracy is upheld, and a democratic society under the rule of law emerges.

Notes

1 This paper has its origin in the Debate on China's Economy in the Reframing China Policy Debate Series of the Carnegie Endowment for International Peace, where I argued for the motion that "Without significantly accelerated reforms and major new policy actions, China's rapid growth will unravel before its economy overtakes the U.S."; see www.carnegieendowment.org/events/.
2 See O'Neill *et al.* (2005).
3 For a review of the debate on how to interpret China's high growth in the period 1978–2000 and why China, unlike the former Soviet bloc, did not experience a recession when it made the switch from a centrally planned economy to a market economy, see Sachs and Woo (2000), and Woo (2001).
4 For example, in the preceding five characteristics of the desired harmonious society, there is no highlighting of a prosperous society. This characterization of the harmonious society is from "CPC key plenum elevates social harmony to more prominent position," *People's Daily Online*, October 12, 2006.
5 "CPC Plenary session calls for developing the economy based on scientific concept," *People's Daily Online*, October 12, 2005; http://english.people.com.cn/200510/12/eng20051012_213891.html.
6 The generation of these additional benefits is discussed in Woo (2005, 2006).
7 "Impromptu remarks reveal the party's pressure for reforms," *South China Morning Post*, Monday, April 16, 2007.

8 To get a sense of how abusive the local leaders could be, the reader should consult Chen and Wu (2006) for documentation on five incidents in the 1990s in Anhui province that suggest that "[many] of China's underclass live under an unchanged feudal system."

9 For example, in 2004, there were 74,000 "mass incidents" involving 3.7 million people compared with 10,000 such incidents involving 730,000 people in 1994 (Pei, 2005).

10 Tanner (2004) pointed out that the "data demonstrate that unrest began rising rapidly no later than 1993–1995 when the rate of economic growth exceeded 10 percent. Protests also show a ratchet effect, remaining quite high (and continuing to rise in at least two provinces) even as the rate of economic growth revived."

11 Tanner (2004).

12 For example, in the same meeting with the Trustees of the Brookings Institution in October 2006, Premier Wen outlined a step-by-step extension of free election from the village level to the provincial level. Whereas such a plan, if proposed, would most likely receive wide societal approval in 2006, it is possible that Chinese society in 2020 might have raised its expectations such that free elections should also be held at the national level.

13 If such escalations in social expectations are natural, then it is likely that, regardless of whether or not the CPC defines "democracy" the same way as the US constitution (or the Taiwanese constitution), the form of the democracy that will finally emerge in China will be closer to the latter's definition. Perhaps, this is why the former Party Secretary Zhao Ziyang warned his colleagues in 1986–87: "Democracy is not something socialism can avoid. The people's demand for democracy is a trend. We must meet their demand to the fullest extent" (quoted in Pei, 2005b).

14 "300,000 people die prematurely from air pollution annually, which is twice the number for South Asia, which has a roughly comparable population" (Economy, 2004, p. 85).

15 Economy (2004, p. 69).

16 "degradation has reduced China's grassland by 30–50 percent since 1950; of the 400 million or so hectares of grassland remaining, more than 90 percent are degraded and more than 50 percent suffer moderate to severe degradation" (Economy, 2004, p. 65).

17 I will not talk about air pollution in this chapter, and this should not be taken to indicate that it is not a serious problem. Of the twenty cities in the world identified by the World Bank as having the dirtiest air, sixteen are located in China. It is shocking that lead and mercury poisoning are more common than expected (see "China's economic miracle contains mercuric threat," *Financial Times*, December 18, 2004; "A Poison Spreads Amid China's Boom," *Wall Street Journal*, September 30, 2006).

18 "Top official warns of looming water crisis," *South China Morning Post*, November 7, 2006.

19 "China may be left high and dry," *The Straits Times*, January 3, 2004. The shortage is reported to be most acute in Taiyuan in Shanxi, and Tianjin (Becker, 2003).

20 "Northern cities sinking as water table falls," *South China Morning Post*, August 11, 2001; and Becker (2003).

21 "Northern China sinking . . . as the south rises," *The Straits Times*, March 18, 2002. "Some 60 percent of the land in Tianjin municipality is plagued by subsistence" (Becker, 2003).

22 "Chinese cities, including Olympic host Beijing, slowly sinking," *Agence France-Presse*, July 23, 2004.

23 "China may be left high and dry," *The Straits Times*, January 3, 2004.

24 "Top official warns of looming water crisis," *South China Morning Post*, November 7, 2006.

25 Examples of serious water pollution are "Main rivers facing a 'pollution crisis',"
    South China Morning Post, June 6, 2003; "Booming cities polluting scarce water
    supplies," *The Straits Times*, September 18, 2003; "Rivers Run Black, and Chinese
    Die of Cancer," *New York Times*, September 12, 2004; " 'Cancer villages' pay heavy
    price for economic progress," *South China Morning Post*, May 8, 2006; and "Rules
    Ignored, Toxic Sludge Sinks Chinese Village," *New York Times*, September 4, 2006.
26 "Quarter of land now desert – and Man mostly to blame," *South China Morning Post*,
    January 30, 2002.
27 This is the average of the 3,800 square miles reported in "Billion of Trees Planted,
    and Nary a Dent in the Desert," *New York Times*, April 11, 2004, and the 4,014 square
    miles reported in "Quarter of land now desert – and Man mostly to blame," *South
    China Morning Post*, January 30, 2002.
28 The number of major sandstorms in China was five in the period 1950–59, eight in
    1960–69, thirteen in 1970–79, fourteen in 1980–89, twenty-three in 1990–99, four-
    teen in 2000, twenty-six in 2001, sixteen in 2002, and eleven in 2003 according to
    Yin Pumin, "Sands of Time Running Out: Desertification continues to swallow up
    'healthy' land at an alarming rate," *Beijing Review*, June 16, 2005.
29 "Billion of Trees Planted, and hardly a Dent in the Desert," *New York Times*, April 11,
    2004.
30 "Quarter of land now desert – and Man mostly to blame," *South China Morning Post*,
    January 30, 2002.
31 "Ambitious canal network aims to meet growing needs," *South China Morning Post*,
    November 27, 2002.
32 "China approves project to divert water to arid north," *South China Morning Post*,
    November 26, 2002.
33 "Massive scheme aims to quench China's thirst," *South China Morning Post*, May 12,
    2003; a lower estimate of 300,000 is given in "China Will Move Waters to Quench
    Thirst of Cities," *New York Times*, August 27, 2002.
34 "China's river plan worries India," *Times of India*, October 23, 2006.
35 "Massive scheme aims to quench China's thirst," *South China Morning Post*, May 12,
    2003
36 "China Water Plan Sows Discord," *Wall Street Journal*, October 20, 2006.
37 "Chinese water plan opens rift between science, state," *American-Statesman*, Septem-
    ber 10, 2006.
38 "China may be left high and dry," *The Straits Times*, January 3, 2004.
39 "Alert sounded over looming water shortage," *The Straits Times*, June 10, 2004.
40 "Water wastage will soon leave China high and dry," *South China Morning Post*,
    March 8, 2006.
41 "Alert sounded over looming water shortage," *The Straits Times*, June 10, 2004.
42 Menon *et al.* (2002), and Streets (2005).
43 "China's poorest worse off after economic boom," *Financial Times*, November 21,
    2006, reported a 2.4 percent drop; and "In China, Growth at Whose Cost," *The Wall
    Street Journal*, November 22, 2006, reported a 2.5 percent drop.
44 Quoted in Kynge (2004).
45 Some past decisive actions were the decollectivization of the agricultural sector
    (which employed 70 percent of the workforce) in a three-year period; the conversion
    of the bulk of the collectively owned rural enterprises to private enterprises in the
    1993–98 period; the restructuring and reduction of the state enterprise sector in the
    period when Zhu Rongji was in charge of economic management; and the entry into
    WTO, an organization that specifies the form that economic institutions must take in
    order for the country to be considered a market economy.

References

Becker, J. (2003) 'The Death of China's Rivers,' *Asian Times Online*, August 26.

Chen, G. and Wu, C. (2006) *Will the Boat Sink the Water? The Life of China's Peasants*, New York: Public Affairs. (Published in Chinese as *Zhongguo Nongmin Diaocha* by People's Literature Publishing House in December 2003.)

Démurger, S., Sachs, J.D., Woo, W.T., Shuming Bao, Chang, G., and Mellinger, A. (2002) 'Geography, Economic Policy and Regional Development in China,' *Asian Economic Papers*, 1 (1), 146–197.

Diamond, J. (2005) *Collapse: How Societies Choose to Fail or Succeed*, New York: Viking.

Economy, E.C. (2004) *The River Runs Black: The Environmental Challenge to China's Future*, Ithaca, NY: Cornell University Press.

Keidel, A. (2006) 'China's Social Unrest: The Story Behind the Stories,' Policy Brief No. 48, Carnegie Endowment for International Peace, September.

Kynge, J. (2004) 'Modern China is facing an ecological crisis,' *Financial Times*, July 26.

Menon, S., Hansen, J., Nazarenko, L., and Luo, Y. (2002) 'Climate Effects of Black Carbon in China and India,' *Science*, 297, 27 September, 2250–2253.

O'Neill, J., Wilson, D., Purushothaman, R., and Stupnytska, A. (2005) 'How Solid are the BRICs?,' Global Economics Paper No. 134, Goldman Sachs, December 15.

Pei, M. (2005a) 'China is Paying the Price of Rising Social Unrest,' *Financial Times*, November 7.

Pei, M. (2005b) 'How Far Has China to Go?,' *Financial Times*, January 18.

Sachs, J.D. and Woo, W. T. (2000) 'Understanding China's Economic Performance,' *Journal of Policy Reform*, 4 (1), 1–50.

Streets, D. (2005) 'Black Smoke in China and Its Climate Effects,' *Asian Economic Papers*, 4 (2), 1–23.

Tanner, M.S. (2004) 'China Rethinks Unrest,' *The Washington Quarterly*, 27 (3), 137–156.

Woo, W.T. (2001) 'Recent Claims of China's Economic Exceptionalism: Reflections Inspired by WTO Accession,' *China Economic Review*, 12 (2/3), 107–136.

Woo, W.T. (2005) 'China's Rural Enterprises in Crisis: The Role of Inadequate Financial Intermediation,' in Yasheng Huang, Anthony Saich, and Edward Steinfeld (eds), *Financial Sector Reform in China*, Cambridge, MA: Harvard University Press, 67–91.

Woo, W.T. (2006) 'China's Macroeconomic Imbalances: The Liquidity Tango Mechanism,' presented at the February 2006 meeting of the Forum of Debt and Development in The Hague, Netherlands.

Woo, W.T., Li, S., Yue, X., Wu, H., and Xu, X. (2004) *The Poverty Challenge for China in the New Millennium*, report to the Poverty Reduction Taskforce of the Millennium Development Goals Project of the United Nations.

3 Environment, health and sustainability in twenty-first-century China

Ian Cook

At the time of writing:

> Fumin County, a hitherto obscure district in south-west China, became the object of international mockery last week when news reached the outside world that the bare slopes of Laoshou mountain had been painted green, to the bewilderment of the villagers, and at a cost of about £30,000.
>
> (Hinton, 2007)

However, this was not the first time that the greening of China had been given a literal expression via a coat of paint: at the time of the final visit by the Olympics vetting panel judging locations for the 2008 Olympics, to Beijing in February 2001, it was suggested that bare areas had also been sprayed with green paint in an effort to brighten up the city at the end of winter (Cook, 2007). Such activities do lead to serious questions about the depth of China's commitment to environmental issues. China is changing rapidly, often for the better, but the overarching emphasis on economic growth is often at a heavy price in terms of environmental degradation, health problems and low quality of life for many. In this chapter I shall attempt to give a flavour of the complexity and impact of contemporary environmental concerns in China via consideration of topics including the problem of water, the quality of the air, health problems and energy use. I will conclude with a discussion of appropriate policy responses.

The problem of water

China is a vast country, in area roughly the size of Europe, and in population the largest in the world (although India's population is expected to outstrip it soon) at approximately 1.3 billion people. Despite the controversy over the Single Child Family Programme introduced in the 1980s, it is generally thought that without it China's population might have been even higher, at 1.6 billion. The combination of such factors as the unevenness of population distribution, the differential impact historically of this emerging population and the variability of soil, bio-geography and climate over China's huge land surface means that it is probably more accurate to talk of China's *environments* rather than a single environment for the whole of China.

Superimposed on the environmental variability across China, following government policy, is urbanization at an almost unprecedented rate, mainly concentrated on China's 'Gold Coast' along its eastern seaboard, sucking in huge amounts of investment from the Chinese state and foreign investors alike, as well as many millions of migrants from rural areas. Thus, what follows may very likely apply to much of China, but not all. Just as one would expect contrast and variability across Europe, so too one finds contrasts across China's huge land mass, as Donald and Benewick (2005), for example, show.

With this caveat in mind, 22 March 2006 was World Water Day. In the People's Republic it was marked among other events by a rather sombre editorial in the influential English-language official-run *China Daily*, entitled 'Water crisis could leave us high and dry'. The editorial considered the grim global situation while also pointing to China's own water profile, arguing that:

> The sad fact now is that many rivers cannot flow into the ocean, as they did before, as the volume of water has so drastically decreased. The Yellow river, China's second longest, stopped flowing into the ocean from early 1970s to late 1990s.
>
> [. . .] In China alone, nearly 1,000 inland lakes dried up in the past five decades.
>
> [. . .] We used to believe that we could change waterways for our immediate benefits, we could build dams to block water for our use and we could treat water in whatever way we thought would bring us immediate benefit.
>
> [. . .] Today desert has conquered or is encroaching on areas that used to be inland lakes or rivers. The biological environment is becoming worse in most delta areas because of less fresh water flowing into the ocean, and degradation of wetland owing to a lack of fresh water from rivers has affected the climate in a negative way.
>
> A proverb says we will never know the worth of water until the well is dry. We hope the reality is not as cruel as it describes, and all of us get to know the worth of water before the well is dry.
>
> (www.chinadaily.com.cn)

This editorial is indicative of the strength of feeling and emotion that environmental issues now evoke in China, even in the official media. After years in which the economy has come a strong first in government priorities there is growing recognition of the need to redress at least some of the imbalance between economic expansion and environmental degradation. This is mainly because of the growing impact and severity of environmental issues across the country. As regards the 'worth of water' it was reported in a symposium held in Beijing later that same day that, even though per capita water consumption in China is currently only a quarter of the world's average at 2,200 cubic metres per year, unless strong steps are taken this will decline to a mere 1,700 cubic metres per capita. Efficiency levels of water use in industry and irrigation will have to be increased, while the fact that 300 million people (some data suggest 360 million) in rural areas still do not have clean drinking water must also be addressed.

However, tackling these and other water issues will not be easy. Seventy per cent of China's rivers and lakes are polluted; so, apart from the problem of rural water quality, even in the capital, Beijing, visitors are advised not to drink the tap water, and, as in other countries, there is a lively trade in bottled water in Beijing's supermarkets. This situation is found in many other cities too, with nearly two-thirds of China's cities, 420, estimated to have water shortage problems, 100 having 'acute shortage', including Beijing itself. Beijing's shortages are due to rapid population increase and economic expansion, overexploitation of underground water from the city's artesian wells, limited usable surface water and huge leakage from pipelines (Qu Geping, cited in Murray and Cook, 2004, p. 79). For some years now, hotel visitors have been exhorted to save water, while residents have been exhorted to listen for the sounds of taps or faucets dripping at night and to fix any drips immediately.

More dramatically, two major projects to control China's water supply are the South–North Water Diversion Project and the Sanxia (Three Gorges) Dam. Both are controversial, and both have proponents and opponents. The diversion project aims to redirect water from the 'water-surplus' Yangtze north to the 'water-deficient' North China Plains. There are three proposed routes, eastern, middle and western (see Woo, Chapter 2), with both the eastern and middle routes currently being progressed (the western route is the shortest and is near the headwaters of both rivers but is the most difficult to construct; being in the uplands of the Qinghai–Tibet Plateau, the technical difficulties are immense). Similarly, the largest and arguably most controversial dam in the world, the Sanxia Dam, is also being built on the Yangtze, in order to reduce flood risks, provide hydroelectric power and improve river transportation to Chongqing upriver. Only time will tell whether these immense and costly projects prove effective (see Murray and Cook, 2002, 2004). Here, I note that there is concern that the delicate balance of the hydrological system of the Yangtze may be destabilized by both these projects, such that the river loses its water surplus and *still* cannot provide large reserves of water to the thirsty north. The loss of water flow with its cleansing and purifying action threatens the river ecology, allowing pathogens to proliferate should a stagnant subtropical ecosystem develop.

Water pollution incidents are also common. In late 2005, a serious incident that caused considerable embarrassment to the Chinese authorities occurred on the Songhua River in the northeast of China. The river begins in Jilin Province then flows through Heilongjiang before entering the Heilong River itself, the river that forms the border with Russia before it in turn merges with the Wusuli River to become the Amur, at Khabarovsk in Russia. On 13 November 2005, there was an explosion in a major chemical plant causing an estimated 100 tons of benzene and nitrobenzene to enter the river, forming a huge toxic slick 180 kilometres in length. At first, the authorities tried, as they have done elsewhere in China in past pollution incidents, to cover it up, and it was ten days later that the Harbin municipality on the river announced that the water supply would have to be shut down for a day on account of the need 'to carry out repair and inspections on the pipe network' (www.pacificresearch.org)!

This announcement caused massive disbelief among the populace, panic buying of water and rumours of an earthquake. Unlike in many situations in the past decades, however, the authorities, as a *China Daily* journalist put it, 'soon realized the stupidity of the false excuse' and then announced the truth of the matter, that the city was endangered by the toxic slick moving downstream. Advice was given about water storage, and regular TV bulletins were made until the danger had passed. Huge numbers of Chinese labourers paid for by the Chinese government were mobilized in sub-zero conditions to build a temporary dam to protect Khabarovsk, in order to prevent an international incident. The winter freeze then ameliorated the crisis, but the danger was not yet over, because it was unknown what chemicals would be left in the river at the spring thaw. In March and April 2006, therefore, the water quality was closely monitored by both Chinese and Russian experts in the affected rivers. Fortunately, it is reported that the readings showed that the danger had passed, and local people could be assured that the water was safe both for irrigation purposes and for drinking. As an important postscript, it seemed at the time that it was the local officials that were deliberately restricting the information about this incident, but it turned out that it was the central authorities in the shape of the State Environmental Protection Administration (SEPA) that were forcing the localities to withhold information, and in the aftermath the Minister of SEPA, Xie Zhenhuan, was forced to resign (Carter and Mol, 2006). I find this particularly ironic given that Murray and I concluded our 2002 book by citing Xie's statement that 'ecological deterioration continues because the endeavour of improvement lags behind the speed of human sabotage' (Murray and Cook, 2002, p. 224).

Serious as it was, the Songhua River incident was only one in a long series of pollution incidents involving industrial plants in China. One month later, in December 2005, there was another major pollution incident in Guangdong Province in the south, with a tributary of the Pearl River being polluted by the dangerous metal cadmium from the Shaoguan Smelting Plant. Seven hundred million cubic metres of water had to be released from a local reservoir in order to dilute the slick to render water once again potable. Such incidents as these have occurred despite growing pressure from the authorities on polluters, and the closure in the late 1990s of thousands of polluting factories around the country. In April 2006, further measures were announced by SEPA against twenty chemical and petrochemical works (including those of CNPC, the largest oil producer, and Sinopec, the state oil company) to force them to reduce pollution hazards. Also, SEPA stopped or postponed approval of forty-four major projects because their location was considered unsafe. The scale of water pollution is shown by the fact that currently only 45 per cent of China's wastewater is treated, although an ambitious target was announced in 2006 to treat 70 per cent of wastewater by 2010 (www.chinadaily.com).

The quality of the air: dust, desertification and air pollution

Other major issues that are refusing to disappear despite huge efforts to reduce their impact are the interrelated problems of dust and desertification, which link to the problem of air pollution more generally. In Beijing in recent years there have been a growing number of 'blue sky days' and pollution is being combated by a wide range of methods, such as use of better quality coal with lower sulphur content, the banning of trucks from the central areas during the day, greater use of liquefied petroleum gas and widespread tree planting (Cook, 2006). West of the capital across north and northwest China, billions more trees continue to be planted in the 'Three-North Shelterbelt Development Programme' (Williams, 2005), known in some localities as the 'Green Great Wall' thanks to its alignment and scale. The target is to plant 35 million hectares by 2050. Such tree planting has been promoted for decades, and this, combined with other measures to hold back the desert, has led to optimism concerning the long-term struggle with the sands of the northwest deserts. For instance, in Xinjiang Province in the northwest, as reported by *China Development Brief* (www.chinadevelopmentbrief.com), a seemingly successful World Bank-funded project was publicized in August 2005. The project is found in China's arid Taklimakan Desert, and is known as 'Tarim II'. Costing US$290 million, the main focus is on lining of canals to prevent water seepage, along with the setting of water quotas for irrigation, improvements to soil quality and crop diversification. The Implementation Completion Report suggests that the project achieved great success on many criteria, has saved 214 billion litres of water per annum and has led to increased incomes for local (Uyghur) farmers and the return of twenty-five species of birds, amphibians, reptiles and fish along 'Xinjiang's Green Corridor'. A final evaluation will be made in several years' time, but at present this may be one of the world's most successful examples of sustainable river management.

Despite such a success story, and there are always such examples to bring some rays of optimism to those concerned over China's environmental problems, there are criticisms of the effectiveness of such projects (Williams, 2005), and yet again, on 16 April 2006, huge sandstorms hit north China. Some 330,000 tons of dust was estimated to have fallen on Beijing that day, and the next saw most of north and northwest China enveloped in sandstorms. Coincident with the Sixth National Conference on Environmental Protection, this was again chastening for the authorities; Premier Wen Jiabao addressed this meeting with the words 'Repeated sandstorms should send a warning to us all, we should feel heavy loads on our shoulders while meeting here to discuss environmental problems'. Despite China's best efforts, nature refuses to be tamed. Much of northwest China is in danger of becoming a dustbowl (the famous lake Lop Nor was swallowed up by 1972 in the Gobi Desert's 'Sea of Death' to become the 'Great Ear' on satellite imagery and many cities on the Silk Road have also been overwhelmed by the desert advance), and desertification has been estimated to cost China, directly and indirectly, US$58.75 billion. Clearly, there is a huge amount still to do, and I note here that there are those who believe that the massive tree planting programme takes too much water from the soil (Walker, 2006), so it is important that what is done is indeed appropriate to deal with the problem.

Meanwhile, as regards the related issue of air pollution, in October 2005 the European Space Agency's satellite data identified Beijing itself as the most polluted city on earth, with the city and neighbouring provinces having the world's worst levels of nitrogen dioxide (Watts, 2005). Similarly, the World Bank notes that sixteen of the world's twenty most polluted cities are in China, and researchers at Yale and Columbia universities ranked China at a low 94 out of 133 countries on an Environmental Performance Index. China is now the second largest emitter of greenhouse gases, including 957 million metric tons of carbon dioxide in 2005, second only to the United States at 1,592 million metric tons, while acid rain is becoming an ever more serious threat, largely because of the record-breaking use of coal as the main power source. By summer 2005, 218 cities were affected by severe levels of acid rain, up from previous years. One-third of the country is thought to be afflicted by acid rain, and the European satellite data show that pollution levels have increased by nearly 50 per cent over the last decade. Indeed, the deputy director of SEPA was quoted by Watts as saying that levels could quadruple within fifteen years unless more was done to curtail energy use and car ownership. The latter is expanding rapidly, contributing further to pollution levels, especially given the fact that, although many Chinese-produced cars are made in partnership with overseas companies such as Volkswagen or Audi, the vehicles are often older models with higher emission rates than would currently be permitted in Europe.

Health problems

The high levels of pollution noted above are having an increasing impact on people's health. Air pollution is thought to have caused 411,000 premature deaths, from respiratory problems or heart disease, with 100 million people living in cities in which the air quality is regarded as 'very dangerous'. But it is not just in cities that respiratory problems are severe. The huge scale of coal burning releases toxins that pose a severe health hazard across the country and respiratory disease has become the main cause of death in rural areas whereas it is fourth in the cities (Cook and Dummer, 2004). Unless there are major changes, the World Bank estimates that by 2020 'China will be paying $390 billion to treat diseases indirectly caused by burning coal . . . an astounding 13 per cent of its predicted GDP at that time. That suggests that something has to give' (Walker, 2006, p. 9). Indeed it has. But the other main threat to people's lungs and heart among other organs comes more voluntarily via smoking. It is forecast by the World Health Organization (WHO) that there could be 2 million deaths per annum from smoking-related diseases by 2025. Perhaps up to one third of China's men could die eventually of smoking-related conditions, according to one estimate (Liu *et al.*, 1998). Nor is this situation helped by the role of the state-owned China National Tobacco Corporation and the big Western tobacco companies, which continue to target such countries as China for their products now that people in the West are beginning to turn away from smoking, and smoking bans in public places become more widespread there.

Apart from respiratory problems, other contemporary health issues in China include resurgent diseases, loss of life via natural disasters, threats from pesticide use, the impact of changing lifestyles and hypertension, HIV/AIDS, severe acute respiratory syndrome (SARS), the widening inequalities of access to health care and, most recently, avian flu.

Here I shall deal only with the most important of these. Further details are found in Cook and Dummer (2004) and Dummer and Cook (2007). First, diseases such as schistosomiasis, leprosy and TB, once thought to have been eradicated or at least under control, are now returning, in part because of the problems of water pollution noted previously but also owing to changes made to health care provision after the Maoist era. Despite criticisms directed at Chairman Mao, the famous 'barefoot doctors' (paramedics in effect, trained in basic hygiene and rudimentary traditional medicines for instance) were a key element in reducing threats to health in rural areas especially, while in the communes health treatment was free or very cheap, as part of the 'Five Guarantees'. The subsequent reform era saw pricing policies introduced that cost health provision and put off many of the poor from accessing rural health services. This and other factors including the dramatic rise of the 'Gold Coast' noted in the introduction, and the increasing residualization of people in remote rural areas, has meant that social and spatial inequalities of access to health care are on the increase. Official statistics released in 2003 showed, for example, that 70 per cent of the population in rural areas consumed only 30 per cent of the country's medical resources. The Chinese government has now recognized this as a major concern and announced in April 2006 that increased funds (RMB4.7 billion) would be put into rural health provision, including the Healthcare Insurance Scheme used in rural areas. It will still cost the farming families some money of their own, however, and it remains to be seen whether this will solve the problems for the poorest in Chinese society. Dummer and Cook (2007) suggest that the health problems in rural areas now constitute a 'crisis', one that is deep-rooted and difficult to resolve.

More funds have also been directed in the last couple of years to the monitoring of infectious diseases. This is owing to concern over not only such 'old' diseases as schistosomiasis but also the new diseases such as HIV/AIDS, SARS and now avian flu. For years the authorities denied that they had a problem with HIV/AIDS, and also denied the existence of SARS (it was first reported in February 2003 but atypical cases of pneumonia had been identified in Guangdong Province in November 2002 and were hushed up). In a growing climate of openness, the new leadership of Hu Jintao and Wen Jiabao have encouraged officials and others to face these issues, and have apologized for hiding the true facts of the SARS epidemic, unprecedented for leaders of a society so concerned with losing 'face'. As regards HIV/AIDS there is conflicting evidence over the current scale of infection. Estimates for HIV have ranged from 1 million infected up to 10 million or even 20 million. Most recently, however, UN estimates have suggested that its own upper figures may have been too extreme and that the lower figures are more likely to be the case, while official figures now show 650,000 infected and the WHO regards the target to restrict HIV/AIDS to 1.5 million by 2010 as a 'good challenge' (Watts, 2006). One feature of tackling this health threat has been at long last an acknowledgement by the authorities that China has a gay community (www.chinadaily.com), after years of denial, and this community is beginning to be involved in educational projects to reduce the threat of transmission of the virus. Another factor to note is that migrants may be particularly at risk from their own high-risk behaviour with regard to sex, smoking and alcohol (Chen *et al.*, 2004; He *et al.*, 2006; Hong *et al.*, 2006; Lin *et al.*, 2005).

The current (2007) major health concern globally is now avian flu, with the threat of a flu pandemic worrying health planners across the planet. At first it was thought that SARS would be of monumental significance, but the response worldwide proved to be adequate to reduce and eventually stop the spread of this virus. Now, the concern is over avian flu, mapped for China in *Beijing Review* as far back as 2004 (Ren, 2004). By the end of March 2006, 103 people had died of the H5N1 virus in Asia and the Middle East, including ten in China. Generally, it seems that the essential policy of openness is holding firm, with the possible bird-flu death of a migrant worker being reported in late March 2006 and another death in Guangdong in early March of that year (www.chinadaily.com). However, bird flu was identified in Hong Kong in February 2006 from Guangdong poultry even though at that time it was reported that there was no bird flu in Guangdong. The tradition of cover-up is embedded at all levels, and it will be vital that openness of reporting is the norm rather than the exception, even with the risk of inducing panic among the people.

Finally in this section, I shall discuss the 'McDonaldization' of Chinese society, shorthand for the Westernization of consumption patterns in China's burgeoning cities. Although the Beijing Olympics of 2008 is being presented as a 'Green Olympics', there are concerns expressed by Dickson and Schofield (2005, p. 170) that 'the main sponsors for the event include 'calorie-dense beverages (Coca-Cola) and food (McDonalds) as well as motorized transportation (Volkswagen)'. Such sponsorship will 'exacerbate' China's growing obesity problem and contribute to 'globesity' – the worldwide epidemic of obesity. Other sponsors such as Samsung or Panasonic produce goods that further contribute to a sedentary lifestyle. Critics argue that 'the world's most populous nation is at the beginning of an explosion in lifestyle-related disease' (cited in Cook, 2007). The increases in wheat and milk products and meat consumption have led to similar problems of obesity, heart disease and other risks to those in Western society. Beijing opened its first 'fat camp' as early as 1994. Strangely, 'intellectuals', journalists and IT profes-sionals are among those groups who are most at risk of reduced life expectancy, with intellectuals having a lifespan of fifty-eight years, ten less than the national average, while IT professionals in Beijing's 'silicon valley' at Zhongguancun can expect only fifty-three years and Shanghai reporters forty-five. A combination of the legacy of upheavals from the Great Leap Forward and the Cultural Revolu-tion, a poor urban environment, increased fat and salt levels in food, plus stressful and sedentary lifestyles can all be implicated in these figures, which sit oddly with the fact that the proportion of the elderly continues to increase in Chinese society, particularly in the cities (Cook and Powell, 2007a,b).

Energy use

Coal may not be King Coal as it once was in the UK but it is certainly King in China. Coal use has never been less than two-thirds of total energy production since 1978 and in 2004 it was 75.6 per cent of the total (National Bureau of Statistics of China, 2006, p. 255). As for consumption it was 67.7 per cent of the total, compared with oil at 22.7 per cent and natural gas at a mere 2.6 per cent, with hydro-power 7.0 per cent. Coal use is more than one metric ton per head of population at present, and is forecast to increase to 2 billion metric tons by 2020 (Walker 2006). In the past much of the coal has been low quality, with high sulphur content, and burned untreated. Increasingly, producers are encouraged to promote high quality coal with low sulphur content and power plants are clean-ing the coal to reduce sulphur or scrubbing it out from emissions, but acid rain remains a major problem. Many small coalmines producing poor quality coal have been forced to close, but others are continually reopening as local officials turn a blind eye to this illegal but lucrative activity. Mining accidents are com-mon and regularly reported; often, it is in these illegal mines that they occur. It is ultimately important to reduce China's dependence on coal but it will be decades before alternatives to coal can be feasible on the scale required. For instance, one reason for the building of the Sanxia Dam is to provide the hydroelectric power equivalent of eighteen nuclear power stations or 100 million metric tons of coal, once thought to be 11 per cent of China's energy needs but now looking like a much smaller proportion given the increased levels of energy use as the economy rapidly expands. Demand is such that energy blackouts have occurred for the last three years, including a 25,000 MW deficit in summer 2005 at peak consumption time (partly due to the now ubiquitous air conditioning equipment).

Growing car ownership is another factor in energy use. Beijing municipality reached car ownership levels by 2003 that were not expected until 2010. Across the country, there are only twenty-two cars per thousand people at present, but the pace of change is such that this figure is expected to rise to 363 by 2050 (com-pared with 500 currently and 555 by 2050 in the US). If petrol remains the main fuel (and this may have to change) where will the oil required come from? China does have major oil reserves and the search for new oil resources continues apace, in Xinjiang for example, or offshore in China's territorial waters. But demand is expected to grow at 8 per cent per annum for the foreseeable future, so China will remain reliant on imports for at least half its oil consumption. Already, at the global level, we saw in early 2006 an increase in oil prices partly because of China's entry to the oil market as a major consumer. China is also operating inter-nationally to secure oil supplies for the foreseeable future, including the following recent activities (Hu, 2006): the signing by Sinopec of a US$300 million deal to develop a natural gas field in Saudi Arabia, a US$70 billion deal struck with Iran to buy 250 million metric tons of natural gas over the next thirty years, the buy-out by CNPC of the Iranian subsidiary of Sheer Energy of Canada for US$121 million, giving the company 49 per cent of the Masjed Soleyman oilfield, and of the Canadian-owned PetroKazakhstan for US$4 billion, visits by President Hu to Indonesia, Brunei, the Philippines and parts of Africa mainly to secure energy supplies, a US$6 billion loan provided to Russia for similar reasons and a US$600 million agreement on energy cooperation signed with Uzbekistan in May 2005.

In his visit to China in March 2006, President Putin noted that Russia became China's fifth-largest energy supplier in 2005, exporting more than 8 million metric tons of crude oil to China. CNPC and Transneft, a Russian pipeline transport company, were working together to explore feasibility studies for laying oil and gas pipelines between the two countries. All this international action has significant implications for geopolitics and geostrategy across the Asia Pacific region, as well as for the earth's carrying capacity more generally, and it was interesting that US Congressional opposition meant that one deal that was not struck was for the Chinese oil company CNOOC to buy the US oil company Unocal, which instead was taken over by Chevron in August 2005.

Other environmental questions

The above summarizes some of the main environmental and health issues that China currently faces. But before addressing key features of the policies that the PRC government is promoting in order to deal with these and other such issues, there are several other problems that must be briefly mentioned, namely floods and illegal logging, melting glaciers, the train on the roof of the world and environmental protests.

The summer months of July and August are when floods on the Yangtze are most likely to take place. One factor in these floods is logging upstream and, as a result, the authorities banned logging of old forests in Yunnan and Sichuan provinces. This law is difficult to enforce but it seems to be having some success within these provinces within China. The problem now, however, is that a flourishing trade in illegal logging in Burma and to a lesser extent eastern Papua in Indonesia has emerged to fill the gap. Exposed in Burma by the charity Global Witness and in Indonesia by the London- and Washington-based Environmental Investigation Agency with its Indonesian partner Telapak, the trade threatens huge areas of remarkable biodiversity. In the Kachin area of Burma for example, where the bulk of the logging takes place, there are ninety-one animal species and 365 bird species under threat. China has now signed an agreement with the Burmese government to tackle this trade, and the Indonesian authorities too have promised to prioritize curbing this activity.

Another potential cause of flooding that has only recently been recognized is the glacial melt on the Qinghai–Tibet plateau, the 'roof of the world'. Reported in China in May 2006, this seemed to add to previous information available in Western media as of September 2004. It seems that glaciers are now shrinking by 7 per cent per annum, with outcomes including flooding of rivers and the turning of tundra into deserts, adding to the likelihood of dust and drought in affected areas. Average temperatures have risen by 0.9°C on the plateau, contributing to the glacial and tundra melts. Perhaps there has been more attention paid to this area because of the new train line constructed to Lhasa across the plateau from Golmud in Qinghai Province. As noted elsewhere:

One of the most sensitive aspects was the plateau region of permafrost, some 500km of which the railway was scheduled to cross. Scientists conducted many experiments to find how the railway might affect the fragile ecology and also how this might be mitigated. They originally worked on the assumption that global warming would produce a temperature rise of 1°C by the middle of the 21st Century. But, other predictions suggested a rise of more than double that amount, bringing greater pressure to bear on the design and construction of the railway. As a result, special aqueducts were built in some areas to raise the tracks off the surface, and experiments were conducted on building up soil layers that could insulate the ground from heat caused by passing trains.

(Murray and Cook, 2004, p. 132)

It remains to be seen whether such innovative measures mitigate sufficiently the impact of the line itself in what is an even more vulnerable environment than was previously thought owing to this new thawing mentioned above.

The last issue with which I wish to deal before turning to the crucial policy dimension is that of protests. In recent years protests across China are on the increase, fuelled by closure of state-owned enterprises and consequent unemployment, protests over increased 'privatization' of vital services, poverty and other causes. A figure of 50,000 environmental pollution protests was officially recognized for 2005 with probably the largest of these being in Xinjiang Province in July. Fifteen thousand demonstrators seeking to close a local pharmaceutical factory clashed violently with police, as did other protesters opposed to a new power plant being built near Dongzhou village in Guangdong Province in December. Here, local residents stated that they had not been compensated for loss of earnings and land nor for future poor air and water quality. It is these events as well as the sheer scale of the many environmental problems of the type noted above that seem to be leading the authorities to take environmental issues more and more seriously. A hotline has been established for people across the country to record their environmental concerns, similar to the process of 'environmental whistle blowing' that I considered essential if a rosy environmental future might be achieved (Murray and Cook, 2002, p. 212). The hotline recorded a massive 600,000 pollution complaints in 2006, including 161 'serious' accidents (Watts, 2007).

Partly in the face of such protests, there does seem to be growing official honesty concerning the dire environmental situation. The government website www.china.org.cn, for instance, notes that 'the country is still struggling to come to terms with environmental issues even though the central government claims expenditure in this domain has grown by 15 per cent every year', and 'imagine a Chinese person stuffing trash into his mother's pockets. Unthinkable, and yet a newly released report by the Yangtze River Water Resources Commission shows water pollution has worsened over the last ten years as billions of tons of waste continue to be dumped into China's "mother river".' Similarly, SEPA announced in April 2006 that the Tenth Five-Year Plan 2000–2005 failed to meet 40 per cent of its environmental targets, as reported in *China Daily* or *China Development Brief* for example, with emissions of sulphur dioxide rising by 27 per cent instead of being cut by 10 per cent. The new plan for 2006–2010 aims to cut energy consumption per unit of GDP by 20 per cent, reduce total discharge of pollutants by 10 per cent, and increase forest cover by 20 per cent. But it is now admitted that, to meet such targets, they will need to be supported by 'the sustained political will' of China's leaders. Certainly, Premier Wen, cited previously, would seem to be serious about tackling these issues, and the rising star in SEPA is Pan Yue, a deputy director who has been outspoken in promoting the environmental protection agenda.

Policy dimensions

Premier Wen Jiabao himself has gone on record as citing Confucius, who said 'facing humiliation borders on bravery', noting that 'the frankness to look at and talk about our problems is a good way to begin solving them'. At the top level of government therefore, and despite China's need to have a growing economy to soak up the ever-rising numbers in the workforce, especially the labour surplus emanating from rural areas, there does now seem to be the will to redress the economy–environment imbalance in which the latter has usually come a poor second to the former. Increased use of Environmental Appraisal, better and more honest information, further development of a 'Green GDP' index, more 'teeth' for SEPA and more power for local environmental watchdogs are some of the measures that will be employed to reduce the many problems of the type outlined in this chapter. Premier Wen stated in 2006 that 'from this year, levels of energy consumption and discharge of pollutants of various regions and major industries should be released to the public every half year to facilitate supervision' (www. chinadaily.com.cn).

So what of the future? I have explored (with Murray) alternative scenarios in the final chapters of *Green China* and *The Greening of China*, noting for example that the 'gloomy' one was more realistic than the 'rosy'. It is indeed difficult to be optimistic when reviewing the vast environmental problems that China faces. And yet the Washington-based Worldwatch Institute in its *State of the World 2006* report, despite noting that two planet Earths would be necessary to sustain China and India at current rates of consumption, argues that these very growth pressures will lead these two countries to leapfrog the West in sustainable energy and agriculture, and the UN China representative Khalid Malik, cited in *China Development Brief*, argues that China's emphasis on *xiaokang* and the 'five balances', one of which includes the balance between economic growth and environment, will also help lead to solutions to these problems. Increased environmental awareness across the country will be a key feature, as will a growing role for environmental NGOs, which are rapidly expanding in number in China, from nine only in 1994 through to 184 student environmental associations alone by 2001 and seventy-three non-student ones by 2002 (Yang, 2005). This is part of the spread of community participation in China, many examples of which are given in Plummer and Taylor (2004).

There are also important roles for the private sector via investment in such areas as recycling, measures to reduce air and water pollution, hybrid cars that use other energy sources as well as petrol, measures to increase energy efficiency and so on. As an example, the British engineering company, Arup, in 2006 signed the joint agreement with Shanghai Industrial Investment Corporation to build China's first 'eco-city' at Dongtan on Chongming Island at the mouth of the Yangtze delta. The plan is to build the first phase for 50,000 people by the time of Shanghai Expo in 2010, with ten times that number of people as the eventual long-term target, by 2040. Another four such cities are also planned, but their locations have not yet been revealed. These eco-cities are meant to be self-sufficient in energy, water and most food products, with the aim of zero emissions of greenhouse gases from transport and an emphasis on ecological harmony. Dongtan alone will cost more than the budget for the Beijing Olympics.

Carter and Mol (2006) suggest that key areas of future research will include a focus on the role of China at the global level, increased political liberalization and stronger civil society, greater environmental capacity building and 'dealing with the large inequalities (and related tensions) with respect to economic opportunities, social welfare, environmental threats and quality of life' (2006, p. 342). Health and welfare will be an important aspect of quality of life. The interweave of health/environment/economy is complex; as the economy develops old health problems can be overcome but as shown above there is a resurgence of some of these, while the country is also becoming vulnerable to new health threats. China will have to operate effectively at and between local, national and international levels if these and similar threats can be resolved. It is fervently to be hoped that that this will indeed turn out to be the case, allowing China's environment, health and quality of life to improve into the next decades of the twenty-first century.

References

Carter, N.T. and Mol, A.P.J. (2006) 'China and the Environment: Domestic and Transnational Dynamics of a Future Hegemony,' *Environmental Politics*, 15 (2), 330–344.

Chen, X.G., Li, X.M., Stanton, B., Fang, X.Y., Lin, D.H., Cole, M., Liu, H.J. and Yang, H.M. (2004) 'Cigarette Smoking among Rural-to-Urban Migrants in Beijing, China,' *Preventive Medicine*, 39 (4), 666–673.

Cook, I.G. (2006) 'Beijing as an "Internationalized Metropolis",' in F. Wu (ed.), *Globalization and the Chinese City*, London: Routledge, 63–84.

Cook, I.G. (2007) 'Beijing 2008,' in J.R. Gold and M.M. Gold (eds), *Olympic Cities: City Agendas, Planning and the World's Games, 1896–2012*, London: E. & F.N. Spon/Routledge, 286–297.

Cook, I.G. and Dummer, T.J.B. (2004) 'Changing Health in China: Re-evaluating the Epidemiological Transition Model,' *Health Policy*, 67, 329–343.

Cook, I.G. and Dummer, T.J.B. (2007) 'Spatial and Social Marginalization of Health in China: The Impact of Globalization,' in H.X. Zhang, B. Wu and R. Sanders (eds), *Marginalization in China: Perspectives on Transition and Globalization*, Aldershot: Ashgate, 215–237.

Cook, I.G. and Powell, J.P. (eds) (2007a) *New Perspectives on Aging in China*, New York: Nova Science Publishers.

Cook, I.G. and Powell, J.P. (2007b) 'Ageing Urban Society: Discourse and Policy,' in F. Wu (ed.), *China's Emerging Cities*, London: Routledge.

Dickson, G. and Schofield, G. (2005) 'Globalization and Globosity: The Impact of the 2008 Beijing Olympics on China,' *International Journal of Sport Management and Marketing*, 1, 169–179.

Donald, S.H. and Benewick, R. (2005) *The State of China Atlas*, second edition, London: University of California Press.

Dummer, T.J.B. and Cook, I.G. (2007), 'Exploring China's Rural Health Crisis: Processes and Policy Implications,' *Health Policy*, in press.

He, N., Detels, R., Chen, Z., Jiang, Q.W., Zhu, J.D., Dai, Y.Q., Wu, M., Zhong, X., Fu, C.W., Gui, D.X. (2006) 'Sexual Behavior among Employed Male Rural Migrants in Shanghai, China,' *Aids Education and Prevention*, 18 (2), 176–186.

Hinton, I. (2007) 'China's Green Pledges are as Deep as a Coat of Paint,' *The Guardian*, 20 February.

Hong, Y., Stanton, B., Li, X.M., Yang, H.M., Lin, D.H., Fang, X.Y., Wang, J., Mao, R. (2006) 'Rural-to-Urban Migrants and the HIV Epidemic in China,' *Aids And Behavior*, 10 (4), 421–430.

Hu, Xiaobo (2006) 'World Affairs: China,' *Britannica Book of the Year: Events of 2005*, Chicago: Encyclopaedia Britannica, 379–382.

Lin, D.H., Li, X.M., Yang, H.M., Fang, X.Y., Stanton, B., Chen, X.G., Abbey, A., Liu, H.J. (2005) 'Alcohol Intoxication and Sexual Risk Behaviors among Rural-to-Urban Migrants in China,' *Drug And Alcohol Dependence*, 79 (1), 103–112.

Liu, B., Peto, R., Chen, Z., Boreham, G., Wu, Y., Li, J. (1998) 'Retrospective Proportional Mortality Study of One Million Deaths,' *British Medical Journal*, 317, 1141–1142.

Murray, G. and Cook, I.G. (2002) *Greening China: Seeking Ecological Alternatives*, London: Routledge.

Murray, G. and Cook, I.G. (2004) *The Greening of China*, Beijing: China Intercontinental Press.

National Bureau of Statistics of China (2006) *China Statistical Yearbook 2005*, Beijing: National Bureau of Statistics.

Plummer, J. and Taylor, J.G. (eds) (2004) *Community Participation in China: Issues and Processes for Capacity Building*, London: Earthscan.

Ren, T. (2004) 'Minor Setback for Poultry Production,' *Beijing Review*, 19 February, 19–23.

Walker, M. (2006) 'A Nation Struggling to Catch its Breath,' *Newscientist*, 190 (2549), 8–9.

Watts, J. (2005) 'Satellite Data Reveals Beijing as Air Pollution Capital of World,' *The Guardian*, 31 October.

Watts, J. (2006) 'HIV Epidemic Less Severe than Feared,' *The Guardian*, 26 January.

Watts, J. (2007) ' Environmental Damage Hit New Heights in 2006,' *The Guardian*, 12 January.

Williams, C. (2005) 'A Land Turned to Dust,' *Newscientist*, 189 (2502), 38–41.

Yang, G. (2005) 'Environmental NGOs and Institutional Dynamics in China,' *China Quarterly*, 181, 47–66.

4 Challenge, governance reform and disharmony in rural society

John Q. Tian

Introduction

The key milestone of China's deepening integration into the global economy was its admission to the World Trade Organization (WTO) at the end of 2001. This event was highly controversial at the time and sparked a fierce debate over the potential impact on the Chinese economy and how China could best cope with the challenges as well as the opportunities. Of particular concern were China's fragile agricultural sector and farmers' welfare. It was feared that, as part of China's WTO commitments, substantial tariff reductions and minimum access opportunities under the tariff-rate quota (TRQ) system and the weakening of other mechanisms of state control and support would bring surging imports of cheap agricultural products, further undermining the sluggish income growth of the Chinese farmers. Many were worried that a sharp fall in farmers' income and sweeping structural changes in the agricultural sector would only exacerbate China's agrarian crisis. These concerns have accentuated the urgency for the Chinese government to revamp its policy towards agriculture and to restructure rural institutions of governance that impose heavy burdens on Chinese farmers and undercut China's only limited support for agriculture.

This chapter examines how rural China has fared more than five years after its WTO entry and the impact of China's deepening integration into the global economy on its rural economy and society. The focus will be on the far-reaching consequences of policy reforms and institutional changes at the local level. Although my initial assessment of China's WTO entry has been largely positive and many of the much feared disruptions have been either absent or minimal, it is important not to ignore many of the existing and new challenges facing the Chinese countryside. While farmers' financial burdens have been alleviated somewhat as a result of the tax-for-fee reforms, abolition of agricultural taxes and initiation of government subsidies, new disputes and even violent clashes over land rights and compensation are on the rise. In addition, the widening income disparities and multifarious inequalities between urban and rural residents in terms of access to the provision of public goods and services like education, health care and employment opportunities and equitable pay continue to pose challenges for the government and could threaten efforts to build a harmonious society in rural China.

I will first review briefly China's WTO commitments regarding agriculture and evaluate how China has fared in the years since WTO entry; then I will look at the challenges posed by further integration into the global economy on rural China and the corresponding policy reforms and institutional changes to cope with these challenges. Furthermore, I will evaluate the impact of these changes and reforms on rural institutions of governance, especially the deepening budget crisis at the local level. Finally, I will analyse the serious consequences of a looming local governance crisis for rural communities. My focus is on the provision of public goods and services, especially the dire situation of rural education and health care provision, and the signs of growing instability in rural society. I will conclude the chapter by examining the long-term implications for China's efforts to achieve harmony and sustainable growth in its rural areas.

WTO and rural China's integration into the global economy

Of all the promises China made in its agreement to join the WTO, its agricultural commitments on tariff reduction and minimum access opportunities under a tariff-rate quota system were the most contentious at the time. They included China's agreement to reduce the average statutory tariff rate for agricultural products from 22.5 per cent to 17.5 per cent by January 2004. By 2005, it was further lowered to 15.35 per cent. For US priority agricultural products, the tariff rate was reduced from 31 per cent to 14 per cent. China also committed itself to make changes regarding non-tariff barriers and agreed to replace its import quota and licensing system with a TRQ system. The introduction of such a system brings the quota tariff rate for major agricultural commodities, such as wheat, corn, rice and cotton, down to an extremely low tariff rate of 1 per cent for a substantial fixed quantity of imports and to no more than 10 per cent for partially processed grain products (X. Wang, 2002, pp. 87–88; Lardy, 2002, pp. 75–79). In addition to its very limited 'green box' supports, China agreed to limit its domestic agricultural support subsidies ('amber box') to 8.5 per cent –between the levels for developed countries (10 per cent) and developing countries (5 per cent) (Lardy, 2002, pp. 92, 156–157). Furthermore, China agreed to eliminate the monopoly of state trading companies over priority agricultural commodity trade such as grains, cotton and soybean oil, which could imply the ending (or at least weakening) of the effectiveness of the government's agricultural policies, including pricing, marketing and distribution (Schmidhuber, 2001, pp. 21–51). Finally, China agreed to eliminate subsidies for agricultural export. This commitment far exceeded those made by other WTO members (Lardy, 2002, p. 92; Gilmour and Brink, 2001, p. 150; Ma and Lan, 2002).

It was worried that China's commitment to such sweeping changes would make China one of the world's most open countries for food imports. Surges of cheap imports of agricultural products might exacerbate the ongoing agrarian crisis because they would further depress farmers' income growth at a time when it was already on a continuous decline from 13.1 per cent in 1996 to only 2.1 per cent in 2000. Slow income growth for farmers has led to widening income disparities between rural and urban residents (Tian, 2001; Sanders *et al.*, 2007).

According to the former director of the State Statistics Bureau, Qiu Xiaohua, the real ratio of urban–rural income disparities in 2001 was about 6:1.[1]

More importantly, it was feared that WTO entry would create severe employment pressures on China's agricultural sector given the number of people still employed there. At the time, it was estimated that more than half of the roughly 312.6 million people still employed in agriculture were redundant (J. Wang, 2002; Pan, 2001, pp. 40–41).[2] This large amount of surplus labour has already fuelled a massive flow of migrant workers estimated currently to be between 120 million and 200 million (State Council, 2006). With the ability of TVEs to absorb new employment declining, many feared that it would be difficult to find alternative employment opportunities for the displaced farmers (Park, 2001), especially at a time of surging urban unemployment and increasing labour unrest in a number of Chinese cities (Eckholm, 2001). Although employment pressures have been reduced somewhat recently by labour shortages in various parts of China, especially the Pearl River Delta, many regard this as a temporary phenomenon that results from a combination of harsh working conditions, stagnant wages for migrant workers and more opportunities near home and in other parts of the country.

However, overall, concerns over the potentially harmful effect of WTO entry on Chinese agriculture have eased greatly today. The impact on Chinese agriculture has so far been moderate. For the first two years after its WTO accession, China imported only relatively small amounts of grain, much less than its quota for the first two years. Indeed, China even incurred a surplus of US$3.88 billion and US$2.5 billion in overall agricultural trade in 2002 and 2003. Although China incurred deficits in 2004, 2005, 2006 and the first quarter of 2007, the deficits have not been large.

In addition, the downward spiral of farmers' income growth was reversed after 2000 thanks to a series of government policies to boost farmers' incomes. These policies included a gradual phasing out of the agricultural tax, programmes to cut the cost of electricity for rural residents, a campaign 'to help migrant workers claim back wages, assistance for the education of migrant workers' children, and a potentially substantial programme to provide welfare for rural residents who have followed the government's birth-control programmes' (D.L. Yang, 2005, p. 21). By January 2005, about 33.1 billion yuan, nearly 98.4 per cent of the arrears owed to migrant workers before 2003 were paid (Xinhuanet, 2005a). Besides, the government began to provide direct subsidies to farmers for grain production. In 2004 the amount was 11.6 billion yuan and it was increased to 14.2 billion in 2006. In addition, in 2004 the central government provided 2.85 billion yuan to subsidize the use of improved seeds. This was increased to 4.7 billion in 2006. Also, in 2004 the government provided another 70 million yuan in subsidies for the purchase of farm equipment. The amount was increased to 600 million in 2006 (CCTV, 2007). Together with a booming economy, recovering agricultural prices and increasing subsidies to farmers, these pro-rural policies have led to the fastest income growth for farmers since 1997. In 2004 farmers' income grew by 6.8 per cent and the momentum has continued ever since. But it is not yet time for euphoria. In 2005, rural income growth dipped to 6.2 percent. While rural income grew by 7.4 percent in 2006, urban income grew even faster at 10.4 percent (Xinhuanet 2007a). As a result, the rural–urban income gap continues to widen.

With rising production costs for farming work, it is not clear how to sustain continuous growth of farmers' income beyond the short-term policy stimuli, especially once the impact of the cancellation of agricultural taxes has tapered off.

Challenges of global integration and policy reforms

Although many of the dire predictions have not materialized, the long-term consequences of rural China's deepening integration into the global economy may lie in a series of government policy responses to tackle the agrarian crises and to restructure local institutions of governance. Even before China's WTO accession, state–peasant relations were already strained. The old problems of excessive taxation, illicit fees, charges and fines caused widespread discontent and growing instability in rural areas (Bernstein and Lu, 2003; Far Eastern Economic Review, 2001). From 1996 to 1997, approximately 380,000 peasants took part in various protests. During the first half of 1998, according to Jonathan Unger's study, a total of 3,200 incidents of collective action occurred in rural China and 7,400 casualties were officially reported, including more than 1,200 local officials and police wounded (Unger 2002, 213; O'Brien 2002, 141). In 2002, there were more than 37,500 cases of public protests in rural areas involving more than 12 million people (Cheng Ming, 2003). China's WTO entry only heightened the urgency for the government to restructure institutions of local governance that imposed heavy financial burdens on farmers and undercut China's only limited support for agriculture.

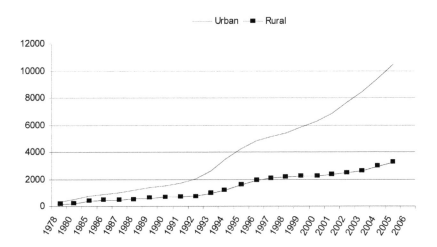

Figure 4.1 Urban and rural net income, 1978–2006 (yuan). Source: *China Statistical Yearbook* (2006, p. 347).

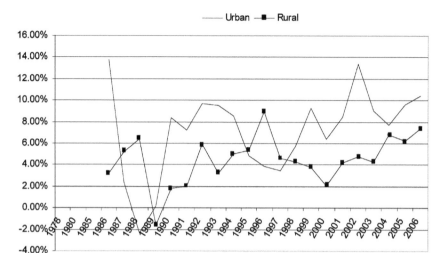

Figure 4.2   Urban and rural net income growth (%). Source: *China Statistical Yearbook* (2006, p. 347).

Ever since the 1990s, the government has held a series of national conferences on agriculture and issued numerous decrees instructing local governments to reduce farmers' burdens, with dismal results. This failure to reverse the deteriorating situation regarding farmers' burdens has raised serious doubts about the effectiveness of central government policies. To tackle this potentially explosive situation and the challenges posed by China's WTO accession, the central government began to adopt and expand local initiatives to reform the institutions of governance at the local level. Politically, the central government has promoted village elections hoping to increase the transparency of village government and curb corruption by local officials. Although it is too early to draw definitive conclusions about the merits and problems of village elections, tentative evidence suggests they have been reasonably effective. For example, Oi and Rozelle (2000) found that, even before WTO entry, some villages have implemented the 'ten opens' demand for publicly posted detailed accounting of village expenditures; in others, the *tiliu* amounts (an elastic 'deduction' that households had to pay for using land and other facilities belonging to the collective) are now openly posted. To the extent that this is true and if these practices can be expanded, they may have the potential to improve the tenuous relations between local governments and peasants, transforming local institutions of governance and promoting rural stability (Oi and Rozelle, 2000).[3]

But the reform with farthest-reaching consequences is the tax-for-fee reform. Initially started in Anhui province in the early 1990s and later extended across the country, tax-for-fee reform (*shuifei gaige*) became especially important in the light of China's WTO accession and of the concerns over its impact on the already stagnant peasant incomes. As mentioned earlier, China's agricultural subsidies at the time of the WTO entry were very low; if one takes account of the various taxes, fees and charges that farmers had to bear, real farm subsidies in China were negative. Given the potential challenges of cheap imports, it was urgent that farmers' burdens be reduced. But the government had tried to do this for years with little success.

Hailed as a third revolution (after land reform and the household responsibility system), tax-for-fee reform, in essence, aimed to replace various taxes, fees and charges with a simplified tax system. Initially only two taxes remained after the reform: a 7 per cent agricultural tax (or an equivalent tax on specialty agricultural products) and an agricultural tax plus (*nongye shui fujia*) which was set at no more than 20 per cent of the agricultural tax. With the two combined, the overall tax fell to about 8.4 per cent. Slaughter taxes, 'expenses' (*tongchou*) imposed and used by local governments, and rural education fees (funding for rural education taken over by higher levels of government) were abolished. Construction of water control projects, bridges, roads and other public projects were to be decided by villages' congresses on a case-by-case basis. *Tiliu* would be collected as the agricultural tax together with no more than 20 percent of the prior agricultural tax. This was to be used to maintain the continuous functioning of the village government and to pay for those rural residents without other forms of support (*wubaohu*). With the expansion of this reform across the country and with various schemes to cut agricultural taxes and abolish taxes on special agricultural products (*nongye techan shui* excluding taxes on tobacco) later, farmers' financial burdens were reduced drastically in many regions across the country (People's Daily, 2004).

With pressures building up to defuse the agrarian crisis following China's WTO entry, the tax-for-fee reform soon built up a momentum of its own. Recognizing the seriousness of the agrarian crisis, Premier Wen Jiabao declared in 2004 at the National People's Congress (NPC) that China would reduce agricultural taxes one percentage point every year with the ultimate aim of abolishing them altogether within five years. But a year later at the 2005 NPC annual meeting, Wen proposed a complete abolition of agricultural taxes in 2006 (Qiao, 2005, pp. 12–14). In addition to the cancellation of agricultural taxes, as I mentioned above, the government also began providing direct subsidies to farmers for grain production, the use of improved seeds and the purchase of farm equipment in major grain-producing areas.

Policy reforms and local governance crisis

Intended to stabilize rural areas, village elections, tax-for-fee reforms and the eventual abolition of agricultural taxes have transformed the local institutions of governance. While these reforms have drastically reduced farmers' burdens, they have also precipitated severe budget crises at the local level that threaten the continuous functioning of many local governments, especially in poor agricultural regions. Since the late 1990s the total accumulated debt at the township level across the country was estimated to be somewhere between 200 billion and 400 billion yuan, an average of more than 4 million yuan for each township (Development

Research Centre, 2002; Lian, 2002; Liu, 2002; Zhu and Ye, 2005). Various reports have estimated that the combined government debt at the township and village levels could be as high as 500 billion yuan and at the county and township levels as high as 1,000 billion yuan, far beyond the 400 billion yuan acknowledged by the Ministry of Finance (Nongbo Wang, 2004a; Economic Reference News, 2005; Chinese Economic Weekly, 2006a). As a result, many township and village governments do not even have funds to pay their employees and teachers.

For many years, scholars and the central government have blamed local governments for the problems in the countryside and have argued for strengthening the capacity of the state to enhance its ability to extract more financial resources (L.C. Li, 2007). Neglected is the spending end of the equation, especially the 'downward trend of dividing expenditure responsibilities among levels of government' (Lee, 2000, p. 1022). Through the 1994 tax assignment reform and the 1996 reform of 'off-budget' revenues, 'central government had augmented its tax base and modified the rules of the game in order to raise the central share of national budgetary revenues, and at the same time transferred expenditure responsibility downwards to lower-level governments' (*'shouru yu zeren weiyi'xianxiang*) (Lee, 2000, p. 1021).

As the central government transfers more and more of its obligations to local governments, including expenditures on education, health, family planning, pension and social welfare funds, price subsidies and fixed capital investment, local budgets – especially those in the poor agrarian regions – become increasingly squeezed between the 'centralization of fiscal revenues and the simultaneous decentralization of expenditure responsibilities' (*caiquan shangshou, shiquan xiayi*) (Lee, 2000, p. 1023). Often, the central government sponsors various programmes without matching funds or without enough funds and therefore requiring matching funds from local governments. In most cases, these unfunded mandates or insufficiently funded projects could only translate into various fees and charges on farmers.

Thus, the recurrent agrarian crises in China can be traced to an imbalance between resource extraction and obligations of service deliveries (*caiquan yu shiquan de bu tongyi*) (Lee, 2000, pp. 1009, 1023; Cao, 2000). For example, although overstaffing of local bureaucracies does exist, the largest item in local budget outlays is education, which, on average, constitutes about half of local budgets. In many of the poor interior regions, it is somewhere between 70 and 80 per cent of local budgets (South Farmers' News, 2002). In a township in Anhui province, it is as high as 93.1 per cent (Zhao, 2001, p. 50; Zhu, 2001, pp. 12–16). Part of the education expenses comes from local obligations to implement central government-sponsored programmes promoting nine-year compulsory education (*pujiu dabiao*). Many counties have fallen deep in debt. Although the central government promulgated a law on compulsory education in 1986 and another law on education in 1995, its share of expenditures on compulsory education by 2002 was only about 2 per cent compared with 78 per cent by township governments, 9 per cent by county governments and 11 per cent by provincial governments (Economic Reference News, 2002; Nongbo Wang, 2003). Although the central government funding rose to 8 per cent in 2004, it is still far from enough to ease the financial burden felt by local governments (Lu, 2005, p. 29), especially given that its share of total government revenues went up to 54.9 per cent in the same year.

Consequently, cancellation of agricultural taxes and various fees has caused serious budget crises at the local level that have pushed local officials to frantically seek new sources of revenue especially through the sale of land to developers and investors. The land grab without proper compensation to farmers has become the main cause of a new wave of disputes and even violent clashes between local officials and farmers in rural China. Throughout 2005 mass protests and riots were frequently reported. In mid-December 2005, thousands of farmers in Shanwei, Guangdong, protested and clashed with police over disputes on land compensation and several villagers were shot dead (French, 2005; Kahn, 2005). On 15 January 2006 another major violent confrontation between police and peasant protestors over a land dispute occurred in Zhongshan, Guangdong, in which more than thirty villagers were reportedly wounded by police (World Journal, 2006; French, 2006a).

The governance crisis at the local level has, in turn, led to pressures to restructure local governments in order to reduce the number of employees. Since 1998, more than 7,400 townships have been either eliminated or merged. In 2005 alone, more than 1,600 townships were eliminated. However, this task is very challenging in the poor agricultural regions in the interior. With limited alternative employment opportunities and continuing pressure from higher-level governments to find employment for college graduates and demobilized military officers, cutting the number of personnel at the township and county levels turns out to be much more difficult than reducing the number of administrative units. Between 2000 and 2003 the central government decided to provide subsidies as an incentive to local governments based on the number of townships reduced and personnel cut. For each township eliminated, the subsidy was 400,000 yuan. For each person got rid of, it was 3,000 yuan (Economic Daily, 2005).

But the focus on the reduction of administrative personnel diverts attention away from pending crises in other important areas, especially in the provision of public goods and services. On account of years of neglect and lack of funding, rural infrastructure such as irrigation, flood control, education and the public health system has deteriorated greatly. For example, according to a survey of 129 townships in Hunan province, 89 per cent suffer from serious debt problems. Strapped with debt burdens, 74 per cent of them rarely provide assistance to the rural poor and needy. Fifteen per cent have never provided any help. Furthermore, 68 per cent of these townships have rarely invested in basic infrastructural projects like country roads and water control systems. Nine per cent have never done so (Chen, 2006). The seriousness of the decay of rural infrastructure is partly reflected in cycles of disastrous floods, ongoing severe drought in most parts of China, overcrowded rural schools and outbursts of public health crises such as AIDS and avian flu. The deepening budget crisis at the local level and the low morale of officials caught in the restructuring of the local administrations only exacerbate the situation.

Rural education and inequality

Given the cancellation of rural education fees and other ad hoc charges and the worsening township government budget crises, tax-for-fee reform and subsequent abolition of agricultural taxes have made the shortage of funding for rural education even worse. Public funding for compulsory education in rural areas as a share of total educational expenditure declined continuously from 22.98 per cent in 2000 to 19.75 per cent in 2001 and then to 18.4 per cent in 2002 (D.P. Yang, 2005, pp. 20–21). What is worse, upper levels of government have often shed responsibility for rural education to lower levels of government at the same time. For example, according to government regulation, funding for the repair of unsafe classrooms in elementary and junior high schools is mainly the responsibility of the provincial level of governments. But according to a government audit of eight provinces, of the 19 billion yuan spent on repairing unsafe classrooms, the central government's share is 25 per cent, provincial governments' 22 per cent, municipal governments' only 4.5 per cent and county governments' 17 per cent. In contrast, the share by township and village governments and funds raised by schools themselves constitute 31.5 per cent (Chinese Youth Daily, 2006a). As a result of rural tax reforms and the subsequent budget crises at the local level, many rural schools have experienced severe financial difficulties. According to a survey by the Ministry of Education Research Centre cited in D.P. Yang's study, 37.8 per cent of rural schools in the western region do not have enough desks, 22.3 per cent do not have safe classrooms or offices and 32.5 per cent lack sufficient funds for purchasing teaching aids, ink, chalk and other supplies (D.P. Yang, 2005, p. 20). According to Kennedy's research in northern Shaanxi, 'the extreme weather takes its toll on the wooden roofs and pane glass (or paper) windows.' Thus, 'the classrooms could get quite cold. . . . and students either freeze in the classroom or skip school altogether to stay warm at home' (Kennedy, 2007, pp. 50–51). Kennedy further points out that teachers' salaries are already low in rural Shaanxi and the elimination of living subsidies as a result of tax reforms only made things worse (Kennedy, 2007, p. 50). Given the 'uncomfortable, even hazardous' conditions, many teachers have left for counties and medium-sized cities where both salaries and living conditions are better (D.P. Yang, 2005, p. 20; Dwnews, 2003). As a result, many rural schools have to hire substitute teachers to teach the students. With extremely low pay and often having to teach multiple classes, these substitute teachers constitute roughly one tenth of all the teachers in rural public schools. The ratio can be even higher in remote and poor mountainous areas (D.P. Yang, 2005, pp. 22–23). All these are likely to lead only to further deterioration in the quality of education in the countryside and further widen the already large educational gap between rural and urban areas.

In response, the State Council decided to put the responsibility for rural compulsory education on county-level governments, especially the payment of teachers' salaries (Xie, 2002; State Council, 2002). But county government budgets are not necessarily any healthier, especially in the poor agrarian regions in the interior. For example, by the end of 2003 the total debt burden for the county-level governments alone in Anhui stood at 18.1 billion yuan with an average of 229 million yuan for each county (Nongbo Wang, 2004b). According to the Ministry of Finance, in 1998 and 1999, 31.8 per cent and 35.5 per cent of county-level government budgets nationwide were in the red (Xue, 2002). By early 2004, about 39.4 per cent of all the counties and county-level cities still faced financial stresses (*caizheng kunnan*) (Zhongxin Wang, 2007). The result is a severe shortage of funding for rural schools.

Thus, the key to the plight of rural education is inadequate funding. In 2004, government budgetary spending on education is only 2.79 per cent of GDP. Although it was increased to 3.38 per cent in 2005, it was still short of the targeted 4 per cent of GDP set for the end of the twentieth century (Figure 4.3).

Government spending on education accounts for roughly 53 per cent of the total educational expenditure and the rest has to be paid by families and private institutions (D.P. Yang, 2005, p. 37). Out of this limited funding for education, in 2002 only 23 per cent went to rural areas where around 60 per cent of the population lives (Peng *et al.*, 2006, p. 50). According to a study, spending on education alone constitutes around 33 per cent of rural household income (Gao and Zhang, 2006). This has been confirmed by another survey of 2,000 rural households conducted by the State Council Development Research Centre in 2005, which finds average expenditure on education was 5,975 yuan, about 30 per cent of total household income in the survey. This makes education the single largest expenditure for these households (Huang, 2005, cited in Yang, 2006, pp. 19–20). With comprehensive fees (including tuition and fees, room and meals) rising up

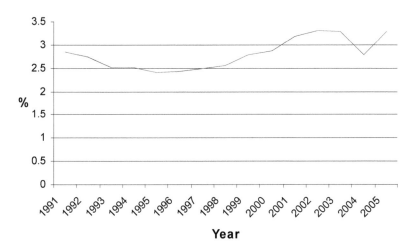

Figure 4.3 Chinese educational expenditure (% of GDP). Source: *Cong renkou da guo mai xiang renli ziyuan qianguo* (Moving from a Country with a large population to a country with strong human resources), *Gaodeng jiaoyu chubanshe* (*Higher Education Press*), 2003, p. 563. Figures after 2000 are taken from materials published by the Ministry of Education (D.P. Yang, 2006, p. 7). *Data for 2005 from Renminwan, July 27, 2005 at http://edu.people. com.cn/GB/1053/3572276.html, retrieved on July 28, 2005.

to more than 10,000 yuan a year, a four-year college education can easily cost an average peasant family more than ten years' income. Education has become a huge burden for many rural families (Xinhuanet, 2005b; Nongbo Wang, 2005; Jin, 2006).

The financial burden as well as low quality of rural education has resulted in a sharp rise in school dropouts in many rural areas, especially in junior high school. According to a study in 2004, in the six provinces or autonomous regions at various economic levels, dropout rates in rural junior high schools varied from 3.66 per cent to 54.05 per cent, far greater than the target set up for compulsory education that requires keeping the dropout rate below 3 per cent (D.P. Yang, 2005, p. 19). According to another study by the Central Party School, in Heishan and Zhangwu counties in Heilongjiang and Kulun in Inner Mongolia, where average rural household income was around 5,000 to 20,000 yuan (which is slightly above the national median level), fewer than 30 per cent of students actually finished junior high school (Pan, 2005).

More importantly, the growing cost of education has become one of the new sources of inequality. With poor quality of rural education, rising dropout rates in rural schools and various obstacles facing children of migrant workers in access to adequate educational opportunities in urban areas, inequality in education leads to different levels of skills and resources that could, in turn, create new barriers for upward social mobility for children from poor rural families.

In response to the growing public outcry for fairness in the educational system and free compulsory education in the countryside, Premier Wen Jiabao announced that, beginning in 2005, all poor students undergoing compulsory education in counties designated by the government for poverty relief would be exempted from book fees and miscellaneous charges and given lodging allowances in boarding schools (*liangmian yibu*). Soon the movement for cost-free compulsory education got a life of its own with several provinces taking the initiative. In January 2005, Hainan cancelled tuition and miscellaneous fees for all the students receiving compulsory education in the province. In September of the same year, Jiangsu province introduced free compulsory education in the poor northern part of the province. In the same month, Suzhou city announced that it would provide free compulsory education for all students from the autumn of 2006. On 19 December 2005, Zhejiang province announced that from the autumn of 2006 it would cancel tuition and miscellaneous fees. Under growing pressure, the State Council decided on 23 December 2005 that from 2006 tuition fees for compulsory education would be eliminated for rural students in the western region and from 2007 this policy would be extended to all students in rural areas across the country. In addition, students from poor families would receive free textbooks and supplementary allowances for their living expenses at boarding schools (D.P. Yang, 2006, pp. 23–25). The funding of these programmes was to be based on a formula according to which the central government would cover 80 per cent of the costs of exemption of miscellaneous fees for the western regions and 60 per cent for the central region in addition to all the costs of free textbooks for the western and central regions. It would provide funding for some eastern regions based on their specific financial conditions. The rest of the funding would be shared by provincial and local governments. So far, more than 50 per cent of this shared funding has been provided by the provincial governments in the central and eastern regions. In many western regions, all the expenses of this shared funding have been provided by the provincial governments (People's Daily, 2007a; Ministry of Education 2007).

Health care and rural poverty

The dire state of local government finance could also have grim consequences for the health care system in China's rural areas, which has already been thrown into turmoil by the dismantling of collective farming and the decline of government support. In 2004 China's total expenditure on health care was 4.75 per cent of GDP, out of which government budgetary spending was only 17 per cent (Figure 4.4).

Government budgetary spending on health care dropped from about 6 per cent of total government expenditure in the 1990s to only 4.5 per cent in 2004 (China Statistical Yearbook, 2006, pp. 57, 281, 882). According to Gao Qiang, Minister of Health, the ratio stayed about the same in 2006 (Gao, 2006).

As Blumenthal and Hsiao point out, the declining government funding has effectively forced medical facilities to privatize their services. With their incomes and other benefits tied to sales of their services and drugs, health providers have begun to charge high fees and overuse high-tech tests for patients (Blumenthal

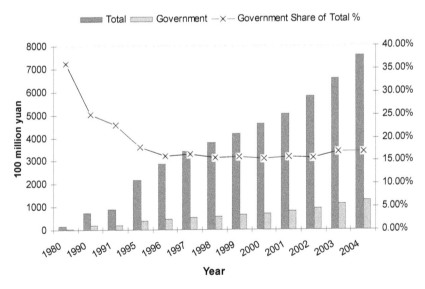

Figure 4.4 Chinese health care expenditure, government budgetary health care spending and share of total/unit (100 million yuan, %). Source: *China Statistical Yearbook* (2006, 882; 2000–2006). Statistics retrieved from Ministry of Health (http://www.moh.gov.cn/open/statistics).

and Hsiao, 2005, pp. 1166–1167). This has effectively pushed up the cost of health care, making it increasingly unaffordable for most Chinese citizens, especially for residents in rural areas. Between 1998 and 2003, the annual average cost of health care for urban and rural residents increased by 13.5 per cent and 11.8 per cent respectively. At the same time, the annual average income growth was only 8.9 per cent and 2.5 per cent. With burgeoning prices and decreasing government support, the proportion of out-of-pocket expenses by individual households increased from 21.2 per cent in 1980 to 58.3 per cent of total health care costs in 2002 (Wu *et al.*, 2006, p. 311).

As central government has transferred more and more responsibilities for providing health care and other public services to provincial and local governments, the costs of these services could only be funded through local taxation or fees. That 'had the immediate effect of favouring wealthy coastal provinces over less wealthy rural provinces and laid the basis for major and growing disparities between investments in urban and rural health care' (Blumenthal and Hsiao, 2005, p. 1166). Whereas urban residents' incomes are triple that of rural residents, they receive 80 per cent of the expenditure on health care. Although most of the population lives in the Chinese countryside, their share of the limited resources spent on health care is only about 20 per cent. As a result, more than 70 per cent of rural residents lack basic health care coverage (People's Daily 2006). As Blumenthal and Hsiao show,

> The rural–urban disparities are reflected in health statistics: In 1999, infant mortality rate was 37 per 1000 live births in rural areas, as compared with 11 percent per 1,000 in urban areas. In 2002, the mortality rate among children under five years of age was 39 per 1000 in rural areas and 14 per 1000 in urban locales. Urban and rural maternal rates in 2002 were 72 and 54, respectively, per 100,000. Perhaps most shocking, in some poor rural areas infant mortality has increased recently, although it has continued to fall in urban centers, and there has been a resurgence of some infectious diseases, such as schistosomiasis, which has nearly controlled in the past.
> (Blumenthal and Hsiao, 2005, p. 1168)

Thus, with the collapse of socialized medicine in the countryside and the staggering cost of health care, farmers have often had to face a difficult choice between health and poverty. According to a survey by Zero Point Poll Company (*Lingdian Diaocha Gongsi*), between October 2004 and October 2005 health care costs took up 21 per cent of rural household income, much higher than the 7.9 per cent and 9 per cent for households in cities and small towns respectively. Health care costs have become the largest item after education in rural household expenditure and one of the important causes of rural poverty. With the average cost of treating a major disease around 7,000 yuan and per capita income only 2,500 yuan, about half of the rural residents in the study said they could not afford treatment when they got sick. Furthermore, roughly 25 per cent of the poor rural households in the survey attributed their poverty to 'having someone sick in the family' (Chinese

Youth Daily, 2006b). According to a study by the Ministry of Health, the number of people forgoing medical treatment when they were ill rose from 36.4 per cent in 1993 to 48.9 per cent in 2003 nationwide. For rural residents in the western region, the rate was 62 per cent in 2003. Nationally, those refusing inpatient care rose to 29.6 per cent. For rural residents, the rate rose from 63.7 per cent in 1998 to 75.4 per cent in 2003. Also, 43.3 per cent of inpatients requested early release from hospital. More than 60 per cent of these resulted from inability to pay the costs. For rural residents, the rate was 75.1 per cent (Gao, 2006; Sukhan *et al.*, 2005, p. 138).

Lack of adequate health care in much of the rural areas 'has sown deep resentment among peasantry while helping to spread infectious diseases like hepatitis and tuberculosis and making the country – and the world – more vulnerable to epidemics like severe acute respiratory syndrome or SARS, and possibly bird flu' (French, 2006b). AIDS patients and HIV positive carriers have reached almost a million. With access contingent on ability to pay, health care expenses resulting from catastrophic illnesses have become one of the leading causes of a resurgence of poverty in rural areas. According to the same study by the Ministry of Health mentioned above, in 2003 more than 33.4 per cent of the rural residents were made destitute or returned to poverty because of serious illnesses (Gao, 2006; Jackson *et al.*, 2005, p. 138). In some poor regions, the rate is even higher. For example, in the western province of Qinghai, in 2002 around 56 per cent of poor rural households fell into poverty or returned to poverty because of major illnesses (Xinghuanet, 2007b).

Faced with growing discontent, the government began experimenting with a new cooperative health care scheme (*xinxing nongcun hezuo yiliao*) in rural areas in 2003. Under the new system, each participating farmer contributes 10 yuan and the central and local government each contribute 10 yuan creating a total of 30 yuan. By 2006, more than 1,451 counties, about 50.7 per cent of all the counties, had experimented with the new cooperative health care scheme in the countryside with more than 410 million rural residents participating, about 47.2 per cent of the total rural population (People's Daily 2007b). In 2007 the central government plans to expand the experiment to cover more than 80 per cent of all the counties in the country. And from 2007 the central government and local government will increase their contributions to 20 yuan each for any participant in the western and central regions. The goal is to set up the basic framework of the new system in 2008, one year earlier than the original plan. Although the central government will supply some help to the eastern region, the funding for the new system in the east region will come mostly from the local governments there.

But the success of this new cooperative medical system in the countryside is far from being assured. In the counties that are experimenting with the new system, only 27 per cent of the funds have been used so far and only 4.2 per cent of rural participants have benefited from the new system (Economic Reference News, 2007). A major complaint is that the reimbursement rate is too low with the maximum around 10,000 yuan or less. Because of the low reimbursement rate, much of the funds do not get used. For example, in Gaizhou, Liaoning province, the total fund accumulated in the second half of 2006 amounted to 20 million yuan. But only 700,000 yuan was reimbursed to rural participants of the plan (Economic Reference News, 2007). In the first twenty-seven counties that experimented with the new cooperative health care scheme in Zhejiang at the end of 2005, only 48 per cent of the participants were satisfied and the participation rate was dropping (Dai *et al.*, 2006). Another complaint by rural residents is that charges at designated hospitals are too high because, with only 40 per cent of their salaries covered by government funding, many township hospitals have to charge higher prices for medicine to make up their income. That is why prices of medicine in rural areas are often higher than in cities (Xu, 2006). In addition, with less than one hospital for 10,000 rural households, there are just too few designated hospitals at the local level. Finally, given lack of funding and the dire conditions of local government finance, many of the local hospitals at the township level are already falling into disrepair. According to a report in the *People's Daily*, 33.6 per cent of the rooms are unsafe at the rural township hospitals in the central and western regions, about 70 per cent of these hospitals need repair and renovation and 60 per cent lack basic medical equipment (People's Daily, 2006). Low pay and poor conditions do not attract well-trained doctors to these places so patients often have to travel to county hospitals for treatment, further increasing financial burdens of rural residents (Blumenthal and Hsiao, 2005, p. 1168).

Governance crisis and disharmony in rural society

More importantly, efforts to restructure power and authority in rural China have precipitated budget crises that threaten the fiscal viability of many local governments, especially those in poor regions. This has, in turn, exposed a deep structural problem of the Chinese political economy in the discrepancy between extraction demands and service obligations. On the one hand, local officials are continuously subjected by the cadre evaluation system to certain performance criteria that requires them to be proactive (Whiting, 2001, pp. 100–118). On the other hand, their ability to live up to these criteria is increasingly restrained by the political and fiscal constraints resulting from recentralization of financial resources and the triple reforms of village elections, tax-for-fee reform and the eventual abolition of agricultural taxes. Consequently, as Prasenjit Duara describes an early period of state building in north China and its impact on the weakening of local authority, 'the symbolic and material rewards of a career in public office were gradually being outweighed by the increasingly onerous nature of the tasks involved' (Duara, 1988, p. 218). Similarly to Duara's account, the plight of many local officials is so unenviable that there are already reports of local officials who choose to relinquish their leadership positions (Nongcun Xinbao, 2002).[4] The vacuum of power and authority caused by local governance crisis may leave the Chinese countryside increasingly unstable as evidenced by the rise of 'incidents of public disturbances' (Zheng, 2007; Xinhua News Agency, 2007). In 2003, 58,000 public protests were reported. In 2004, the number jumped to 74,000. In 2005, the number reached an all-time high of 87,000 (Lum, 2006, pp. 1–2). Furthermore, the scales of the protests are increasing. For example, in November 2004, 100,000 farmers in Sichuan seized Hanyuan County government offices to stop the work of a dam project for days and 10,000 paramilitary troops had to be called in to quell the unrest. A month later tens of thousands of angry people swarmed the central square of Wanzhou, Sichuan, to protest against the beating of a porter by an official (Kahn, 2004). More importantly, unrest can occur quite randomly. For instance, on 19 March 2007, riots erupted over the hike of fares at the bus station in a town in Yongzhou, Hunan province. More than 20,000 people and about 1,700 police were involved. Buses were burned and many people were reported injured (World Journal, 2007).

In addition, increasing instability and weakening of local governance have created ample room for the rise of lineage, religious, cult, gambling (*majiang*) and even criminal organizations (Du, 2007; Liaowang, 2007). Various researches have shown that in many places local governments have been taken over by local bullies (*heie shili*) (Yu, 2003; Zhao, 2003). According to a researcher in Henan province, no more than 15 per cent of village level governments can be regarded as good.[5]

Another disturbing development is the sharp increase of crime rates in the countryside. The rates of violent crimes such as homicide, theft, robbery and rape are all much higher than in urban areas. According to the Vice Minister of Public Security, in the first nine months of 2006 there were 8,031 homicides, 59,000 injury cases and more than 880,000 cases of theft and robbery of crops, livestock and farming tools and materials (Liu 2006). When I returned to visit the villages where I grew up in central China in the autumn of 2006, I was struck by the absence of farm animals. My childhood friends told me that thieves steal farm animals almost as a form of open robbery so that not many people still raise these animals nowadays.[6]

Also, with most young and middle-aged men migrating out of the countryside to search for jobs in cities, many women and children left behind in the villages (*liushou funu yu liushou ertong*) have fallen prey to sex offenders and kidnappers. According to a police station chief in north Jiangsu province, investigation of a rape case in 1999 led to the discovery of more than ninety rape cases in a single village. In a nearby town, around 6 per cent of the women admitted that they had been raped (Chinese Economic Weekly, 2006b). Similar cases have also been reported in other regions (Xing, 2006; Xinhua Daily Newswires, 2006). When I visited a village in Dingzhou, Hebei province, in the autumn of 2006, most of the people I saw were women, children and senior citizens. Most of the houses in the village were surrounded by high walls and thick doors. The cab driver told me that if it was not during daytime, he would not be willing to drive me to the villages from the county just before the corn was harvested because there were so many criminals roaming around in the corn field that he might fall victim to robbery. These reports may be an indication that, in some rural areas, order is gradually yielding to lawlessness (Eckholm, 2002). Given the weakness of local institutions of governance and subsequent instability in rural areas, Luyi county in central Henan province is experimenting with contracting local public security to collective and private security providers to patrol their villages (Song, 2006).

Conclusion

More than five years after its entry into the WTO, Chinese agriculture and farmers have fared better than expected and the many feared disruptions have not occurred, thanks to a combination of a favourable international market situation, various policy measures and institutional changes. Ironically, it could be argued that it has been the very pressure of deepening integration into the global economy that has forced the Chinese government to revamp many of its policies towards agriculture and to restructure rural institutions of governance that impose heavy burdens on Chinese farmers. In 2004 and 2005, the central government twice issued an all-important 'No. 1 Document' (*yi hao wen jian*) that emphasized the importance of increasing food production and farmers' incomes through the strengthening of overall agricultural production capacity, improving infrastructure and the use of science and technology. The 2005 document also required coordinated development between urban and rural areas (*chengxiang tongchou fazhan*).

Although these policies may have helped avert a pending crisis in China's rural areas, many of the challenges facing Chinese agriculture and farmers still remain. First, for a rural household government subsidies of different varieties amount to only a few hundred yuan at best. In most cases they are even less, given the small size of Chinese farms. Albeit helpful, it is truly doubtful if this limited amount can really make a huge difference. There are already debates over whether this money can be better used to fund public projects and improve the provision of public goods and services in rural areas instead of doling it out in small pieces to each household. So far, the central government has not budged because it fears that the fund might be diverted to other illicit uses such as the purchase of new cars, the building of new offices or even funding big feasts for local officials. Also, the stimulating effect of the abolition of agricultural tax and subsidies on farmers' income growth may well turn out to be only temporary. The recent increase in farmers' income has already been threatened by higher prices of production materials like fuel and fertilizer. It is also unrealistic to expect grain prices to remain high as happened in 2004 when a drop in grain production in previous years led to a rebound in price. Indeed, bumper harvests and increased imports in 2004 caused a slight fall in the grain price in 2005 in which farmers' income growth dipped to 6.2 per cent. Although farmers' income growth rebounded to 7.4 per cent in 2006, it was still below the 10.4 per cent of urban income growth. More importantly, to date, it is still not clear how to sustain farmers' income growth once the effect of the cancellation of agricultural tax tapers off. Meanwhile, as an increasingly important source of rural household income, the remittances paid back to rural areas from migrant workers in cities remain low despite long hours and harsh working conditions. Notwithstanding the rhetoric, discrimination against migrant workers remains prevalent (China Today, 2005). Finally, the deteriorating situation in terms of the provision of public goods and services in China's rural areas and the rising costs of education and health care are already eating away some of the recent increases in farmers' income growth. Two recent studies have confirmed a drop in investment in rural infrastructure at the village level (Luo *et al.*, 2006; Sato 2006).

All these may undercut the potential of rural development. Given the limited effectiveness of a series of policies to raise farmers' income and signs of continuing instability in rural areas, the Chinese government launched a new initiative to 'build a socialist new countryside' with the issuing of two more No. 1 Documents at the beginning of 2006 and 2007. The goal of this new policy is to reverse the widening of urban–rural disparities and to fundamentally transform rural China through the development of modern agriculture, increasing farmers' income, improvement of the rural infrastructure and environment, the reconstruction of rural health care and the social welfare system and the cultivation of a new generation of farmers.

This new policy initiative to build a socialist new countryside has already created a momentum that may lead to far-reaching institutional changes. As I have mentioned above, the government has already increased its funding for rural compulsory education and the new cooperative health care system in rural areas. Also, discussions are now under way over how to restructure and increase the presence of financial institutions in rural areas. More importantly, under increasing pressure, twelve provinces, autonomous regions or municipalities have already abolished the dual *hukou* system that separates urban and rural residents and denies rural residents the rights to equal access to employment, education, health care and other social benefits (People's Daily, 2007c).

Although this new policy initiative has been elevated as the government top priority, its success is far from being guaranteed. One of the obstacles is the weakened nature of rural governance. As a large number of young people have migrated to search for work in urban areas, and with financial difficulties at the local level, few capable people are now available or willing to assume leadership positions in rural communities. With the deterioration in the quality of human resources and declining organizational capacity of local governments, it is hard to imagine how to mobilize farmers in rural areas to bring about a transformation on a sufficient scale.

The weakness of local institutions of governance and the lack of initiative from rural communities has led to an increasing sense of dependence. Expecting funding to build the new countryside to come from upper-level governments, farmers tend not to contribute to projects that could serve the interests of their own local communities (C. Li, 2007). This passivity may undercut efforts to transform rural China through the creation of an environment that encourages entrepreneurship, especially from those farmers who have worked in cities as migrant workers and accumulated experiences and vision to set up businesses in their home communities. Lack of initiative, a sense of dependence and the dire situation of rural education, especially for the tens of millions of children left behind in many rural areas as their parents migrate to work in cities, may not bode well for the nurturing of a new generation of farmers who are designated as the key to the success of this new campaign to transform rural China into a new harmonious society.

Notes

1   According to a figure released by the government, the ratio of rural and urban income rose to 1:3.24 in 2003 (People's Daily, 2003). According to a report in *Caijing Magazine* (Finance), the rural–urban income gap increased to 1:3.28 in 2006 (www.aweb. com.cn, 9 March 2007); however, according to Qiu Xiaohua, about 40 per cent of rural residents' income is in kind, and cash income is only about 1,800 yuan a year, or about 150 yuan a month. After deducing costs on agricultural inputs, rural per capita disposable income (PDI) is only about 120 yuan a month; while at the same time urban PDI is about 600 yuan. If we add various urban social welfare benefits, the real urban–rural PDI gap is about 6:1 (see Chinese Youth Daily, 2002). This last figure is confirmed again by the report in *Caijing Magazine* mentioned above.
2   According to one estimate, Chinese agriculture at current technology levels needs a labour force of only 130 million and therefore over 200 million or 60 per cent of the employment in agriculture now is redundant (see Wang, 2002).
3   Also see other articles in this Special Issue: Elections and Democracy in Greater China. *The China Quarterly*, 162 (June 2000).
4   Interviews by author, summer of 2003 and autumn of 2006.
5   Interview by author, 30 September 2006.
6   Interview by author, 2 October 2006.

References

Bernstein, T. and Lu, X. (2003) *Taxation Without Representation in Contemporary Rural China*, Cambridge: Cambridge University Press.
Blumenthal, D. and Hsiao, W. (2005) 'Privatization and Its Discontents – The Evolving Chinese Health Care System,' *The New England Journal of Medicine*, 353 (11) (15 September), 1165–1170.
Cao, J. (2000) *Huanghe bianshang de zhongguo: yi ge xuezhe dui xiangcun shehui de guancha yu shikao* (China by the Yellow River: a scholar's observation and analysis of rural society), Shanghai: Shanghai wenyi chubanshe.
CCTV (2007) *China Focus*, March 12, Online. Available <www.aweb.com.cn> (accessed on 15 March 2007).
Chen, W. (2006) 'Jingti xiangcun zhaiwu yingxiang shehui wendi' (Township and village debts may threaten social stability), *Zhongguo fazhan guancha* (China development review), 7, Online. Available <http://finance.aweb.com.cn/2006/7/7/9170027.htm> (accessed on 7 July 2006).
Cheng Ming (2003) 'Hu Warns: Corruption Pushes People to Revolution,' 306 (April), 9.
China Statistical Yearbook (2006) Beijing: China Statistics Press.
China Today (2005) 'Rural Workers Tell Their Own Stories', May, 58–60.
Chinese Economic Weekly (*Zhongguo Jingji Zhoukan*) (2006a) 'Xiangcun caizheng Kunnan' (Financial difficulties facing township and village governments), Online. Available <http://finance.aweb.com.cn/2006/4/4/6171214.htm> (accessed on 4 April 2006).
Chinese Economic Weekly (*Zhongguo Jingji Zhoukan*) (2006b) '5,000 wan "liushou cunfu" fei zhengchang shengcun diaocha' (An investigation of the abnormal living conditions of the 50 million rural women left behind in the villages), Online. Available <www.people.com.cn> (accessed on 16 October 2006)
Chinese Youth Daily (*Zhongguo qingnian bao*) (2002) 'Chengxiang jumin shouru guoda zhide jingti' (Widening urban–rural income gap calls attention), 2 November, Online. Available <www.aweb.com.cn/2002/11/2/2002112110109. htm> (accessed on 2 November 2002).

Chinese Youth Daily (Zhongguo qingnian bao) (2006a) 'Nongcun shisheng gaobie weifang, gaizao touru xiang jiceng zhuanyi' (Farewell to unsafe classrooms, funding borne mostly by local governments), 28 June, Online. Available <http://edu.aweb.com. cn/2006/6/28/8592148.htm> (accessed on 2 July 2006).

Chinese Youth Daily (Zhongguo qingnian bao) (2006b) 'Jiaoyu chengwei chengxiang jumin zhipin shouyin' (Education becomes major cause of poverty for urban and rural households), 8 February, Online. Available <http://society.people.com.cn/GB/1063/4083129. html> (accessed on 19 February 2006).

Dai, Q., Jie, H. and Yang, S. (2006) 'Xin nonghe jinfang jigong jinli' (Some issues with the new rural cooperative healthcare), *Jingji cankao bao (Economic reference news)*, 29 March, Online. Available <http://finance.people.com.cn/GB/4249322/html> (accessed on 8 June 2006).

Development Research Centre, State Council (2002) 'Xiangzhen caizheng chizi yu Zhaiwu yanjiu baogao' (Research report on township budget deficits and debts), Online. Available <www.aweb.com.cn/2002/11/1/200211182716.htm> (accessed on 1 November 2002).

Du, P. (2007) 'Zhongguo zongjiao fuxing shi haoshi hai shi huaishi' (Is China's religious renaissance good or bad?), *Lianhe Zaobao (United Morning Post)*, Online. Available <www.zaobao.com/yl/y1070209_501.html> (accessed on 9 February 2007).

Duara, P. (1988) *Culture, Power, and the State: Rural North China, 1900–1942*, Stanford, CA: Stanford University Press.

Dwnews (2003) 'Dalu nongcun jiaoshi xindi liushi, duoxuexiao wufa kaike' (Many rural schools stop classes as teachers leave due to low pay), Online. Available <www.chinesenewsnet.com> (accessed on 11 April 2003).

Eckholm, E. (2001) 'Leaner Factories, Fewer Workers Bring More Labour Unrest to China,' *The New York York Times*, Online. Available <www.nytimes.com> (accessed on 19 March 2001).

Eckholm, E. (2002) 'Order Yields to Lawlessness as Maoism Recedes in China', *The New York York Times*, 29 May, Online. Available <www.nytimes.com> (accessed on 29 May 2002).

Economic Daily (Jingji Ribao) (2005) 'Zhongyang caizheng chuzi huanjie xianxiang caizheng kunnan' (Central government budget to help alleviate county and township financial difficulties), Online. Available <http://news.aweb.com.cn/2005/6/8/9201815. htm> (accessed on 8 June 2005).

Economic Reference News (Jingji cankao bao) (2002) 'Nongcun yiwu jiaoyu caiquan yu shiquan bu duicheng' (Compulsory education in rural areas: the imbalance between financial resources and service obligations), Online. Available <www.aweb.com. cn/2002/8/5/200285151937.htm> (accessed on 5 April 2002).

Economic Reference News (Jingji cankao bao) (2005) 'Zhongguo xianxiang zhengfu zhaiwu tupo 1 wangyi, fuzhai jianguan yigai poti' (Chinese government debt at the county and township level reachs 1,000 billion yuan. It's time to tighten supervision and regulation), Online. Available <http://news.aweb.com.cn/2005/3/23/8021189.htm> (accessed on 23 March 2005).

Economic Reference News (Jingji cankao bao) (2007) 'Xingnonghe ruhe rang nongmin gengduo shouhui' (How to make new rural cooperative health care benefit more farmers), 14 February, Online. Available <http://nc.people.com.cn/GB/61154/5398978. html> (accessed on 13 March 2007).

Far Eastern Economic Review (2001) 'Agriculture: how to build a rebellion,' 29 September, Online. Available <www.feer.com> (accessed on 29 September 2001).

French, H. (2005) '20 Reported Killed as Chinese Unrest Escalates,' *The New York Times*, 10 December, Online. Available <www.nytimes.com> (accessed on 10 December).

French, H. (2006a) 'Police in China Battle Villagers in Land Protest,' *The New York Times*, 17 January, Online. Available <www.nytimes.com> (accessed on 17 January).

French, H. (2006b) 'Wealth Grows, but Health Care Withers in China,' *The New York Times*, Online. Available <www.nytimes.com> (accessed on 14 January).

Gao, Q. (2006) 'Liu da yuanyin daozhi laobaixing kanbing nan, kanbing gui' (Six Causes for high cost and low accessibility of health care), *Zhonghua Wang*, 2 February 2006, Online. Available <http://news.china.com/zh_cn/domestic/945/20020219/13105322. html> (accessed on 19 February 2006).

Gao, Y. and Zhang, R. (2006) '1998–2002 wuoguo gaoxiao xueza fei cengzhang 5.34 bei' (Cost of higher education rose 5.34 times), *Xiaokang* (*Comfortable Living Magazine*), 11 July 2006, Online. Available <http://edu.people.com.cn/GB/8216/4580454.html> (accessed on 17 July 2006).

Gilmour, B. and Brink, L. (2001) 'China in the WTO: Implications for International Trade and Policy Making in Agriculture', in OECD, *China's Agriculture in the International Trading System*, Paris: OECD, 71–88.

Huang, H. (2005) 'Luoshi "liangge qushi" de zhongda panduan' (The momentous decision to put the 'two trends' into action), *Liaowang* (*Outlook Weekly*), 3 October 2005.

Jackson, S., Sleigh, A., Li, P. and Liu, X. (2005) 'Health Finance in Rural Henan: Low Premium Insurance Compared to the Out-of-Pocket System', *The China Quarterly*, 181 (1), 137–157.

Jin, S. (2006) 'Bei daxue xuefei tuokua de nongmin jiating' (Rural families bankrupted by college fees), *Shichang bao* (*Market News*), 17 July, Online. Available <http://edu. people.com.cn/GB/4596152.html> (accessed on 17 July 2006).

Kahn, J. (2004) 'China's "Haves" Stir the "Have Nots" to Violence', *The New York Times*, 31 December, Online. Available <www.nytimes.com> (accessed on 31 December 2004).

Kahn, J. (2005) 'Police Fire on Protestors in China, Killing Several', *The New York Times*, 9 December, Online. Available <www.nytimes.com> (accessed on 9 December 2005).

Kennedy, J.J. (2007) 'From the Tax-for-Fee Reform to the Abolition of Agricultural Taxes: The Impact on Township Governments in North-West China,' *The China Quarterly*, 189 (March), 43–59.

Lardy, N. (2002) *Integrating China into the Global Economy*, Washington, DC: Brookings Institution Press.

Lee, P. (2000) 'Into the Trap of Strengthening State Capacity: China's Tax-Assignment Reform', *The China Quarterly*, 164 (December), 1007–1024.

Li, C. (2007) 'Xinnongcun jianshe zhongde caizheng yilai wenti yiren shengsi' (Some thoughts on the sense of dependence in the reconstruction of new rural China), *Xuexi shibao* (*Study Times*), Online. Available <http://nc.people.com.cn/GN/61160/5632219. html> (accessed on 18 April 2007).

Li, L.C. (2007) 'Working for the Peasants? Strategic Interactions and Unintended Consequences in the Chinese Rural Tax Reforms', *The China Journal*, 57 (January), 89–106.

Lian, J. (2002) 'Dalu jiceng zhengfu caizheng xian kunjing' (Local governments' budget crisis in mainland China), *Gongshang shibao* (*Commercial times*) (Taipei), 12 August, Online. Available <www.chinatimes.com> (accessed 12 August 2002).

Liaowang (*Outlook Weekly*) (2007) 'Xibu nongcun chuxian "xinyang liushi", xiejiao liliang kuaisu kuozhang' (The collapse of the belief system in rural North West and the rapid spread of cults), 5 February.

Liu, J. (2006) 'Zhongguo gongan jiguan jiang zhongdian daji nongcun liumang eshili' (Chinese policies will strike at criminals in rural areas), Online. Available <www.people.com.cn> (accessed on 7 November 2006).

Liu, Z. (2002) 'Xiangzhen caizheng chizi yuanyin yu duice' (The cause and policy response to township budget deficits), *Jingji ribao* (*Economic Daily*), 9 July, Online. Available <www.economicdaily.com.cn> (accessed 9 July 2002).

Lu, R. (2005) 'When Will Chinese Children Enjoy Free Compulsory Education?,' *China Today*, 54 (6) (June), 29.

Lum, Thomas (2006) 'Social Unrest in China,' Congressional Research Service, Online. Available <www.fas.org> (accessed on 8 May 2007).

Luo, R., Zhang, L., Huang, J. and Rozelle, S. (2006) 'Elections, Fiscal Reform and Public Goods Provision in Rural China,' paper presented at Beijing Forum 2006: Toward a Harmonious Urban–Rural Relations, 27–29 October, Centre for Chinese Economic Studies, Peking University, Beijing, China, 200–243.

Ministry of Education (2007) 'Press Conference,' Online. Available <www.people.com.cn> (accessed on 27 February 2007).

New York Times (2001) 'Leaner Factories, Few Workers Bring More Labor Unrest in China,' 19 March, Online. Available <www.nytimes.com> (accessed)..

New York Times (2006) 'China Seals Off Villages after Protest Violence,' 16 January, Online. Available <www.nytimes.com> (accessed)..

Nongbo Wang (2003) 'Nongcun jiaoyu: loudou jingji xia de jiandaocha' (Rural education: the scissor situation under a filter economy), Online. Available <www.aweb.com.cn/2003/2/22/2003222105807.htm> (accessed on 22 February 2003).

Nongbo Wang (2004a) 'Xiangzhen jiceng caizheng fuzhai 5000 yi, tizhi gaige hushing rijing poqie' (Local government debt at 500 billion yuan, institutional reform urged), Online. Available <www.aweb.com.cn/2004/4/4/200444103913.htm> (accessed on 4 April 2004).

Nongbo Wang (2004b) 'Guanyu Anhui xianxiang caizheng qingkuang de diaocha' (A survey of county and township finance in Anhui), Online. Available <http://news.aweb.com.cn/2004/7/31/2004731112716.htm> (accessed on 31 June 2004).

Nongbo Wang (2005) 'Nongmin peiyang yige daxuesheng xu 18 nian de shouru' (A four-year college education costs farmer 18 years' income), Online. Available <http://news.aweb.com.cn/2005/12/19/8243750.htm> (accessed on 19 December 2005).

Nongcun Xinbao (*Rural News*) (2002) 'Jiceng diaocha: xiangcun ganbu dui shuifei gaige "sanpan" "sanpa"' (Local survey: township and village officials' 'three hopes and fears'), Online. Available <www.aweb.com.cn/2002/5/26/200252693639.htm> (accessed on 26 May 2002).

O'Brien, K. (2002) 'Collective Action in the Chinese Countryside' (Review Essay), *The China Journal*, 48 (July), 139–154.

Oi, J. and Rozelle S. (2000) 'Elections and Power: the Locus of Decision-Making in the Chinese Villages,' *The China Quarterly*, 162 (June), 513–539. Special Issue: Elections and Democracy in Greater China.

Pan, W. (2001) 'Woguo nongcun shengyu laodongli de zhuangyi qianjing' (Prospect of transferring redundant rural labour in China), *Liaowang* (*Newsweek*), 13 (26 March), 40–41.

Pan, Y. (2005) 'Nongcun yiwu jiaoyu de xianshi kunjing' (Plight of rural compulsory education), *Zhongguo Jingji shibao* (*China Economic Times*), 18 January, Online. Available <http://news.aweb.com.cn/2005/1/18/10404957.htm> (accessed on 16 February 2007).

Park, A. (2001) 'Trade Integration and the Prospects for Rural Enterprise Development in China', in OECD, *China's Agriculture in the International Trading System*, Paris: OECD, 186–196.

Peng, G., Dai, H., Liu, X., Zhu, S. and Feng, X. (2006) 'An Open Letter by Five Veteran Educators Appealing for Fairness in Education,' reprinted in D.P. Yang (2006), 49–57.

People's Daily (2003) 'Dangqian zhongguo de nongcun jingji he nongcun zhengce' (Current Chinese rural economy and policy), 9 February, Online. Available <www.peopledaily.com.cn/GB/jingji/1037/ 2327776.html> (accessed on 9 February 2003).

People's Daily (2004) 'Nianzhong nongcun jingji shuping: Nongmin Shouru jiaoda fudu zengzhang' (End of year comment on rural economy: great income growth of farmers' income), 27 December, Online. Available < www.aweb.com.cn/2004/12/27/8532166.htm> (accessed on 27 December 2004).

People's Daily (2006) 'Shuxie nongcun yiliao' (Injecting blood into rural health care), 22 September, Online. Available <www.aweb.com.cn> (accessed on 22 September 2006).

People's Daily (2007a) 'Nongcun wa shangxue buyong zaijiao qian' (Free compulsory education for rural kids), overseas edition, 2 January.

People's Daily (2007b) 'Xinxing nongcun hezuo yiliao huanjie kanbing gui' (New rural cooperative healthcare system to reduce the cost of health care), Online. Available <http://politics.people.com.cn/GB/1026/5464176.html> (accessed on 13 March 2007).

People's Daily (2007c) 'Zhongguo wenjian tuidong chengxiang hukou tongyi' (China to steadily promote a unitary urban–rural hukou system), 9 April, Online. Available <http://news. aweb. com.cn/2007/4/9/117200704090857120.html> (accessed on 9 April 2007).

Qiao, T. (2005) 'Sharing Economic Fruits with 900 Million Farmers' (Special Report), *China Today*, 54 (5) (May), 12–14.

Sanders, R., Chen, Y. and Cao Y. (2007) 'Marginalisation in the Chinese Countryside: the Question of Rural Poverty,' in Heather Zhang, Bin Wu and Richard Sanders (eds), *Marginalization in China: Perspectives on Transition and Globalization*, Aldershot: Ashgate (forthcoming), 15–34.

Sato, H. (2006) 'Public Goods Provision and Rural Governance,' paper presented at Beijing Forum 2006: Toward a Harmonious Urban–Rural Relations, 27–29 October, Centre for Chinese Economic Studies, Peking University, Beijing, China, 245–270.

Schmidhuber, J. (2001) 'Changes in China's Agricultural Trade Policy Regime: Impacts on Agricultural Production, Consumption, Prices, and Trade,' in OECD, *China's Agriculture in the International Trading System*, Paris: OECD, 21–51.

Song, X. (2006) 'Nongcun zhian chengben qineng zhuanjia gei nongmin?' (Why should farmers bear the cost of rural public safety?), *Nongmin ribao* (*Farmers' Daily*), 6 November, Online. Available <http://nc.people. com.cn/GB/61160/5000180.html> (accessed on 14 March 2007).

South Farmers' News (2002) 'Nongmin zenshou xiancong jianshui rushou' (Tax reduction to boost peasant income), 29 March.

State Council, China (2002) 'Quebao xin nongcun yiwu jiaoyu guangli tizhi jinnian Quanmian yunxing' (To ensure smooth running of the new management system of rural compulsory education), Online. Available <www.aweb.com.cn/2002/5/17/200251783822.htm> (accessed on 17 May 2002).

State Council, China (2006) *A Research Report on China's Migrant Workers*, Beijing: Yanshi Chubanshe (in Chinese).

Tian, Q. (2001) 'China's New Urban–Rural Divide and Pitfalls for the Chinese Economy', *Canadian Journal of Development Studies*, 22 (1), 165–190.

Unger, J. (2002) *The Transformation of Rural China*, Armonk, NY: M.E. Sharpe.

Wang, J. (2002) 'Sannong wenti de xingcheng yuanyin' (The causes of the agrarian crisis), Online. Available <www.aweb.com.cn/2002/9/29/2002929104034.htm> (accessed on 29 September 2002).

Wang, X. (2002) 'The WTO Challenge to Agriculture,' in Ross Garnaut and Ligang Song (eds), *China 2002: WTO Entry and World Recession*, Canberra: The Australian National University, Asia Pacific Press, 81–95.

Whiting, S. (2001) *Power and Wealth in Rural China: The Political Economy of Institutional Change*, Cambridge: Cambridge University Press.

World Journal (Shijie ribao) (2006) 'Violent Clashes over Land Dispute and More than 30 were Wounded,' 15 January, Online. Available <www.worldjournal.com> (accessed on 15 January 2006).

World Journal (Shijie ribao) (2007) 'Yongzhou shijian' (Yongzhou incident), 14 March, Online. Available <www.worldjournal.com> (accessed on 14 March 2007).

Wu, P., Mau, Z. and Liu, J. (2006) 'Zhongguo nongcun yiliao weisheng gaige de licheng yu zhanwang' (The history of reforming the Chinese rural health care system and prospect), in Lei Guang (ed.), *Gaige zhong de nongcun, nongmin he nongye (The State of Rural China: Peasants, Agriculture and Rural Society in the Reform Era)*, Hong Kong: Tidetime Publishing, 310–341.

Xie, Y. (2002) 'Nongcun yiwu jiaoyu: zhongyang qianzhang taiduo' (Rural compulsory education: the central government owes too much), Online. Available <www.aweb.com.cn/2002/12/18/2002121884651.htm> (accessed on 18 December 2002).

Xing, Z. (2006) 'Subei liushou funu diaocha, qiangjian an pinfa fudanzhong' (A report of women left behind in the villages in northern Jiangsu), *Xiandai kuaibao (Modern Daily News)*, 22 November 2006.

Xinhua Daily Newswires (Xinhua Meiri Dianxun) (2006) 'Shuifu jingcheng nan, quefa anquangan: liushou funu 4700 wan' (47 million left-behind women: hard to move with husband and lack of security at home), 8 November, Online. Available <www.people.com.cn> (accessed on 8 November 2006).

Xinhua News Agency (Xinhua She) (2007) 'Buduan gaijin xinfang gongzuo, niuzhuan qunti xing shijian gaofa shitou' (Improve the work on petitions to reverse the rise of public incidents), Online. Available <http://poliitcs.people.com.cn/GB/1026/5534382.html> (accessed on 28 March 2007).

Xinhuanet (2005a) 'Gedi qingqian gongcheng kuan he mingong gongzi shijian biao' (Timetable for paying back arrears of construction projects and back wages for migrant workers), Online. Available <http://news.xinhuanet.com/banyt/2005/01/21/content_2491549.htm> (accessed on 21 January 2005).

Xinhuanet (2005b) 'Jiaoyu fudan: nongmin buke chengshou zhizhong' (Education: too heavy a burden for farmers), Online. Available <http://news.aweb.com.cn/2005/6/22/8123498.htm> (accessed on 5 July 2005).

Xinhuanet (2007a) 'Zhongguo chengxiang jumin shouru 2006 nian jiasu zengzhang' (Incomes for China's urban and rural residents see faster growth in 2006), Online. Available <www.aweb.com.cn> (accessed on 25 January 2007).

Xinhuanet (2007b) 'Xinxing nongcun hezuo yiliao huanjie nongmin "yibing zhipin" wenti' (New rural cooperative health care system to ease 'poverty by illness'), Online. Available <http://finance.aweb.com.cn/2007/3/8/10372454.htm> (accessed on 10 March 2007).

Xu, L. (2006) 'Jiejue nongmin kanbing nan yaokua jidao kan' (How difficult to solve health care problem for farmers), *Shichang bao (Market News)*, 5 June, Online. Available HTTP:<http://news.aweb.cn/2006/6/5/9000685.htm> (accessed on 5 June 2006).

Xue, X. (2002) 'Caizheng ying jiada dui nongcun jichu jiaoyu zhichi: fang Su Ming' (Central budget should increase support for rural basic education: interview with Su Ming), *Jingji ribao (Economic Daily)*, 8 October, Online. Available <www.economicdaily. com.cn> (accessed on 8 October 2002).

Yang, D.L. (2005) 'China's Looming Labor Shortage,' *Far Eastern Economic Review*, 168 (2) (January/February), 19–24.

Yang, D.P. (2005) 'China's Education in 2003: From Growth to Reform,' *Chinese Education and Society*, 38 (4) (July/August), 11–55.

Yang, D.P. (2006) 'Pursuing Harmony and Fairness in Education,' *Chinese Education and Society*, 39 (6) (November/December), 3–44.

Yu, J. (2003), 'Nongcun heie shili he jiceng zhengquan tuihua' (Rural criminal forces and the decay of local governance), *Zhanlue yu guangli*, 60 (5), 1–14.

Zhao, S. (2003) 'Xiangcun zhili: zuzhi he chongtu' (Village governance: organization and conflicts), *Zhanlue yu guangli*, 61 (6), 1–8.

Zhao, Y. (2001) 'Nongcun shuifei gaige: baogan daohu yilai youyi zhongda zhidu Chuangxin' (Tax-for-fee reform in the countryside: another major institutional innovation since household responsibility system), *Zhongguo nongcun jingji* (*Chinese Rural Economy*), 6, 45–51.

Zheng, Y. (2007) 'Zhongguo qunti xing shijian de jueqi shuoming liao shenme?' (The meaning of the rise of 'public incidents' in China?), *Lianhe zaobao* (*United Morning Post*), 16 January, Online. Available HTTP:<www.zaobao.com/special/forum/pages5/ forum_zp070116.html> (accessed on 16 January 2007).

Zhongguo qingnian bao (Chinese Youth Daily) (2002) 'Chengxiang jumin shouru guoda zhide jingti' (Widening urban–rural income gap calls attention), Online. Available <www.aweb.com.cn/2002/>.

Zhongxin Wang (2007) 'Caizheng kunnan xian jinnian jiben jiejue' (Financially strapped counties to be eliminated this year), 19 March, Online. Available <www.aweb.com.cn> (accessed on 19 March 2007).

Zhu, B. (2001) 'Nongcun shuifei gaige shidian de jinzhan, nandian ji sikao' (Tax-for-fee reform: progress, difficulties and analysis), *Zhongguo nongcun jingji*, (*Chinese Rural Economy*), 2, 12–16.

Zhu, M. and Ye, Z. (2005) 'Kunrao nongcun shufei gaige de sange wenti' (Three problems troubling tax-for-fee reforms), *Remmin ribao (People's Daily)*, 8 June, Online. Available <http://theory.people.com.cn/GB/40764/48184/3450846.html> (accessed on 8 June 2005).

5 Exit of involution[1] in rural China

An alternative development path?

Yang Chen

Introduction

This chapter first identifies the positive relationship between industrialization in the form of the development of township and village enterprises (TVEs) and the unique 'localized urbanization' in coastal provinces in China. The research findings indicate that, where there has been successful development of TVEs, the extent of urbanization of rural townships and counties has been far greater than in those rural regions where TVEs have remained largely underdeveloped. After a substantial review of the literature in the area, this chapter attempts to identify institutional factors that have put a brake on agricultural involution and underpinned industrial evolution in coastal provinces in China.

Second, the chapter suggests that de-involution is more likely occur in regions where rural industrialization and local urbanization have already taken place. However, the *de-involution* occurring in coastal regions has inflicted unexpected impacts on agricultural production and rural development in inland provinces, where a tendency towards involution remains. Finally, the chapter argues that the development path through industrialization and urbanization undertaken by the coastal rural regions of China may not be feasible for inland rural areas to adopt given the institutional and environmental constraints on the potential for economic growth in the less developed parts of China. An alternative development path is therefore indispensable to lift inland rural China out of its involutionary tendency.

The evolution of township and village enterprises (TVEs) and the de-involution of rural China

Phillip Huang's involutionary theory is derived from his research on the Chinese small-scale peasant economy in two of his classic works: *Small Scale Peasant Economy and Social Change in Northern China* in 1985 (2000a) and *Small Scale Peasant Household and Village Development in the Yangtze Delta* in 1990 (2000b). In these two works, Huang applied the concept of diminishing marginal returns to analyse the nature of the small-scale peasant economy with empirical data from northern China (mainly from Hebei province) and from the Yangtze

Delta. The key theme of his involutionary theory is that highly developed small-scale farming leads to low levels of agricultural growth that do not bring about improved per capita crop yields or substantial economic development.

Since the end of the 1970s, the most fundamental change in rural China has been the large-scale movement of rural labour to cities and a transformation of commune-based agricultural labour into industrial waged labour. By the end of 2003, it was estimated that roughly 100 million peasant workers were employed in cities, classified as *litu lixiang* peasants (peasants who were no longer engaged in agricultural production and reallocated from their origins to cities). In addition to this group, there were over 100 million *litu bu lixiang* peasants – those who worked in local TVEs as employed manufacturing labour but remained living where they had always done (Zhang, 2004; Lu, 2005). As a result, out of approximately 500 million rural workers 200 million (40 per cent) were engaged in non-agricultural production while 300 million (60 per cent) were still engaged in farming, if only part-time (Chinese Rural Statistical Yearbook, 2004, p. 31). In the 700,000 (administrative) villages in China, on average, 300 out of 700 workers per village no longer worked in the agricultural sector in 2003 at all (ibid.).

Thus, it is important to answer a number of key questions: has *de-involution* taken place as consequence of this fundamental change in rural China over the past two decades? If so, how did it take off? Has the change brought about growth with development? What were the characteristics of the change?

One of the unique experiences of change in rural China since the reforms of the early 1980s has been the rise of township and village enterprises (TVEs). Farmers benefited from the implementation of the 'household responsibility system' (HRS), which, most commentators have argued, significantly boosted farmers' incentives to produce and, as indicated in Figure 5.1, allowed the take-off of TVEs, which absorbed large amounts of surplus rural labour in the countryside. TVEs provided the initial dynamo for the Chinese reform process in the 1980s and the first half of the 1990s, particularly in rural areas, allowing substantial growth in terms of industrial employment and productivity across the Chinese countryside, *both in agriculture and in industry.*[2]

The numbers of TVEs grew rapidly, with double-digit growth rates throughout the 1980s and 1990s, employing only 7 per cent of rural Chinese in 1978 and 11 per cent in 1984 but, at their peak, 28 per cent in 1996.[3] Thereafter, however, the numbers employed began to decline, mainly as a result of the decline of purely collectively owned TVEs as indicated in Figure 5.1 facing losses and cutting jobs. Employed persons in private TVEs and self-employed individuals (see Figure 5.1), this notwithstanding, kept rising after 1996 and these trends provided new dynamos for the further growth of enterprise employment and income. As a result, the numbers of employed persons in TVEs, which dropped between 1996 and 1999, picked up again subsequently. Over the past two decades, TVEs have created jobs for 70 per cent of the 130 million workers who have migrated from rural areas to urban regions.

TVEs sprang up in manufacturing and even expanded into the tertiary sector. Measured by employed persons in TVEs by industrial sector, most jobs were cre-

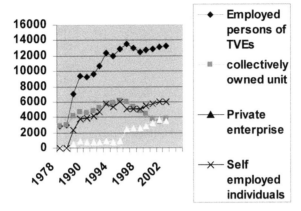

Figure 5.1 Number of people employed by TVEs at year-end according to the type of the enterprise (10,000 persons). Source: Compiled by the author from data taken from *Chinese Statistical Yearbook* (2004, p. 448).

ated in secondary industry, while the numbers of employed persons in tertiary industries doubled between 1992 and 2002 (Figure 5.2). The number has kept rising in the last few years and is likely to increase further in the future.

The growth of TVEs was remarkable throughout the 1980s and the first half of the 1990s with an average annual growth rate of production of over 20 per cent. The contribution of TVEs to total GDP increased so fast that, by the early 1990s, it was contributing a similar share of GDP to the state-owned sector. At the same time it absorbed surplus rural labour and alleviated employment pressure in the agricultural sector, allowing the numbers engaged purely in agriculture to fall. Thus, as agricultural employment fell while farm output rose, an opportunity for agricultural de-involution was brought about as a result of *increases* in marginal returns in agricultural production, thereby increasing TFP in rural China. However, continued fast rates of growth in the population in the Chinese countryside, despite the strict population control associated with the 'one child policy', compromised this opportunity as rural labour engaged in 'farming, foresting, herding and fishing' continued to increase from 298 million in 1980 to 324 million in 1989, with the total rural labour force increasing from 318 million in 1980 to 409 million in 1989 (Chinese Statistical Yearbook, 2004, pp. 473–474).

Since the mid-1990s onwards, instigated by accelerated integration into international markets, urbanization and industrialization have been intensified as global capital has been invested in China with great intensity. As a consequence, robust economic growth has created over 100 million new jobs for *litu lixiang* peasants in the past decade. However, since population pressure in the countryside has not been alleviated, the numbers of rural labourers engaged in 'farming, foresting, herding and fishing' have remained constant, being 313 million in 2003, not significantly less than the level of 324 million pertaining in 1989 (ibid.).

The size of the total rural labour force and the share of employment in the primary sector as a percentage of total employment have both been declining

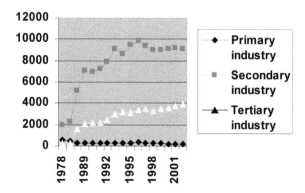

Figure 5.2   Number of people employed by TVEs at year-end by industrial sector (10,000 persons). Source: Compiled by the author from data taken from *Chinese Statistical Yearbook* (2004, p. 448).

since the middle 1990s. The total rural labour force fell from 348 million in 1997 to 339 million in 2005 while the share of employment in the primary sector as a percentage of total employment fell from 49.9 per cent to 44.7 per cent in the same period. Meanwhile, the contribution of the primary sector to GDP fell by 5.6 per cent from 18.1 per cent in 1997 to 12.5 per cent in 2005 (Ye, 2006). When the contribution of agricultural sector to GDP declines at a faster rate than the fall in the share of agricultural employment as a percentage of total employment, structural dislocation occurs: with technological development in the agricultural sector lagging behind the level of the non-agricultural sector, the comparative productivity of the agricultural sector falls while at the same time the Engel coefficient falls,[4] leading to insufficient demand for agricultural goods. Partly as a result, the urban–rural income gap has continued to widen, the urban–rural income ratio growing from 2.47 in 1997 to 3.22 in 2005 as indicated in Figure 5.3. Moreover this ratio has continued to rise in the last few years despite the central government reforming the two-tier urban–rural governance structure and introducing a raft of policies in the countryside – 'more investment and subsidy, less tax and more flexibility' – which have included the abolition of agricultural taxes, the lifting of constraints on the free movement of peasant farmers and direct subsidies to grain farming. These observations do not suggest that de-involution has taken place in the countryside nationwide as a consequence of fundamental industrialization and urbanization in China over the past two decades.

Regional diversity: the formation of two types of 'semi-industrial, semi-farming' rural society in the Chinese countryside

In that the growth of TVEs in the 1980s (and the accelerated industrialization, commercialization, international trade and urbanization associated with that growth) absorbed over 200 million rural workers, transforming them into industrial waged labour, to what extent did such change enable *development* in rural

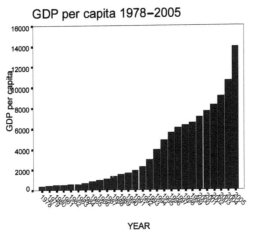

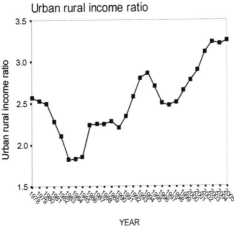

Figure 5.3 Urban and rural income ratio (GDP per capital): 1978–2005. Source: Compiled by author from data taken from *Chinese Statistical Yearbook*.

China? In practice, the impact was limited as the successful development of TVEs was not only regionally diverse but also patchy even within the same region. Three distinctive types of TVEs evolved through the 1980s: (i) the Sunan/Shandong collectively owned TVEs, (ii) the Zhejiang privately owned TVEs and (iii) the Zhujiang Delta export-oriented TVEs. Each of them has distinctive characteristics in terms of property rights arrangements, organizational structure, position in the supply chain, the degree of achievement of economies of scale and management strategies. The Pearl River Delta export-oriented TVEs developed into industrial clusters mainly as production bases for multinational companies. The Sunan and Shandong TVEs have grown as a result of the transition of state-owned enterprises in traditional local industrial centres such as Shanghai, Qingdao and Tianjin. By 2003, the numbers of people employed in TVEs in Shandong province alone was over 15 million, the highest number for any province in China. Guangdong province had the second highest number with 12 million, while over 10 million were employed in TVEs in Zhejiang province (third highest) and 9.8 million in Jiangsu province (fourth highest) (Chinese Statistical Yearbook, 2004).

From 1997 onwards, collective TVEs have experienced shareholder restructuring and private and self-employed businesses have become the new dynamos of growth for TVE employment. As indicated in Table 5.1, which measures the shares of private businesses in terms of number of enterprises, employment and registered capital, the eastern provinces of China, including Jiangsu, Zhejiang, Guangdong and Shandong, accounted for roughly 70 per cent of each category in 2003, while the central provinces, including Hunan, Hubei, Anhui and Sichuan, all with very large rural populations, accounted for only about 17 per cent. Moreover, as indicated further in Table 5.2, the four provinces of the east of China mentioned above substantially outperformed other inland provinces in terms of the number of employed persons in private enterprises, the size of registered capital and the number of enterprises.

The Chinese economy has been integrating into the international marketplace at an accelerated pace since the middle 1990s. China is one of the few developing countries who have benefited from globalization (Sachs, 2005). As indicated in Figure 5.4, the delivery value of exported goods of TVEs has doubled over the past decade and reached 120 billion yuan in 2003.

Table 5.1 Ratio of private business by region in 2003

	% of enterprises	% of employed persons	% of registered capital
East	69.34	68.33	70.90
Middle	17.15	18.28	16.09
West	13.51	13.38	13.01

Source: *Chinese Private Business Annual Book*, 2002–2004, p. 73.

Table 5.2 List of the development level of private enterprises in 2003

	Number of enterprises	Employed persons	Registered capital (10,000 yuan)
1	Jiangsu 343,680	Zhejiang 4,143,100	Guangdong 45,227,995
2	Guangdong 323,007	Jiangsu 3,865,466	Shanghai 41,737,629
3	Zhejiang 302,136	Shandong 3,063,831	Jiangsu 36,326,092
4	Shanghai 291711	Guangdong 2,849,621	Zhejiang 29,240,602
5	Shandong 228,554	Shanghai 2,557,064	Beijing 23,395,283
6	Beijing 186,805	Beijing 2,191,735	Shandong 21,725,496
7	Liaoning 114,415	Liaoning 1,823,366	Fujian 13,175,161
8	Sichuan 110,359	Hebei 1,603,665	Liaoning 12,589,057
9	Fujian 87,510	Sichuan 1,214,519	Hubei 10,720,929
10	Hubei 86,155	Shanxi 1,096,587	Sichuan 10,419,164

Source: *Chinese Private Business Annual Book*, 2002–2004, p. 73.

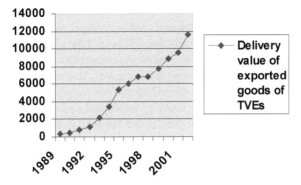

Figure 5.4   Delivery value of goods exported by TVEs (100 million yuan). Source: *China Statistical Yearbook* (2004, p.452). Figure shows the independent Theil index as well as its decomposition.

Guangdong, Zhejiang, Jiangsu and Shandong provinces contributed 67.5 per cent of the total delivery value of exported goods of the TVEs. In 2003, the delivery value of exported goods from TVEs in Guangdong province was over 28 billion yuan alone, the highest in the country, with Zhejiang coming second with over 26 billion yuan and Jiangsu and Shandong coming third and fourth with values of 17 billion yuan and 10 billion yuan respectively.

The initiation of TVEs was not designed by the government but was a grass-roots experience developed by trial and error. Whereas the growth of TVEs has without doubt transformed the Chinese countryside, the changes instigated by the development of TVEs also have distinctive regional features which can be understood and interpreted appropriately only on a case-by-case basis.

And the pace of industrialization, commercialization, international trade and urbanization in coastal provinces has been much more intensive than in inland provinces. Has such intensive change brought about 'growth with development' in rural areas in coastal provinces and what impacts has it had in the countryside in inland provinces? To address these questions, this paper identifies two types of change in rural China.

Type 1 change: semi-industrial, semi-farming: de-involution brought about by industrial evolution characterized by local urbanization and 'litu bu lixiang' peasant workers – the case of Zhejiang industrial clusters

In those rural regions with highly developed TVEs but remaining as rural adminis-trative units, farmers have become labourers with jobs in manufacturing factories while remaining farmers on their allocated plots of land, creating the phenomenon of *litu bu lixiang* peasant workers for whom non-agricultural waged labour in factories has become the major source of income while income from agricultural production has become secondary and merely complementary. In some counties in the Pearl River Delta and Yangtze Delta regions with a high degree of localized urbanization, a significant number of local rural households no longer engage in any form of agricultural production and rent out their allocated lands to migrant agricultural workers from inland provinces (Huang, 2006). The economic growth in these rural regions has certainly broken the constraints of involution and led to the enjoyment of 'growth with real development'. One of the most remarkable rural forms of development has cropped up in certain regions of Zhejiang province. These regions used to be agricultural towns and counties before the 1980s. Now, not only are they completely urbanized but they have also developed into international manufacturing centres over the past two decades.

The majority of TVEs in industrial clusters have been developed from scratch by peasant entrepreneurs who used to make a living on thin agricultural production. Most peasants in these regions are either self-made entrepreneurs or waged peasant workers working in TVEs. The income received from agricultural production is now minor and complementary for peasant workers. The Anglo-American experience of rural capitalist development that Huang applied as the benchmark for 'growth with development' in his studies has indeed taken place in these regions. Thus, de-involution is more likely to occur in rural regions where local urbanization is achieved with *litu bu lixiang* peasant workers comprising a majority of the labour force.

Industrial clusters which have evolved in Zhejiang province have a distinctive growth mode, combining 'rural industrialization' with the development of a distinct market for a specific product, with each district (either at county or township level) specializing in the production and trade of a certain type of good. Rural industrialization in Zhejiang has developed on the basis of the local socio-economic network of 'market–village–rural household' (Zhang, 2006). The most distinctive characteristic of this mode is that it is not the large-sized companies or even the SMEs that have become the key players in the industrial cluster but the individual rural households.

Phillip Huang's research suggests that individual rural households engaged in handicraft production in the Yangtze Delta region in 1930s experienced involution as rural households constrained by surplus labour were less likely to behave as rational enterprises but act accordingly to the cost–benefit logic of the family, producing frequently at levels at which marginal costs exceed marginal revenue. However with the industrialization in the 1990s, with the accelerated pace of technology diffusion and the access to international markets, the abundant supply of rural labour led not to agricultural involution but to industrial evolution (Zhang and Zhao, 2006). In this new mode of rural industrialization, individual rural households have become the basic production unit often with as little as one unit of capital (e.g. a sock weaving machine). Almost all individual households in the county or township engage in the production of a part of a certain type of good in which the district specializes. Having received orders from local agents or trade companies in the relevant market division, sometimes in the form of face-to-face or telephone agreement, individual households produce the goods and deliver them on time to the agents. Thereafter, the products are sold worldwide through cluster markets such as the international market in Yiwu (see Chapter 12 of this volume). Personal computers and broadband internet have become an indispensable part of individual household production as most orders are given in electronic format and machines are computer controlled.

Over the past two decades, Zhejiang's rural townships and villages in Shaoxing, Xiaoshan, Yiwu and Wenzhou have been industrialized and rural counties upgraded to cities. The per capita income has risen from less than 200 yuan in 1978 to over 30,000 yuan in 2003. De-involution has indeed taken place in these regions, implying 'growth with development'. As the Zhejiang mode is different from the Jiangsu and Shandong modes of industrial evolution, which have relied much less on individual rural households, a relevant hypothesis is proposed as follows: de-involution is more significant in the regions with higher levels of self-employed *litu bu lixiang* peasants.

Rural workers receive on average 7.3 years of education, which is much less than the average of 10.3 years for urban workers. Among rural workers, the illiteracy rate is 7.4 per cent; 31.1 per cent of them merely received primary education and only 0.52 per cent[5] received higher education and professional training. By having a higher level of self-employed *litu bu lixiang* peasants, the well educated skilled workers remained in the countryside in Zhejiang province, whereas in inland provinces the well educated skilled workers left the countryside and moved to cities as *litu lixiang* peasant workers (migrant workers).

Type 2 change: semi-industrial, semi-farming: intensified involution characterized by limited urbanization and 'litu lixiang' peasant workers

In addition to factors such as the local social network, the access to international market and fast technology diffusion, Wang (2005) suggests that local networked entrepreneurship, shrewd local governance and astute policies have led to the rise and development of Zhejiang private industrial clusters (see also Chapter 12 of this volume). Nonetheless the low cost of production of clustered enterprises has been their core competitive advantage. Abundant supplies of *litu lixiang* waged peasant workers who have come from less developed inland provinces have kept labour costs continuously low over the past two decades. The development of industrial clusters in Zhejiang has not only created job opportunities for local peasant workers but also absorbed a significant amount of rural labour from inland provinces. It has consequently led to a population boom in newly urbanized counties in Zhejiang and other developed coastal provinces. The size of the population increased from fewer than half a million in 1980s to over 1.7 million by the end of 2005, 1 million of which are migrant peasant workers. This process should have helped inland peasant workers to increase their income and, with the remittances back home, should have propped up rural development in less developed regions. However, the successful evolution of TVEs in coastal regions has inflicted unexpected impacts on agricultural production and rural development in inland provinces.

The household responsibility system (HRS), introduced in 1978, has provided the framework by which social stability in the countryside has been maintained ever since. The household has become the dominant agricultural production unit and, given the small size of plots allocated to each household, economies of scale are difficult if not impossible to achieve. In 2003, per capita cultivated land was 2.4 *mu* and the average household was allocated 9.2 *mu*. Every unit of labour engaged in agricultural production worked an average 7.3 *mu* of land nationwide, this average number being significantly lower in provinces in the centre and east of China, where the agriculture sector has traditionally been important and where refined farming has been well developed: in 2003 in Hunan the average allocation of land was 2.1 *mu* per head, in Hubei it was 2.7 *mu* per head, in Anhui 2.7 *mu* per head and in Sichuan 2.0 *mu* per head (Chinese Statistical Yearbook, 2004, pp. 33, 139). As a result, the HRS has institutionalized small-scale farming in rural China. Population pressure and small-scale farming have become, *ipso facto*, the institutional arrangements which have allowed the reintroduction of involution in the Chinese countryside. By 2003, the per capita income of an agricultural worker was 1344 yuan (roughly US$165) when China's per capita GDP exceeded US$1000 (Huang, 2006).

Provinces in the middle of China are the most densely inhabited areas, with abundant rural labour, and these provinces have become major labour 'exporters'. Inland provinces such as Sichuan, Hunan, Anhui, Henan and Hubei are well known in China as *dagong* (waged labour) provinces with large numbers of *litu lixiang* peasant workers who have left home and gone to work in factories in coastal regions. The *litu lixiang* peasant workers are mostly strong young workers. As they work in cities, their agricultural plots are left for the old or young members of the households to cultivate; in some regions, female members of the family have completely taken over agricultural production at home. In these inland regions, a two-tiered agricultural production system thus has come into being – *nangong nugeng* (males working as waged industrial labour, females working on the land) and *zhuanggong laogeng* (the young and strong working as waged industrial labour while the old and fragile work on the land). In inland provinces, the majority of people, 58 per cent according to a recent survey (Lu, 2004, pp. 308–309), still engage only in agricultural production to make a living, 15 per cent of them being semi-industrial, semi-farming peasant workers with 10 per cent jobless (ibid.).

In 2003, the average per capita crop yields of grain of agricultural workers was 1,362 kg, only 18 per cent (294 kg) being commodity grain and sold in the marketplace, the rest being for their own consumption (Huang, 2006; China Statistical Yearbook, 2004, pp. 502–503). These statistics imply that most of those peasants who stay at home in inland provinces are still engaged only in small-scale farming for domestic consumption. As the population grows, the agricultural plots cannot provide sufficient jobs, which therefore leads to rising rates of 'hidden unemployment' in the countryside, referring to those agricultural workers who do not work full-time. On average, agricultural workers worked only 130 days in 2003 (Chinese Agricultural Yearbook, 2004). Since the average income for an agricultural worker was 11 yuan per day, such a worker could expect to receive only 1,430 yuan for the whole of 2003 (Huang, 2006). As the average waged industrial worker received much higher levels of income, it was a rational choice for young male rural workers to leave home and work as *litu lixiang* peasant workers in cities.

The booming economy and successful development of TVEs in coastal provinces were the key factors that relieved the pressure of involution and brought about opportunities for achieving 'growth with development' in local rural regions. However, these factors, combined with others including the HRS, which has institutionalized small-scale farming, have inflicted poignant changes in agricultural production and rural development on inland provinces: the constraints of involution on agricultural production has not been alleviated and those rural households who are engaged purely in agricultural production have been marginalized and left in relative poverty in an otherwise booming Chinese economy. The rural community in inland provinces has consequently been locked in a new form of involution – semi-farming, semi-industrial involution.

This new form of involution has discouraged engagement in agricultural production, dismantled traditional family structures in rural communities and reduced the self-esteem and morale of peasants. It is one of the key evolutionary institutional factors that has instigated the *san nong* problems – deprived countryside, bitter peasants and endangered agricultural sector. Agricultural production has tottered in the past few years and total grain crop yields have declined since 1998, reducing from 500 million metric tons in 1998 to 430 million metric tons in 2003. Crop yields per agricultural worker have slipped from 1,574 kg to 1,362 kg in 2003 (Chinese Agricultural Statistical Yearbook, 2004) while crop yields per *mu* have stagnated over the last decade: 324 kg in 1995, 342 kg in 2000, 344 kg in 2003. It suggests that involution remains as peasants merely uphold production capacity at a subsistence level. I therefore derive a hypothesis from the above analysis which can be stated as follows: de-involution is unlikely to take place in those rural regions where a majority of the local labour force has become *litu lixiang* migrant workers.

An alternative path of development: non-economic cooperatives

It is acknowledged by the Chinese leadership and think tanks (Ren, 2006; Zhang, 2004) that the involutionary tendency in Chinese agriculture will be more likely to exist in the long term and that growing social polarity in the countryside remains a major concern in China. Increasing numbers of Chinese farmers, marginalized in a country where national income per head has been rising by 9–10 per cent a year for two decades, have engaged in violent protests at their lot (Sanders, Chen and Cao, 2007; see also Chapter 4 of this volume), leading to disturbing levels of social instability in the countryside. State policy maximizing GNP at all costs has been held responsible for this state of affairs,[6] as have the lack of political rights for farmers, deficiencies in local government and rampant corruption of cadres. Thus, China's development policy has been modified recently to prioritize redistribution and has shifted towards sustaining the living conditions of the poor (Ye, 2006). Since 2004 the central government has moderated detrimental effects on farmers by policy initiatives including the abolition of fees and charges by the state at all levels, the curtailment of the scale of government presence at village level[7] and the promotion of the New Countryside Movement officially initiated by central government in February 2006 (Wen, 2005).

The implementation of the New Countryside Movement has so far been a state-led mass programme, yet with forms of discretionary policy associated with welfare economics. The mainstream policymakers and scholars (Zhang, 2004) believe that the exit of involution for less developed rural China can be achieved only through substantial economic growth and they thus emphasize the importance of developing economic institutions in the countryside. The key concepts and government propaganda associated with the New Countryside Movement can be summarized as *nongye chanye hua* (industrialization of agricultural production), *nongye xiandai hua* (materialization of agricultural sector), *nongye jixie hua* (mass agricultural production with the widespread use of machinery and new technology) and *nongmin sixiang xiandaihua* (modernization of peasants' thoughts).

This school believes that, so long as farmers in less developed rural China can be transformed to *litu bu lixiang* peasant-workers in local enterprises, de-involution would be achieved by following the development path of coastal rural regions through industrialization, localized urbanization and access to international markets. In 2006, Xu Guangchun, the Governor of Henan province, the largest rural province, with a population over 100 million, identified the following as essentials for the success of his government's New Countryside Movement policy: (a) a resilient local leadership (at village level), (b) a good business initiative for the local community, (c) a key product with great commercial potential, (d) a rural community with entrepreneurial spirit and (e) an effective and efficient local government providing sufficient support to the local community. This government strategy clearly reflects the mainstream thoughts and policy priorities centred around three key concepts, marketization, industrialization and globalization.

Along the same lines, different forms of economic cooperative initiatives have been encouraged nationwide in the New Countryside Movement. In prosperous rural regions in China where industrialization and urbanization has taken place on a wide scale (Chen, 2005), economic cooperatives such as the Farmers Association of Production, Marketing and Finance in Zhejiang province are the most popular form of ongoing cooperative initiatives. The pilot establishment of a self-governing Farmers Association was initiated by a politician-scholar in 2005 and received endorsements from the Zhejiang provincial government. The aim was to reduce the vulnerability of individual farmers in the market economy by rejuvenating key rural *economic* cooperatives including rural small finance cooperatives – *xinyong she* – sales cooperatives – *gongxiao she* – and production cooperatives – *hezuo she*, integrating them into a new form of association.

However, as this chapter has identified, the intensive industrialization and urbanization that has taken place in Chinese countryside over the past two decades has been uneven with significant regional disparities and a widening urban–rural income gap. Coastal developed provinces and less developed inland regions are at different points along the Kuznets curve. Given the level of socio-economic regional disparities, central policy initiatives need to be adjusted to take the local conditions into consideration. The divergence of de-involutionary forms in developed coastal provinces reflects different the rural development paths that have been undertaken.

The key question is to what extent could the Zhejiang model be copied and repeated in inland rural provinces? In the less developed inland provinces where the agricultural sector still makes a significant contribution to local GDP, unexpected, *negative* side-effects have resulted, however. Li Changping (2006), who in 2003 appealed to Premier Zhu Rongji to abolish fees and charges in the countryside, now agonizes at the collapse of public infrastructure after the abolition of fees and charges and the vacuum of governance resulting from frequently dysfunctional village committees elected through open elections (*hai xuan*). Other researchers (e.g. Pan Wei, 2006) argue that the policy of self-governance has not only been insufficient to lift marginalized farmers out of poverty but, in many cases, has intensified their problems as fundamental impediments to change are beyond the scope of the villagers themselves to deal with.

These impediments include the fact that the involutionary tendency of agricultural production (Huang, 2002a,b) has not been alleviated as the rural population keeps rising, leading to a vicious circle of insufficient employment and declining marginal returns in agricultural production. Farmers, locked into small-scale farming, have found themselves increasingly vulnerable to the vagaries of the market. Meanwhile the establishment of the household responsibility system (HRS), re-establishing, through strong individual incentives, small-scale family farming as the principal mode of production in the countryside in place of the communes, has had destructive effects on *public* institutions,[8] weakening agricultural infrastructures and reducing farmers' participation in public affairs (He Xuefeng, 2004). As a result, *nongye chanye hua* (industrialization of agricultural production), *nongye xiandai hua* (materialization of agricultural sector) and *nongye jixie hua* (mass agricultural production with the widespread use of machinery and new technology) are unlikely to be realized without substantial investment, in both the short and the long term, in infrastructure construction in the countryside.

Moreover, both foreign observers (Woo, 2006) and domestic think tanks are deeply concerned about the extent to which the capacity of the natural environment can cope with further mass urbanization at the scale of 200 million migrants leaving the land in the next twenty years. Furthermore, recent research (Hutton, 2007) argues that the effect of globalization, which was the indispensable factor in the successful de-involution of the coastal regions in China, may not last, as the global market cannot accommodate the increase of Chinese exports at an average rise of 20 per cent annually, which has occurred in the recent past, into the next decade. The appreciation of the RMB and the upgrading of the economic structure in China are the other two key factors which may compromise the competitiveness of China's exports in international markets. Therefore, the de-involution path of the past, relying on rural industrialization, local urbanization and globalization, may not be possible for the development of inland rural provinces with high levels of *litu lixiang* migrant workers.

An alternative path has been proposed by one school of Chinese scholars, the *Huazhong Xiangtu Pai* (School of the Native of Middle China), that development paradigms should be shifted to accommodate changing contextual circumstances reflecting the geographic, economic and institutional divides in different parts of rural China. Compared with the mainstream school of thought, which believes in both the power and the strength of economic growth and thus emphasizes the importance of the development of economic institutions in the countryside, the School of the Native of Middle China is skeptical of the tenets of economic growth and attempts to find an alternative path of development through the construction of public institutions which hopefully would provide a sense of identity and belonging to those who have been marginalized.

In these less developed regions with large number of *litu lixiang* peasant workers, trials have been introduced to find an alternative path to rural development through the construction of *cultural* cooperatives including associations for the elderly, women's associations and local youth trusts. For example, the initiators in Hubei province, including intellectual elites with strong agricultural backgrounds, acknowledge both the long-term existence of the involutionary tendency in Chinese agriculture (Huang, 2006) and the environmental constraints on economic growth and are therefore attempting to develop a programme to build up a rural community above all *at ease with itself* with a moderate level of material self-sufficiency.

This alternative paradigm favours localization than globalization, emphasizes the development of post-industrialization sectors rather than unbridled industrialization, promotes lifestyles based on the provision of sufficient means to meet basic necessities rather than middle-class lifestyles 'coded' within the global commercial village and encourages spiritual fulfillment rather than materialism. It purports to provide wise and sensible principles to guide the further development of rural China. The journey to search for an alternative exit of involution in inland rural China, as previous reforms and changes have indicated, will be a muddy process full of dilemma and uncertainty.

Notes

1 Involution can be defined as 'growth without development', i.e. growth in total production which does not lead to rise in per capita incomes. Alternatively, it can be defined as short-run production which is carried on beyond the equilibrium point such that marginal cost is greater than marginal revenue. De-involution can thus be defined as 'growth with development', i.e. growth in total production which also brings about improved per capita income.

2 The nature of a TVE at the start of this period was largely 'collective': a form of publicly owned enterprise regarded by many scholars as a remarkably successful institutional adaptation to the Chinese economic environment of the time (Naughton,

1994, pp. 266–270). Through the 1990s, however, more and more TVEs were established as forms of 'private' enterprise.

3   Calculated with the data from *Chinese Statistical Yearbook*, 2001, pp. 110–111: Number of Employed Persons at the Year-end by Residence in Urban and Rural Areas.

4   By the end of 2000, the Engel coefficient for China's urban and rural residents had dropped under 50 per cent.

5   According to the fifth national population survey.

6   State policies towards agriculture were designed not to encourage rural development merely for its own sake, but to link agriculture and other sectors of the rural economy into an overall economic strategy which benefited industrialization (Sanders, Chen and Cao, 2007). Peasants were trapped in poverty by the internal system of household registration (*hukou*), which meant that the rural population was denied rights of migration to urban areas, alongside the planned labour allocation system, which denied them rights to work in factories, and the social welfare system, which merely covered urban residents' needs and denied to farmers the entitlement to equivalent welfare in terms of education, medical treatment, retirement and pension benefits that urban residents enjoyed (Du, 2001).

7   The number of administrative villages was reduced from 800,000 in 2000 to fewer than 600,000 in 2005 (Zhang, 2006).

8   The main cooperative institutions comprised three main economic cooperatives – *xinyong she* (rural small finance cooperative), *gongxiao she* (sales cooperative) and *hezuo she* (production cooperative).

References

Chen, Lin (2005) 'The Implication of the Development of New Form of Cooperatives,' *Twenty First Century Economic Report*, October, Ruian: Ruian City Government Documents.

Chinese Agricultural Statistical Yearbook (*Zhongguo nongye tongji nianjian*) (2004) Beijing: Ministry of Agriculture (Zhonghua renmin gongheguo nongye bu).

Chinese Private Business Annual Book (*Zhongguo saying jingji nianjian*) (2002/2004) Beijing: China Industry and Business Alliance Press (Zhonghua gongshang lianhe chubanshe).

Chinese Rural Statistical Yearbook (*Zhongguo nongcun tongji nianjian*) (2004) Beijing: State Statistical Bureau Department of Rural Social and Economic Investigation (Guojian tongjiju nongcun shehui jingji diaocha zongdui).

Chinese Statistical Yearbook (*Zhongguo tongji nianjian*) (2001) Beijing: China Statistical Press (Zhongguo tongji tubanshe).

Du, Rensheng (2001) 'We are Heavily Indebted to Peasants,' in Li Changping, *I Tell the Truth to Primer*, Beijing: Guangmin Daily Press, 2.

He, Xuefeng (2004) *The Contextual Circumstance in the Study of Chinese Countryside*, Wuhan: Hubei People's Press.

Huang, Zongzhi (2000a [1985]) *Huabei de xiaonong jingji yu shehui bianqian* (Small-scale peasant economy and social change in Northern China), Beijing: Chinese Press Bureau (Zhonghua shuju).

Huang, Zongzhi (2000b [1990]) *Changjiang sanjiaozhou xiaonong jiating yu xiangcun fazhan* (Small-scale peasant household and village development in Yangtze Delta), Beijing: Chinese Press Bureau (Zhonghua shuju).

Huang, Zongzhi (2006) 'Institutionalized Involutionary Agriculture Sector with the Feature of "Semi Semi Farming",' *Dushu*, 10, 118–130.

Hutton, Will (2007) *The Writing on the Wall: Why We Must Embrace China as a Partner or Face It as an Enemy*, London: Little, Brown.

Li, Changping (2006) 'Following Up Recommendation to Agricultural and Rural Problems: Agricultural Tax Should be Replaced with Land Rent,' *Sang Nong Zhong Guo*, 1, 103.

Lu, X.Y. (2004) *Social Flow in Contemporary China*, Beijing: Chinese Academy of Social Science, Centre for Social Strata in Contemporary China, Social Science Literature Press.

Lu, X.Y. (2005) 'The Effective Governance of Peasant Workers,' Online. Available <www.yannan.cn/data/detail/phpid=3084>.

Naughton, B. (1994) 'Chinese Institutional Innovation and Privatization from Below,' *American Economic Review*, 84 (2), 266–270.

Pan, Wei (2006), 'A Discussion on Different Mechanism of Villagers Self-Governance,' *SangNong ZhongGuo*, 2, 5–17.

Ren, X. (2006) 'The Reciprocated Forces in the Process of Institutional Change: Local Government Resolve in the Privatisation – A Hypothesis and the Test of "Wenzhou" Model,' *Social Science Research*, 1, 68–74.

Sachs, J. (2005) *The End of Poverty: How We Can Make It Happen in Our Lifetime*, London: Allen Lane.

Sanders, R., Chen, Yang and Cao, Yiying (2007) 'Marginalisation in the countryside: the question of rural poverty,' in H. Zhang, B. Wu and R. Sanders (eds) *Marginalisation in China: Perspectives on Transition and Globalisation*, Aldershot: Ashgate, 15–34

Wang, Z.Q. (2005) 'Jiqunshi minyin qiye fazhang xianzhuang yu qushi de shezheng yanjiu – yi zhejiang weili de diaochao yu fenxi' (An empirical study of the status quo and development trend of clustered private enterprises – Investigation and analysis in Zhejiang province), *Shanghai Jingji Yanjiu* (*Shanghai Economic Studies*), 12, 78–87.

Wen, Tiejn (2005) 'Why do we Need Countryside Construction in the New Era?' *Sang Nong Zhong Guo*, 2, 83.

Woo, W.T. (2006) 'A Harmonious Socialist Society or Bust: China's Quest for Sustainable Development,' Carnegie Endowment 12/1.

Ye, X.Q. (2006) 'Four Suppositions of Urban–Rural Income Gap and Three Routes in Boosting Coordinated Rural–Urban Development,' paper presented at the Fourth International Symposium on Agricultural Modernisation, Yiwu, China.

Zhang, X.S. (2004) 'Analysis of the Shortage of Peasant Workers in China,' *China Youth Daily*, 19 October.

Zhang, Y.X. (2006) 'Positive Research on the Developing Mechanism of Zhejiang Model from Involution to Evolution – A Case of Datang Socks Industrial Clusters in Caijiafan Village, Zhuji, Zhejiang Province, China,' paper presented at the Seventeenth CEA (UK) annual conference, London.

6 Regional vulnerability, inequality and asset growth

An analysis using an asset-based framework

Yiu Por Chen and Richard Schiere

Introduction

The issue of vulnerability has become a prominent study for poverty researchers (Dercon, 2001; Mansuri and Healy, 2000; Wood, 2003), in particular in developing and transitional countries like China. In this chapter, regional income vulnerability is defined as the risk of events in which a bad outcome could move the household into poverty on a regional level.[1] This approach aims to identify which regions are more vulnerable than others. The operationalization of this definition involves the estimation of vulnerability with average household expenditure at the provincial level, and the explanatory factors involve the Theil inequality index of the composition of various assets (liquid assets, human capital and health care). The objective of this research is to analyze the composition of assets in China as well to present the evolution of vulnerability by region. This is done by using provincial-level data from 1985–2001. By presenting a methodology to estimate the evolution of vulnerability, this chapter provides a new perspective on poverty and aims to contribute to the development of a harmonious society in China.

China's reform and opening-up period, which started at the beginning of the 1980s, has led to dramatic economic growth and reduction of poverty. This coincides with the growth in regional disparities as well as urban–rural inequality, particularly after the 1990s. The issue of vulnerability has been studied only on a limited basis in China (Jalan and Ravallion, 1999, 2001; Fan, Zhang and Zhang, 2002; McCulloch and Calandrino, 2003), but, in general, only household-level data were used and the studies did not focus on provincial-level evolution of vulnerability as well as its asset composition. More specifically, the research in this paper complements the debate on poverty in China by presenting a methodology to estimate vulnerability by region.

There are several reasons why there is a growing interest in vulnerability in China. First, although China is rapidly evolving economically, inequalities on a regional and social level are also on the rise. In these kinds of circumstances, it is important to estimate vulnerability, as this provides a more dynamic poverty perspective, instead of using absolute poverty measurements, which often focus on income and expenditure variables (Lipton and Maxwell, 1992). Second, vulnerability plays an important role in the decision-making of the poor because their resilience to negative shock is low (Wood, 2003). Therefore, vulnerability not only results from poverty, it can also reinforce poverty. Third, a relative small number of households in China have an average consumption below the poverty line, but a much larger number of households are just above the poverty line (McCulloch and Calandrino, 2003).

This paper takes a two-step approach to estimate vulnerability in China. First, asset composition is estimated by a one-stage Theil decomposition index with one liquid assets variable (savings deposit in banks per capita), two human capital variables (people with at least secondary education and people with at least college education) and two health care variables (amount of beds in hospitals and the amount of medical personnel in hospitals). The one-stage Theil method provides an opportunity to distinguish inequality between three main regions (eastern, western, and interior) as well as between regions and individual provinces. Asset inequality is related to vulnerability as higher inequality leads to: (i) lower access to public services for the poor, as they are more dependent on the state than richer people, and (ii) an increasing gap of social development, which will reduce the trickle-down effect of economic growth on poverty reduction and increase the risk of staying in poverty. For example, it is hard for an illiterate person to benefit from rapid economic development.

Second, the one-stage Theil decomposition index is introduced into a logistic regression whereby a geographical area is identified as being poor or non-poor, based on 80 percent of the median disposable household income. To ensure the validity of results three control variables are introduced (mortality rate, rural food expenditure, and urban food expenditure). Furthermore the *average marginal effects* of the coefficient of the logistic regression are calculated, which are used to estimate the evolution of vulnerability in China by region (eastern, interior, and western) as well as its decomposition between regions (i.e. between the three regions) and within regions (i.e. between province and regions).

Measuring vulnerability through asset ownership

Although the issue of vulnerability in the economic literature is gaining attention, it is often analyzed at the household level. However, in the traditional vulnerability literature, vulnerability is also used to identify social groups, or regions that are more vulnerable than other regions. For example, a well accepted definition of vulnerability in the field of food security/famine is "an aggregated measure, for a given population or region, of the risk of exposure to food insecurity" (Downing, 1991). As such, vulnerability in a geographical area is a function of exposure to shock and of resilience of households, correlating positively with the probability and impact of a shock and negatively with the resilience and its determining factors. Vulnerable regions are extremely sensitive to shocks such as seasonal events or unforeseen circumstances because the capacity of households to manage a shock in these areas is weak (Misselhorn, 2005). Another example of how vulnerability could apply to a geographical area is the Economic Vulnerability Index (EVI), which is based on a country analysis of risks faced to its sustainable development by unforeseen exogenous factors. The EVI is important as lower vulnerability enhances growth, reduces poverty, and increases economic security simultaneously. In addition, the EVI is used by the United Nations as an indicator to identify Least Developed Countries (Guillaumont, 2006).

The conceptionalization of vulnerability has led to a closer examination of the role of assets as a means of mitigating negative shocks. In this regard, assets are often associated with 'wealth' and 'money income'. Sometimes assets are interpreted in broad terms and defined as the value of wealth of all household resources, both human and non-human. In terms of vulnerability, financial assets are essential to reduce vulnerability as they are the first buffer to cope with stressful situations as well as providing the opportunity to benefit and participate in economic growth. The initial distribution of assets is also important from a capital market perspective, as it is the physical assets base that is likely to influence the extent to which poor people can take part in economic growth. If they cannot do so, this leads to underutilization of productive and growth potential as a lot of (poor) people are excluded. Therefore, greater initial inequality in asset distribution will mean that the growth that does occur is less (income) poverty reducing (World Bank, 2006).

Research in China also highlights the importance of wealth distributions in determining poverty levels as well as poverty changes in rural China (Wan, 2006). Additionally, China as a whole became much more unequal between 1995 and 2002. This latter was reinforced by urban housing reform, in which public apartments, which can be considered fixed assets, were sold to urban households at extremely low prices. The effect of this was an increase in inequality in wealth between urban and rural households (Li and Zhao, 2007), with regrettable effects on inequality in redistribution of assets and an increase in inequality. The likely

Table 6.1 Comparison of assets wealth distribution within countries, PPP values in percentages (2000)

Proportion of the population	China	India	Africa	Europe	America
Decile 1	2.99	13.60	29.53	6.12	2.30
Decile 2	6.28	14.18	18.42	6.19	4.27
Decile 3	6.50	16.32	14.40	6.80	5.75
Decile 4	14.71	11.72	9.36	6.12	5.42
Decile 5	16.47	10.56	7.51	6.25	5.75
Decile 6	15.02	10.23	6.79	8.07	6.57
Decile 7	14.23	9.20	6.28	9.48	8.54
Decile 8	12.91	7.51	5.45	12.17	10.18
Decile 9	9.09	5.18	–	15.27	15.76
Decile 10	1.80	1.49	2.26	23.54	35.47
Total	100	100	100	100	100

Source: UNU-Wider.

outcome is that the poor will have less chance to participate in economic growth as well as having fewer assets to mitigate negative shocks, which would both translate into higher vulnerability.

The capacity to cope is not only linked to monetary wealth but also related to non-tangible assets.[2] Researchers on vulnerability emphasize that mitigating factors with regard to reducing vulnerability are not only assets such as disposable items (classically, jewelry and livestock), but also social networks or public interventions (Hulme and Shepherd, 2003). Other studies show how the composition of assets influences livelihood opportunities (Bebbington, 1999). Vulnerability is also inversely related to health, education, income, and the capacity to sell assets (Misselhorn, 2005). For example, descending households often have income shocks arising from ill health (Jalan and Ravallion, 1999; Sen, 2003) or natural disasters, which result in the decline of household fortunes (Sen, 2003). Therefore the advantage of an asset base analysis is that it can focus on how household assets can be used to manage risk. This could be an "asset vulnerability framework," which includes elements of tangible assets such as labor and human capital, and productive assets, such as housing, as well as intangible assets like household relations and social capital (Moser, 1998).

The asset framework presented in the paper is applied on a provincial level with the aim of identifying which regions are more vulnerable than other regions. Theoretically this should be positively relating liquid assets, human capital, and health care; i.e. the more assets the lower the vulnerability. This could also be considered an analysis of "proximate" vulnerability and not "structural" vulnerability as this research focuses mainly on productive assets (liquid assets and human capital) in a given year for an individual province and not on structural vulnerability variables such as headship, age, households with old and infirm members—similar to concepts of structural poverty (Davies, 1996). As such, it builds upon similar approaches in Latin America (Bebbington, 1999) as well as a study using an asset framework in various urban areas in Zambia, Ecuador, the Philippines, and Hungary (Moser, 1998).

Data description

To estimate the evolution of the asset base of households in China the dataset covers 1985–2001. This dataset is based on the China Statistical Data Compilation of Michigan University[3] as well as on that of Belton M. Fleisher and Min Qiang from Ohio University on human capital in China.[4] Both are datasets on provincial levels and by year. The following five variables are used to measure assets (A_i) on a provincial level:

1   *Liquid assets* (L): Per capita savings deposits by individuals in banks that have interest. The savings deposit is calculated by adding demand deposits, times deposits, savings deposits, other deposits, and foreign currency deposits. This is deflated by the Consumer Price Index (CPI). Liquid assets are key components in reducing vulnerability as they can be used as a buffer for

short-term negative income shocks, in particular as liquid assets are easily accessible.

2, 3 *Human capital* (H_1 and H_2): The amount of people with at least secondary education (H_1) and amount of people with at least college education (H_2). These human capital variables are important as they influence the capacity to seek employment or engage in productive activities as well as to recover from crises. The role of human capital in the reduction of poverty is well documented in the literature (Adam and Jane, 1995; Campa and Webb, 1999).

4, 5 *Health* (HC_1 and HC_2): The number of hospital beds per 10,000 persons per province (HC_1) and the number of medical personnel per province (HC_2). The definition of hospitals includes hospitals, health centers, sanatoriums, maternity, child care centers, and other health institutions. Health care is important as illness, especially chronic illness, is a major factor in making people poor (Jalan and Ravaillion, 1999; Sen, 2003).

To identify poor and non-poor provinces, we adopt a relative measurement of disposable income on a provincial level:

6 *Poverty* (*P*): Disposable income on a provincial level. This measurement is weighted by urban disposable income of the non-agricultural population and by rural income of the agricultural population (see equation 6.1). Disposable income in China is the total income of household minus taxes.[5] This is deflated by CPI. The poverty rate is set at 80 percent of the median, which means that provinces that fall below 80 percent of the median are considered poor (value 1) and if the province is higher than 80 percent of the median the region is considered non-poor (value 0).

$$I = \gamma_{rt} * (I_{urb} - I_{urblivexp})_{rt} + (1 - \gamma_{rt}) * (I_{rural} - I_{rurallivexp})_{rt} \qquad (6.1)$$

With the following annotations: I is disposable income, γ_{rt} is urbanisation rate, I_{urb} is urban household income, $I_{urblivexp}$ is living expenditure in urban areas, I_{rural} is rural household income, $I_{rurallivexp}$ is living expenditure in rural areas, γ is the non-agricultural–agricultural population coefficient, r is region of China and t is year.

Ideally, the use of the poverty measure would be to compare income or expenditure variables with the official poverty rate. However, the official poverty rate in China is set rather low and so only a few provinces were poor, which was insufficient for a statistical analysis. Therefore, we have chosen to use a relative measurement of poverty, which is traditionally more widely used in rich countries than in developing countries (Wong, 1995). There are several reasons for using relative poverty measurements. First, China is rapidly developing and some development variables are more like middle-income countries whereas others are more like low-income countries.[6] Therefore absolute measurements would fail to capture the inequality between these regions (Osberg and Kuan, 2006). Second, in terms of policy formulation, relative poverty provides a tool to target certain regions.[7] For these reasons relative poverty measurements, such as the median income variables, have been used in other developing countries and low-income countries, for example in Mexico (Salas, 2003) and Nepal (Wagle, 2006).

To ensure that the results of this research are valid, three control variables are introduced, which are:

7 *Death rate* (D): The number of people that die per 10,000.[8] As the risk of poverty increases, it is highly likely that death rate will also increase. The control variable of the death rate is strongly linked to the probability of becoming poor as the ultimate result of vulnerability could be death. In addition, the death rate could not be directly linked to variables used to measure liquid assets, human capital, and health care. For example, the number of beds or doctors at provincial level does not directly affect the death rate. This is because the death rate in a developing country such as China is influenced by a wide range of issues such as working conditions, accidents and distance to hospital.

8 *Rural food expenditure* (RF): Expenditure on food in rural areas by province by year deflated by the CPI. A person is counted as rural if he/she was born in a rural area or has lived in rural areas for at least one year. This could be a control variable as a reduction of food consumption is clearly linked to vulnerability to poverty, as this is the last expenditure item that would be influenced. In addition, food intake is often used as a variable for vulnerability in the original food insecurity literature (Downing, 1991).

9 *Urban food expenditure* (UF): Expenditure of food in urban areas by province by year, which is deflated by CPI. As with rural food expenditure, urban food expenditure could be a control variable as a reduction of food consumption is clearly linked to vulnerability to becoming poor, as this is the last expenditure item that would be influenced. In addition, food intake is also used as an indicator for vulnerability in the original food insecurity literature (Downing, 1991).

Overall there is therefore one variable to measure poverty at 80 per cent of the median (P), five assets-based variables (L, H_1, H_2 HC_1, and HC_2) and three control variables (D, UF, and RF). All variables are the average of the provincial level by year.

Methodology

This paper takes a two-step approach to estimating vulnerability through an assets-based framework. The first step is to construct a one-step Theil decomposition index for the various asset variables so as to estimate vulnerability. The one-step Theil decomposition index provides the opportunity to distinguish the contribution of inequality between regional component (i.e. between regions) and within a region. For this research, the provinces of China are divided as followed: eastern and northeastern (Beijing, Tianjin, Hebei, Shanghai, Jiangsu, Zhejiang, Fujian, Shandong, and Guangdong-Hainan; Liaoning, Jilin, and Heilongjiang), interior (Shanxi, Inner Mongolia, Anhui, Jiangxi, Hubei, Hunan, Henan, Guangxi, Sichuan-Chongqing, Guizhou, Yunnan, and Shaanxi), and western (Gansu, Qinghai, Ningxia, and Xinjiang). Tibet is excluded for lack of data. The provinces of Guangdong-Hainan and Sichuan-Chongqing have been merged to make compatible the datasets on Human capital provided by Belton M. Fleisher and Min Qiang from Ohio University. The observation years are 1985–2001 for every individual year and for every individual province.

The measurement of inequality in the hierarchical structure of a country (i.e. between region and province) can be done by using the province as the basic unit. The standard Theil equation that measures inequality is:

Theil inequality index = $\Sigma_i \Sigma_j (Y_{ij}/Y) \log (Y_{ij}/Y/N_{ij}/N)$ (6.2)

An inequality index can be decomposed if total inequality is the sum of between-group and within-group inequalities. In addition, the mean independence implies that the index remains unchanged if every province income is changed by the same proportion, and population-size independence means that the index remains unchanged if the number of people in each region is changed by the same proportion (i.e. the index depends only on the relative population of each region, not the absolute population).

To obtain a decomposition of the Theil index into a between regional component (T_{BR}) and a within regional (T_{WR}) component would require the following (see Akita, 2000):

Decomposed Theil $(Th) = T_{BR} + T_{WR}$

$T_{BR} = \Sigma_r (A_{ir}/A_{ic}) \log (A_{ir}/A_{ic}/N_r/N_c)$ (6.3)

$T_{WR} = \Sigma_r (A_{ir}/A_{ic})T_{PI}$ (6.4)

$T_{PI} = \Sigma_p (A_{ipr}/A_{ir}) \log (A_{ipr}/A_{ir}/N_{pr}/N_r)$ (6.5)

With the following annotations: T_{BR} is the between regional component of the Theil index of vulnerability variable, T_{WR} is the within regional component of the Theil index of vulnerability variable, T_{PI} is the between province income inequality, A_i are the individual Asset variables (L, H_1, H_2, HC_1, and HC_2), A_{ipr} is the individual Asset i, in province p and region r, A_{ir} is the sum of the asset i, in region r, A_{ic} is the sum of the individual asset variables i, in the country, N is the population, N_{pr} is the population in province p and region r, N_r is the sum of the population in region r, N_c is the sum of the population in the country of China.

The second step is to introduce the one-stage Theil index into a logistic regression whereby a region is measured on binary based (poor and non-poor) with disposable income as dependent variable (see equation 6.1), five independent vulnerability variables (as estimated with the Theil index) and three control variables, which means that:

The dependent variable is poverty (P), which is calculated by disposable income on the provincial level by 80 percent of the median. This means that a province becomes poor if the disposable income becomes less than 80 percent of the median income. This 80 percent threshold of median income was chosen for two reasons. First, the average incomes of households on a provincial level are relatively close to each other, which means that at 60 per cent or lower there are hardly any poor provinces. This was insufficient for a thorough statistical analysis. Second, the 80 percent threshold is used in other countries as this could include out-of-pocket medical expenditures in poverty, a relevant issue in China.[9]

The independent variables are the assets-based Theil index of the following variables: liquid assets (L), human capital 1 (H_1), human capital 2 (H_2), health care 1 (HC_1) and health care 2 (HC_2).

The control variables are death rate (D), rural food expenditure (RF) and urban food expenditure (UF).

The core logistic regression is as follows:

$$\text{Logit}(p) = \log(p/1 - p) = \beta_0 + \beta_1 X_1 + \beta_2 X_2 + \ldots + \beta_k X_k \tag{6.6}$$

This logistic regression is adapted in this paper to include the following variables:

$$\text{Logit}(p) = \log(p/1 - p) = \beta_0 + \beta_1 T_L + \beta_2 T_{H1} + \beta_3 T_{H2} + \beta_3 T_{HC1} + \beta_3 T_{HC2} + \beta_4 D + \beta_5 RF + \beta_6 UF \tag{6.7}$$

With p as the percentage of the odd ratio: $\begin{cases} 1 = province - poor \\ 0 = province - nonpoor \end{cases}$

The equation has the following annotation: T_L is Theil of liquid assets, T_{H1} is Theil of human capital 1, T_{H2} is Theil of human capital 2, T_{HC1} is Theil of health care 1 and T_{HC2} is Theil of health care 2, D is death rate, RF is rural food expenditure, and UF is urban food expenditure. β_X are the coefficients of the respective variables. The results of this logistic regression are demonstrated in Tables 6.2, 6.3 and 6.4.

Finally we estimate the *marginal effect* of the coefficient of the vulnerability variables so as to estimate the evolution of vulnerability in China over the years. This can be done by introducing the averages into the nonlinear function (Wooldridge, 2002). With the marginal effect of coefficients (dF/dx) it is possible to estimate the evolution of assets in China on a regional level from 1985 to 2001. The results of *average marginal effect* of the assets coefficient are presented in Table 6.5. These averages can be weighted by adding up all the coefficients (β_L, β_{H1}, β_{H2}, β_{HC1}, and β_{HC2}), see equation 6.8:

Table 6.2 Statistical summary

Observations		N
Selected observations	Observations in analysis	423 (88.7%)
	Missing observations	54 (11.3%)
	Total	477 (100.0%)
Unselected observations		0 (0.0)
Total		477 (100.0%)

Table 6.3 Predictability of logistic regression of poverty at 80% of median level

		Predicted		
		Poverty		
Observed		*Non-poor (0.00)*	*Poor (1.00)*	*Percentage correct*
Poverty	Non-poor (0.00)	302	26	92.1
	Poor (1.00)	35	60	63.2
Overall percentage				85.6

Table 6.4 Results of logistic regression analysis with poverty at 80% of median level as dependable variable

Asset variables	B	SE	Wald	Significance
Theil liquid assets	−13.14	7.29	3.29	0.072**
Theil human capital 1	−42.55	14.20	8.99	0.003*
Theil human capital 2	−51.31	12.97	15.65	0.000*
Theil health care 1	13.16	4.29	9.61	0.002*
Theil health care 2	26.46	10.03	6.96	0.008*
Death rate	0.85	0.22	14.65	0.000*
Rural food expenditure	−0.05	0.00	34.22	0.000*
Urban food expenditure	0.04	0.00	2.87	0.090**
Constant	2.49	1.58	2.47	0.116

Notes:
*Correlation is significant at the 0.01 level (two-tailed).
**Correlation is significant at the 0.1 level (two-tailed).

$$\beta_{TOT} = |\beta_L| + |\beta_{H1}| + |\beta_{H2}| + |\beta_{HC1}| + |\beta_{HC2}| \tag{6.8}$$

With the following annotations: β_{TOT} is total sum of coefficient, β_L average coefficient of liquid assets, β_{H1} average coefficient human capital 1, β_{H2} average coefficient human capital 2, β_{HC1} average coefficient health care 1 and β_{HC2} average coefficient health care 2. The weighted coefficient can be introduced into a

Table 6.5 Results of logistic regression analysis (dF/dx) with poverty at 80 percent of median level as dependable variable to measure the marginal effect of the coefficient

Asset variables	dF/dx	SE	z P>|z|	Significance
Theil liquid assets (T_L)	$-0.14\ (\beta_L)$	0.0991	-1.74	0.081**
Theil human capital 1 (T_{H1})	$-0.45\ (\beta_{HC1})$	0.404	-3.06	0.002*
Theil human capital 2 (T_{H2})	$-0.53\ (\beta_{H2})$	0.401	-3.94	0.000*
Theil health care 1 (T_{HC1})	$00.14\ (\beta_{HC1})$	0.133	3.14	0.002*
Theil health care 2 (T_{HC2})	$0.27\ (\beta_{HC2})$	0.238	2.59	0.001*
Death rate	0.01	0.0081	3.99	0.000*
Rural food expenditure	-0.00	0.0004	-6.28	0.000*
Urban food expenditure	0.00	0.0000	1.78	0.090**
Constant	2.49	1.582	2.473	0.116

Notes:
*Correlation is significant at the 0.01 level (two-tailed).
**Correlation is significant at the 0.1 level (two-tailed).

function to estimate the evolution of vulnerability (V). The control variables have been excluded as the average impact is negligible (>0.01).

$$V = (\beta_L/\beta_{TOT})\,T_L + (\beta_{H1}/\beta_{TOT})\,T_{H1} + (\beta_{H2}/\beta_{TOT})T_{H2} \\ + (\beta_{HC1}/\beta_{TOT})T_{HC1} + (\beta_{HC2}/\beta_{TOT})T_{HC2} \tag{6.9}$$

$$V = (-0.09)\,T_L + (-0.29)\,T_{H1} + (-0.35)T_{H2} \\ + (0.09)T_{HC1} + (0.18)T_{HC2} \tag{6.10}$$

With the following annotation: V is the level of vulnerability, T_L is Theil of liquid assets by year, T_{H1} is Theil of human capital 1, T_{H2} is Theil of human capital 2, T_{HC1} is Theil of health care 1, and T_{HC2} is Theil of health care 2. Finally, the Theil index can be decomposed into a between regional component and a within regional component (decomposed Theil $(Th) = T_{BR} + T_{WR}$). The weighted coefficient of the average marginal effect can also estimate vulnerability by a between and within regional component through assets:

$$\text{Theil }(T) = T_{BR} + T_{WR} = V_{BR} + V_{WR} \tag{6.11}$$

$$V_{BR} = (-0.09)TBR_L + (-0.29)\,TBR_{H1} + (-0.35)TBR_{H2} \\ + (0.09)TBR_{HC1} + (0.18)TBR_{HC2} \tag{6.12}$$

$$V_{WR} = (-0.09)\,TWR_L + (-0.29)\,TWR_{H1} \\ + (-0.35)TWR_{H2} + (0.09)TWR_{HC1} + (0.18)TWR_{HC2} \tag{6.13}$$

With the following annotation: T_{BR} is the between regional component of the Theil index, T_{WR} is the within regional component of the Theil index, V_{BR} is the between regional component of vulnerability, V_{WR} is the within regional component of vulnerability, TBR_L is the between regional component of Theil of liquid assets, TWR_L is the within regional component of Theil of liquid assets, TBR_{H1} is the between regional component of Theil of human capital 1, TWR_{H1} is the within regional component of Theil of human capital 1, TBR_{H2} is the between regional component of Theil of human capital 2, TWR_{H2} is the within regional component of Theil of human capital 2, TBR_{HC1} is the between regional component of the Theil of health care 1, TWR_{HC1} is the within regional component of the Theil of health care 1, TBR_{HC2} is the between regional component of the Theil of health care 2 and TWR_{HC2} is the within regional component of the Theil of health care 2. The results are reflected in Figure 6.1.

Results

This section presents results of inequality measurements from the logistic regression in which the 80 percent median of income poverty is the dependent variable, with five variables that estimate assets (L, H_1, H_2, HC_1, and HC_2), as well as three control variables (D, RF, and UF). The statistical summary of the regression is indicated in Table 6.2, and the predictability of the logistic regression analysis can be viewed in Table 6.3.

In Table 6.2 on the statistical summary, it is noted that that 423 (88.7 percent) of the observations are included in the analysis, and 54 are excluded (11.3 percent). In Table 6.3, it is noted that the 423 observations were divided into 328

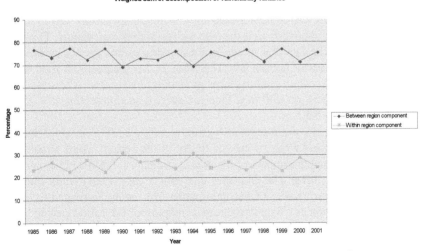

Figure 6.1 Decomposition of asset vulnerability index with a between region component and a within region component (equations 6.12 and 6.13). Source: Data provided by Belton M. Fleisher and Min Qiang, Ohio University and China Data Centre of the University of Michigan

non-poor (77.5 percent) and 95 poor (22.5 percent). The predictability of logistic regression with the median dependent variable of 80 percent is correctly predicted in 85.6 percent of the cases. This is the average prediction of both non-poor (63.2 percent) and poor (92.1 percent). This means that, 85.6 times out of 100, the predicted y_i matches the actual y_i. However, this can be misleading as a goodness-of-fit statistical test, as it is simply an average of the outcome of the non-poor and poor. Therefore, a Pseudo R2 measurement is introduced, which is based on the log likelihood and is 0.4549. The 85.6 percent correctly predicted in combination with a Pseudo R2 of 0.4549 leads to a robust result.

Table 6.4 indicate that the asset variables are significant at the 0.01 (in the case of human capital 1, human capital 2, health care 1, and health care 2 as well as the control variables, death rate and rural food expenditure) and the 0.1 level (in the case of liquid assets and urban food expenditure). In addition, liquid assets, human capital 1, and human capital 2 have a negative impact, which means that a higher Theil index leads to lower odds ratio probability of becoming non-poor (i.e. more risk of poverty). However, health care 1 and 2 have a positive impact, which means that a higher Theil index leads to a higher odds ratio probability of becoming non-poor (i.e. less risk of poverty), which is counter-intuitive.

There are also three control variables to ensure that the results of the logistic regression are valid. The first control variable, death rate, has a positive impact, which indicates that higher inequality in death rates leads to higher probability in the risk of becoming poor. The second control variable, rural food expenditure, has a negative impact, which indicates that a lower inequality in rural food expenditure leads to an increase in the odds ratio of becoming non-poor (i.e. less risk of poverty). The third control variable, urban food expenditure, has a slightly positive impact (0.004), which indicates that a higher inequality in urban food expenditure leads to lower probability of poverty. This is contrary to intuition, which would indicate that higher inequality in food expenditure would lead to higher probability of poverty as is the case with rural food expenditure. This could be explained by the fact that urban food expenditures are already sufficient to meet the basic needs of households. Therefore, higher inequality in food expenditure does not necessary lead to lower probability of poverty. After discussing the different impacts, we will now focus on average marginal effects, which are indicated in Table 6.5.

Table 6.5 presents the results of logistic regression (dF/dx), which indicate the *average marginal effect* of the coefficient of the various assets variables. It should be noted that the impact of the human capital 1 (−0.45) and human capital 2 (−0.53) are strong. This indicates that human capital is strongly linked to the reduction of probability of becoming poor. This could be related to human capital accumulation as China introduced a compulsory Education Law in March 1986, which requires free education for all for the first nine years of schooling. In addition, the importance of human capital accumulation is confirmed by other researchers who demonstrate the strong relationship between education and poverty reduction (Adam and Jane, 1995; Campa and Webb, 1999).

Liquid assets also contribute to the reduction of poverty, although this has a much smaller impact than human capital. However, health care 1 and health care 2 have a positive impact. This indicates that this variable would increase the risk of poverty as inequality in medical personnel and beds in hospitals increases. This could be linked to decentralisation as more health care staff means a higher wage bill, transferred to the users by service fees. As user fees would make it difficult for the poor to get access to health care, the probability of poverty might increase as inequality in health care 1 and 2 is reduced. In practical terms, this would mean that the overall quality of health care could increase but benefiting only a small portion of the population, while the poor are excluded by the introduction of fees. The health care results are contrary to those of the education sector. The fact that a law to increase access to schooling for all was introduced might explain the difference in results between the health care variables and the education variable.

Figure 6.2 demonstrates that the eastern region is less vulnerable than the western and interior regions. However, the eastern region does seem to have an increase in vulnerability until 1995, after which it stabilizes. The unequal evolution in vulnerability could be linked to different patterns of growth in China. In particular, the eastern region benefited from economic growth while the western and interior region did not have high economic growth rates. This could explain why vulnerability is lower than in the other two regions as well as the successful evolution of the eastern region between 1985 and 2001.

Figure 6.1, the decomposition of inequality, indicates that the between regional component contributes roughly 70–80 percent to the inequality in vulnerability

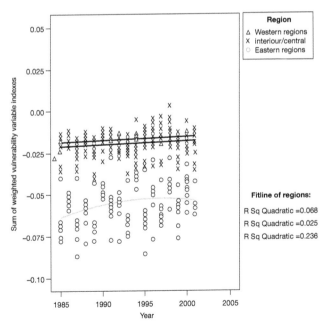

Figure 6.2 Result of the weighed vulnerability variables (equation 6.10). Source: Data provided by Belton M. Fleisher and Min Qiang, Ohio University, and China Data Centre of the University of Michigan.

variables, whereas the within regional component contributes roughly 20–30 percent to the inequality in the vulnerability variables. Again, this indicates that inequalities between regions are large and is linked to the growth process in China that has focused on the eastern region while the interior region and western region have been left out.

Conclusion and policy implications

The objective of this research has been to analyze the composition of assets in China as well as to present the evolution of vulnerability by region between 1985 and 2001. The conclusion is threefold: First, liquid assets and human capital contribute to the reduction of vulnerability, whereas health care does not contribute to the reduction of vulnerability. Second, the interior and western regions have higher degrees of vulnerability as their populations have a higher probability of becoming poor, whereas the eastern region has a lower degree of vulnerability, which peaks around 1995. Third, the inequalities *within* regions (i.e. between individual regions and their provinces) contribute about 20–30 percent to vulnerability, while inequality *between* regions contributes about 70–80 percent to vulnerability (i.e. between the three regions). Therefore any policy that focuses on the reduction of vulnerability in China should aim at supporting the accumulation of human capital and liquid assets as well as addressing inequalities at the regional level.

However, we have to interpret our results with caution in regard to their impact on vulnerability. First, this paper focuses on "proximate" vulnerability and not "structural" vulnerability, as this research mainly emphasizes productive assets (liquid assets, human capital, and health care) of entitlements in a given year and not on structural vulnerability variables such as headship, age, informal networks as well as family networks (i.e. *guanxi*), households with old and infirm members – similar to concepts of structural poverty (Davies, 1996). Second, the assets variables focus on "resilience" of households and not on external risks. For example, some regions might be more prone to natural disasters, floods, or economic downturns than other regions. These external threats have not been taken into account in this paper. Third, distinctions between urban and rural areas that are likely to affect vulnerability should ideally be taken into account. Unfortunately, the dataset does not allow it to be disaggregated in this manner. Fourthly, the variables that measure assets of households may not reflect the reality, as the variables do not necessary measure effectiveness and accessibility. This is particularly the case with regard to the health care variables, but could also be the case for the education sector, which would have negative implications for human capital. Finally, there is a problem of the direction of causalities between vulnerability and poverty. One could assume that having a low level of exposure to vulnerability is the *source* of an assets build-up. For example, at the beginning of the 1980s, everybody was guaranteed a minimum level of free health services. Nowadays, an individual would have to gain access to these same health services. Therefore asset build-up could also be seen as a coping mechanism in regard to rising exposure to vulnerability.

Despite these limitations, we believe the research to be sufficiently robust to argue that the reduction of vulnerability would ensure the population of a province or region in China would have greater resilience to poverty in the case of a negative economic shock. This would decrease social tension and contribute to the development of a harmonious society in China. To further reduce vulnerability, the Chinese government could take the following policy measures into consideration:

1 Encourage human capital accumulation in an equitable manner. The research indicates that human capital formulation is closely linked to the reduction in the probability of becoming poor. Therefore, stimulating the accumulation of human capital, at secondary school as well as university level, would increase the resilience of a region as it increases the capacity to cope with stress as well as to recover from crisis situations. An entry point could be to introduce an amendment into the compulsory education law, extending the current nine-year period of free education by several years.
2 Increase accessibility to health care as the current system does not reduce vulnerability. This could be done by introducing a law that would compel health care institutions to provide free basic medical care for everybody. Such an intervention would increase accessibility and would have two advantages. The first would provide a safety net for households whose members fall ill or have work or traffic accidents. The second advantage is that health care would encourage human capital accumulation that, as previously described, would increase resilience. Providing such a safety net is particularly important as the strong employment inflows and outflows are not symmetrical (Wu and Yao, 2006), resulting in those adversely affected being poor for a long period of time.
3 Develop regional strategies to address underdevelopment in the interior and western regions. This would reduce inter-regional disparities, thereby contributing 70–80 percent to the reduction of vulnerability. Such development strategies could be modeled on the eastern region (through, for example, the provision of tax incentives, and the establishment of export processing zones and encouragement of industrial development), as vulnerability in this region is lower than the interior and western regions. However, this should be accompanied by major investments in infrastructure to ensure linkages between, on the one hand, the coastal areas and, on the other hand, the western and interior regions.

With these measures, vulnerability in China would be reduced by increasing the resilience of the population at the provincial level. This would contribute to the strengthening of social cohesion as well as to the wellbeing of households in China. Moreover, in any potential future economic downturn households would have the capacity to absorb negative income shocks, thereby reducing the prospect of civil strife and enhancing political stability. These are all key elements in the development of a harmonious society in China.

Notes

1 This definition combines two elements: (i) the risk of an event in which a bad outcome could move the household into poverty (Alwang *et al.*, 2001); and (ii) the identification of a geographical area that is more vulnerable than other areas (Downing, 1991; Guillaumont, 2006).

2 An example of the multidimensional approach is the poverty pyramid, which indicates traditional income poverty measurements at the top of the pyramid, with at the bottom a broad set of poverty variables including dignity, assets, common resources, state-provided commodities, and autonomy (Baulch, 1996).

3 This dataset is officially certified by the Statistical Bureau of China.

4 This dataset was provided by Belton M. Fleisher and Min Qiang, but originated from Sylvie Demurger. Figures for college education were based on the 1982, 1990 and 2000 censuses, as well as the annual Population Change Survey (1996, 1998, 1999, 2002 and 2003). Data on secondary education were based on Sylvie Demurger's work and was extended by Belton M. Fleisher and Min Qiang.

5 Disposable income is based on spot checks.

6 Some areas in some coastal provinces in China have development indicators that perform more like a middle-income country (such as in the areas of literacy and infant mortality), while in western China these variables are more like low-income countries (Kanbur and Zhang, 2005).

7 For example in the allocation of funds, it is important to identify which areas need to be targeted.

8 The national total death rate excludes the populations of Hong Kong, Macau, and Taiwan.

9 The 80 percent median income as poverty rate measurement has been proposed by the US Census Bureau (Bavier, 2005) as a means to incorporate out-of-pocket medical expenditures, which is one of the main sources of poverty in the United States of America and is, in a sense, similar to other developing countries. In addition, some states, like the state of Oregon, use the 80 percent median income to define low income (Housing and Income data, 2005).

References

Adam, H. and Jane, J. (1995) 'Sources of Income Inequality and Poverty in Rural Pakistan,' International Food Policy Research Institute Research Report 102.

Akita, T. (2000) 'Decomposing Regional Income Inequality Using Two-Stage Nested Theil Decomposition Method,' Working Paper No. 2, presented at the Sixth World Congress of the Regional Science Association International, in Lugano, Switzerland.

Alwang, J., Siegel, P.B., and Jørgensen, Steen L. (2001) 'Vulnerability: A View from Different Disciplines Social Protection,' Discussion Paper No. 0115, World Bank.

Baulch, B. (1996) 'The New Poverty Agenda: A Disputed Consensus,' *Institute of Development Studies Bulletin*, 27 (1), 36–42.

Bavier, R. (2005) 'Medical Out-of-Pocket Spending Poverty Thresholds in Poverty Measurement Working Papers,' US Census Bureau, Housing and Household Economic Statistics Division, Online. Available <www.census.gov/hhes/www/povmeas/altmoop.html>.

Bebbington, A. (1999) 'Capitals and Capabilities: A Framework for Analyzing Peasant Viability, Rural Livelihoods and Poverty,' *World Development*, 27 (12), 2021–2044.

Campa, M. and Webb R. (1999) 'Mobility and Poverty Dynamics in the 1990's,' paper presented at IDS/IFPRI Workshop on Poverty Dynamics, Institute of Development Studies, University of Sussex.

Davies, S. (1996) *Adaptable Livelihoods: Coping with Food Insecurity in the Malian Sahel*, London: Palgrave Macmillan.

Dercon, S. (2001) 'Assessing Vulnerability to Poverty,' paper prepared for the Department for International Development (DFID), London.

Downing, T. E. (1991) 'Assessing Socio-Economic Vulnerability to Famine: Frameworks, Concepts and Applications,' Final Report to US Agency for International Development, Famine Early Warning System Project, Washington DC.

Fan, S., Zhang, L., and Zhang, X. (2002) 'Growth, Inequality, and Poverty in Rural China: The Role of Public Investments,' International Food Policy Research Institute (IFPRI) Research Report 125, Washington, DC.

Guillaumont, P. (2006) 'Economic Vulnerability Still a Challenge for African Growth,' document de travail de la série Etudes et Documents (E.2006.41), CERDI.

Housing and Income Data (2005/6) *City of Ashland in Oregon State*, Online. Available <www.ashland.or.us/Files/Housing_Income_Data.pdf>.

Hulme, D. and Shepherd, A. (2003) 'Conceptualizing Chronic Poverty,' *World Development*, 31 (3), 403–423.

Jalan, J. and Ravallion, M. (1999) 'Are the Poor Less Well Insured? Evidence on Vulnerability to Income Risk in Rural China,' *Journal of Development Economics*, 58 (1), 61–81.

Jalan, J. and Ravallion, M. (2001) 'Behavioral Responses to Risk in Rural China,' *Journal of Development Economics*, 66 (1), 23–49.

Kanbur, R. and Zhang, X. (2005) 'Spatial Inequality in Education and Health Care in China,' *China Economic Review*, 16 (2), 189–204.

Li, S., and Zhao, R. (2007) 'Changes in the Distribution of Wealth in China, 1995–2002,' Research Paper No. 2007/03, UNU WIDER.

Lipton, M. and Maxwell, S. (1992) 'The New Poverty Agenda: An Overview,' Discussion Paper 306, Institute of Development Studies.

McCulloch, N. and Calandrino, M. (2003) 'Vulnerability and Chronic Poverty in Rural Sichuan,' *World Development*, 31 (3), 611–628.

Mansuri, G. and Healy, A. (2000) 'Assessing Vulnerability: An Ex Ante Measure and its Application Using Data from Rural Pakistan,' mimeo, Development Research Group, World Bank, Washington, DC.

Misselhorn, A. (2005) 'What Drives Food Insecurity in South Africa? A Meta-Analysis of Household Economy Studies,' *Global Environmental Change*, 15 (1), 33–43.

Moser, C. (1998) 'The Asset Vulnerability Framework: Reassessing Urban Poverty Reduction Strategies,' *World Development*, 26 (1), 1–19.

Osberg, L. and Kuan, X. (2006) 'How Should We Measure Global Poverty in a Changing World,' UNU WIDER Research Paper No. 2006/64, United Nations.

Salas, J. (2003) 'Poverty in Mexico in the 1990s,' Working Paper No. 357, Maxwell School of Citizenship and Public Affairs, Syracuse University, NY.

Sen, B. (2003) 'Drivers of Escape and Descent: Changing Household Fortunes in Rural Bangladesh,' *World Development*, 31 (3), 513–534.

Wagle, U. (2006) 'The Estimates and Characteristics of Poverty in Kathmandu: What do Three Measurement Standards Suggest?,' *The Social Science Journal*, 43 (3), 405–423.

Wan G. (2006) 'Poverty Accounting by Factor Components,' Research Paper No. 2006/63, UNU WIDER.

Wong C. (1995) 'Measuring Third World Poverty by the International Poverty Line: The Case of REFORM CHINA,' *Social Policy & Administration*, 29 (3), 189–203.

Wood, G. (2003) 'Staying Secure, Staying Poor: The "Faustian Bargain",' *World Development*, 31 (3), 455–471.

Wooldridge, J. (2002) *Econometric Analysis of Cross Section and Panel Data*, Cambridge, MA: MIT Press.

World Bank (2006) *World Development Report 2006: Equity and Development*, Washington, DC: World Bank.

Wu, Z. and Yao, S. (2006) 'On Unemployment Inflow and Outflow in Urban China,' *Regional Studies*, 40 (8), 811–822.

Part 2

China's Post-Reform Economy

Sustaining growth

7 China's banking reform

Problems and potential solutions[1]

Charles Goodhart and Xiaosong Zeng

Introduction

China's financial system has been undergoing major reforms during the last decade, with the aim of establishing a modern commercial banking system and the development of stock market(s). In recent years there have been large capital injections into ailing state-owned banks, and currently encouragement for them to explore initial public offerings (IPOs), as well as bail-outs of bankrupt securities firms by state-owned investment companies. We acknowledge the considerable progress already made in reforming the banking system, but we feel that there are still questions that need to be asked. For example, exactly what is the core of the fundamental problem(s) with the banking system in China? What is the best path to take to address such problems?

Key problems of China's banking sector

Despite recent reforms, we note that there remain worrying current developments including the following:

1 The asset quality of state-owned banks is still a concern

Based on the latest statistics, released in July 2005 by the China Banking Regulatory Commission (CBRC), the regulator of commercial banks and lending institutions in China, as of 30 June 2005, the non-performing loan (NPL) balance of state-owned banks was RMB1,013.5 billion, which is RMB903.3 billion less than the RMB1,916.8 billion as of 31 December 2003. However, after adjusting for the transfer of NPLs of RMB634 billion from the Industrial and Commercial Bank of China (ICBC), RMB254 billion from the Bank of China (BOC), and RMB9.5 billion from the China Construction Bank (CCB), the NPL balance of state-owned banks would be RMB1,911.0 billion, not significantly lower than its 2003 level.

Moreover, we are concerned about the soaring totals of special mention (SM) loans, which can be used to hide NPLs. Taking the three forefront banks in the restructuring, CCB, BOC, and Bank of Communications (BoComm), as examples, we observe that the combined balance of their SM loans rose 22.4 per cent, to RMB731 billion, in 2004. Also, if the NPLs transferred to AMCs are included back into the NPLs, the combined impaired loan balance (i.e. NPLs plus SM loans) would grow by RMB190 billion from the end of 2003. Accordingly, their impaired loan ratio would grow by 2.21 percentage points to 28.47 per cent from 26.27 per cent during the same period.

The NPL increase in the first half of 2005 was primarily related to new loans made in 2003 and 2004, when the economic cycle of China peaked. In 2003, annual GDP growth was over 9 per cent and banks made roughly RMB3,000 billion new loans, among which RMB1,679 billion was made by the 'Big Four' state-owned banks. In addition to their desire for profitability (which also enables them to make larger provisions for NPLs without being forced to show an accounting loss), banks benefit from making new loans because, by doing so, the NPL ratio is diluted. Indeed, there are some suggestions that bank expansion has been partly driven by pressure from regulators to reduce NPL ratios. But, if such new loans then generate the same proportion of NPLs or, even worse, a higher ratio, the strategy will be self-defeating.

In any case such a strategy of trying to grow out of trouble came to an end in April 2004, when the central government took action to cool down the overheated economy, and to curb the bubble in the real estate market. We are concerned about the banking system's vulnerability to a credit cycle downturn, since their NPL ratios could further deteriorate if the economy should grow significantly less fast, and if the real estate market in metropolitan cities like Shanghai should encounter price declines.

2 Taxpayers and depositors continue to subsidize state-owned banks

In any case, an easing of the government's 'Macro-Adjustment' might not be helpful in alleviating the NPL levels of commercial banks if the fundamental problem is not properly solved, and NPLs incurred on new loans remain large. Moreover, in early August 2005, several state media reported that commercial banks would increase the rate of new lending in the second half of 2005, thanks to increasing deposit and newly injected capital. The target for new loans in 2005, set by the People's Bank of China, was roughly RMB2,500 billion, and commercial banks made RMB1,450 million, or 58 per cent of the annual target, during the first half of 2005, lower than the historical average of 60 per cent; so commercial banks were expected to be more aggressive in their lending policy subsequently. A potential concern is the new NPLs generated for the next several years by current new lending.

The government has injected substantial capital into the 'Big Three' state-owned banks, and took over a large proportion of their NPLs. The next in line for rescue is the fourth largest bank in China. After that all state-owned banks in China will have been rescued with money from tax payers, many of whom are also depositors in these banks. The rescue of state-owned banks is followed by the government's bail-out of bankrupt securities firms. Will such government rescues solve the fundamental problems of China's banking system? How far, if at all, do such rescues and subsidies solve the basic problems of China's banking system? Might they not even make them worse by reducing banks' concern to check and monitor the viability of existing and proposed loan business (moral hazard and adverse selection)? Depositors at the Big Four state-owned commercial banks already enjoy implicit 100 per cent deposit insurance, but moral hazard issues might range more widely should a deposit insurance scheme (DIS) be launched in the near future.

3 Banks' loan margins are too low to generate a proper return on capital and strengthen the capital adequacy ratio

The revenue of commercial banks in China is highly dependent on corporate loan business; it accounted for over 80 per cent of the Big Four state-owned banks' revenue in 2004 on average. But the loan margins on such business are too low to generate a sufficient risk-adjusted return (e.g. risk adjusted return on capital or RAROC) and capital adequacy ratio. Given the rapid growth of deposits, due to the high savings rate of individuals and lack of alternative financial investment opportunities, bank capital must also increase in line to maintain capital adequacy. Net revenues have been too low to generate sufficient profitability to maintain RAROC. Part of the solution must be to increase margins by some combination of reduction on deposit interest and/or increase in lending rates. But this latter could raise NPLs ever further via adverse selection.

4 Capital adequacy ratio is low

The CAR of Chinese banks is low, with the highest no more than 12 per cent, and the highest among the five A-share banks no more than 10 per cent, in contrast to the average ratio over 18 per cent of Hong Kong listed banks.

Though CBRC is requiring all Chinese banks to achieve a CAR no lower than 8 per cent by the end of 2006, we are not sure whether these banks can achieve this goal by the due date. The current temporary freeze of secondary offers in the A-share market will cut off another route for raising equity.

5 Reliability of data is still questionable

The reliability of accounting data, such as the loan classification and loan loss provisions, is critical for the assessment of the soundness of banks. The widespread doubts over Chinese banks' financial data are due to concern over the quality of banks' auditing procedures, standards and controls.

What are the fundamental problems with China's banking system?

In our view, the fundamental problems with China's banking system are the inter-dependence between banks and state-owned enterprises (SOEs), the way that banks are run as SOEs, and government's improper influences on the operations of SOEs and banks. Though these problems have been around for a long time and are deeply rooted, we do not believe that they have been really solved. In our opinion, without a thorough reform of the SOEs and the way that banks are run as SOEs, the problems with China's banking system will never be really solved, even after the banks are (partially) relieved of current NPLs, invested by minority foreign bank shareholders, and listed on the stock exchange.

The history of China's SOEs has made them very different from the profit-maximizing firms of market economies. Traditionally, SOEs provided a set of social services to their employees and their families, and have usually been used to solve the unemployment problem and alleviate the social burden on the govern-ment; in developed economies enterprises are less influenced by local government and have a better corporate governance structure and less social burden. Whereas China has been trying to establish a 'modern enterprise system' by transforming many SOEs into shareholding companies and also to shift the provision of social security to the state, the SOE reform has been only partial and incomplete. Profit maximization is still not the sole objective for an SOE; besides initially fulfilling the quantitative objectives of the production plan (not necessarily profit plan) set by either the central government (if the SOE is large enough and is categorized as a 'Central Level Enterprise') or local government, SOEs also shoulder the burden of providing tax (and other, sometimes dark) revenues and employment (from time to time to retiring government officials).

For all these reasons, the ability of an SOE to generate profits is not the sole criterion of success nor determines its ability to continue in existence. SOEs have rarely been subject to a hard budget constraint, neither are they subject to bankruptcy if they cannot meet their debts. The state control of ownership also makes the take-over of an underperforming SOE less likely (unless the enormous loss of a SOE affects the employment target, makes it lose its various values for the government, or it is perceived to be too weak to be turned around by the government-appointed management team). Nor is the management of a typical SOE subject to a well-structured incentive plan, which rewards the management based on the performance of the firm. Also, the management of SOEs and typical banks usually carry a political rank comparable to government officials, and they participate in political activities from time to time, so political influence on SOEs and banks is virtually unavoidable. Moreover, general managers of SOEs may be politically more senior than those of banks in the system, making it very difficult for banks to say no to borrowing requests from these SOEs.

The inefficiency of SOEs have had fiscal/financial consequences. Under a cen-trally planned system, the banking system plays little role in allocating capital, and state-owned banks extend loans as, and when, required to finance plan allocations.

So there was originally little concern in the banks for managing the risk of loan losses or non-performing loans. Even after the move towards a market-oriented economy, there was a continuing, in part politically driven, desire to enable many (perhaps most, as represented by total employment) loss-making SOEs to continue in operation.

The problem has been how to finance this. The Big Four commercial banks traditionally have done much of this, a (hidden) form of fiscal subsidy. Given the difficulties, and disadvantages, within China of raising additional tax revenues to take over the remaining social functions from SOEs (and of paying unemployment benefits to ease the redeployment of labour from inefficient, closed SOEs), the incentive to local governments to continue using the commercial banks as an informal fiscal piggy-bank was enormous.

Indeed this syndrome went further. The stock market has been seen as another way to provide a quasi-fiscal subsidy to SOEs, (not so much as a means of allocating capital efficiently). Many, though not all, of the SOEs chosen for listing and IPOs were so selected not because they were the best performing SOEs, but because they were most in need of an infusion of extra funding. The result of this has been that many of the SOEs listed on the Shenzhen and Shanghai stock exchanges have failed to make profits or to distribute any dividends, with many becoming the target of speculative trading and finally becoming 'shell' companies. The management of many listed companies, no matter how poor is their performance, are not subject to the risk of being replaced, as the majority shares are still controlled by the government or legal entities affiliated to the government. Partly as a consequence, equity prices on the two stock exchanges have tended downwards, causing upset (to say the least) amongst their investors, and making the regulator unwilling to authorize any further new listings (of whatever quality) and even opposed to other initiatives (such as controlled portfolio outflows into foreign assets, via Qualified Domestic Institutional Investors (QDII) that might provide alternative (and better performing) investments than the local stock exchanges. So, despite the stock markets having been operating for the better part of ten years, neither the equity nor, partly for other reasons, the corporate bond market (i.e. the capital markets) has played an efficient role in the intermediation of saving and investment, or in the allocation of capital in the PRC. This government has realized this problem and has tried to permit the sales and trading of such 'non-tradable shares' of domestically listed companies, as we will discuss in the later part of this chapter.

Since making losses did not (quasi-automatically) lead to closure and the dismissal of the management, SOE managers have been in many cases effectively on a soft budget constraint. Moreover, the bigger an enterprise, the harder it usually is to close, because of the resultant effects on the local economy. So the management of SOEs usually has had an incentive to invest and to expand, in some large part without much concern for relative prices, notably interest rates. If the investment is successful, they – the managers – obtain much of the benefit. Losses, and failures, can be largely passed on to the banking system – banks and equity investors. There is a built-in incentive to expand output and employment, but not the return on capital.

Given their historical background in financing SOEs, the banks accumulated a large proportionate volume of NPLs, which, if on a rigorous accounting basis, could endanger the solvency of the main commercial banks. This has meant that state-owned banks too have been on a soft budget basis. From time to time the authorities have tried to 'clean up' the banks by transferring old NPLs to asset management companies (AMCs, which have their own incentive problems – not discussed here), and shifting strategic investment financing onto the policy banks (whose operations appear neither well-defined nor transparent – also not discussed further here), and injecting new assets – most recently US Treasury bonds – into the banks in the place of the transferred NPLs.

This has been, at best, a partial success. One reason for this is that the banks have only in practice been able to transfer a proportion of their existing NPLs to the AMCs. Much more important is that the incentive of the government and bank to make new loans to (potentially or probably) underperforming SOEs remains strong. Not only are the banks still on a soft budget basis, but in the event of a bankruptcy, or closure, a bank ranks low amongst creditors. 'Ever-greening', i.e. carrying loss-making SOEs, avoids political ructions and making large losses concrete on the books. Banks have become what is known as 'passive creditors'.

Even when the government sets some goals, such as the minimum capital adequacy ratio (CAR) and maximum NPL ratio, for banks receiving capital injections, banks can use creative accounting and other measures to achieve such goals. For example, to achieve the goal of CAR, some banks consider temporarily selling some risky assets at the end of the year to other banks without such CAR pressure (say, banks with higher CAR or very low CAR). And, as we discussed in the earlier part of this chapter, many banks try to rapidly increase their asset size, which is not only helpful to dilute the NPL ratio and to expand the amount of profits (but not the profitability, such as net interest margin and return on average asset (ROA).

We are concerned about the rapid growth of bank loans, which, measured by the ratio of total loans/GDP, has been higher since 2003 than that of Thailand, Indonesia and Korea in 1997, the year immediately prior to the Asian Financial Crises in 1998, and just slightly lower than that of Malaysia in 1997, as shown in Figure 7.1.

Moreover, state-owned banks, like SOEs, are majority owned and run by the government. In particular senior management is appointed by the government based on various factors and considerations, instead of being selected from the market, based on track records and experience in bank management. And we do not believe that this will be fundamentally changed even after their respective IPOs, based on the listings of several banks either domestically or overseas. As the management of state-owned banks and SOEs are generally colleagues within the governmental or political system, it is not an easy job for state-owned banks to decline making loans to many SOEs. It is actually not unusual for state-owned banks to favour even loss-making SOEs against better performing non-SOEs (NSOEs) such as private enterprises, which sometimes have to either borrow from an 'underground banking house' or restrict the scale of investment. That being said, we are not arguing that SOEs always underperform NSOEs, or that SOEs are the only source of PRC banks' problem loans.

Also, the compensation of SOE and state-owned bank's management, as we previously discussed, could distort the incentive structure of SOEs (see Zeng, 1995). If, as usual in China, political cadres are transferred by the government to banks, and the reward to a successful banker in a state-owned bank is promotion/transfer by the government to a senior position within the political system, it will be difficult for the management of state-owned banks to set return on equity (ROE) maximization and risk control as their foremost objectives and resist political pressure or benefit to make loans to support local economic growth. Bankers grown from the political system are also less professional in banking skills and risk management, which are more and more complicated and challenging in today's financial world.

This conjuncture also reduces the effectiveness of market-oriented monetary policy. Since they are subject to soft budgets, the SOEs (and the banks) pay relatively little attention to price signals, i.e. to the level of interest rates. Indeed in China from time to time a rise in interest rates has the perverse effect of shifting resources to relatively low-return enterprises such as SOEs, who may ignore rising interest rates, and away from other NSOEs who do respond to price signals.

Last but not least, we note that the management of SOEs and state-owned banks who violated lending policies and procedures, or even broke laws, were not always disciplined via the legal means – many of them were disciplined via the government's internal political system instead. Prosecutions and imprisonments were usually related to scandals involving foreign jurisdictions (e.g. in the US and Hong Kong) and revealed by foreign media.

Some proposals for banking reform in China

China has done much to reform SOEs, ranging from the establishment of a 'Modern Enterprise System' to the listing of some SOEs in the stock markets, domestically and even internationally. Nevertheless there remain outstanding questions whether underperforming firms have been penalized by higher financing costs, management restructuring and even bankruptcy. And have good firms been rewarded by a reduced cost of capital? If not, the capital market did not properly play its role in disciplining the corporate sector through its lending and fundraising functions. We believe that the ultimate success of reforms of SOEs and banks will require an effective capital market.

The most recent efforts of the government to make state-owned shares of listed companies tradable in the stock market appears a move in the right direction, even though the ways to implement the reform, fairness in valuation for the holders of tradable shares versus non-tradable shares, as well as the freezing of secondary offerings or overseas listing, are widely debated. The effectiveness of this reform remains to be seen.

There are, of course, many pre-conditions for the establishment of an effective capital market, but the following need to be emphasized:

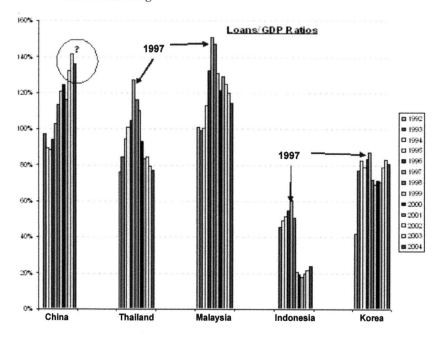

Figure 7.1 Loans/GDP ratio of China compared with countries affected by the Asian Financial Crises, 1992–2004. Source: Garg and Zeng, 2005.

1 Improve the information infrastructure

There must be adequate information disclosure and enforcement of that by regulators. The quality of information disclosure is dependant on the professional infrastructure, notably the availability of clearly defined accounting standards and the establishment of a financial professional system, within which professionals, such as well-trained accountants and security analysts, can adequately analyse the financial conditions of a company. If accurate public information on the financial position of enterprises is scarce and of uncertain reliability, it will be difficult for investors to allocate funds efficiently. This uncertainty may serve to divert funds from capital markets to the banks, which are (correctly and properly) perceived as having implicit 100 per cent protection.

Financial regulators should focus on surveillance of disclosure quality, strictly enforce disclosure rules, and make the management shown to be responsible for false disclosure or fraudulent practice accountable for their actions (Zeng, 1997a). Whereas numerous security rules and regulations have been enacted in China, their enforcement, in particular their timeliness, strictness and effectiveness, is critical. Financial regulators should also try to establish an effective incentive structure in financial regulation (Goodhart, 1995; Zeng, 1997b).

2 Strengthen creditors' rights

There is a need to establish an effective legal system for the enforcement of bankruptcy laws. In many emerging soft budget countries, the law, especially bankruptcy law, is strongly biased towards debtors, and/or the legal system is lax in enforcing the law. The weakness of banks' positions as a creditor of a failed company has already been mentioned. Furthermore the ability of a secured creditor to foreclose on a defaulting mortgage is strictly limited. Unless bond holders possess covenants that enable them to control and replace management and to realize collateral before all the assets are depleted, such bond holders stand at severe risk of being dispossessed. In the case of bonds issued by SOEs in China, it is far from clear what security a bond holder would have, and there may be many grey areas in the enforcement of bondholder's claim against such security in a bankruptcy. Under such conditions it is, perhaps, not surprising that no corporate bond market has yet developed. We recognize that the government has taken a more proactive approach to develop the corporate bond market, such as the recent approval by the State Reform and Development Commission for several 'Central-Level' SOEs to issue bonds in the second half of 2005; it remains unclear, however, why the debt issuance quota, which is perceived as a scare resource in China, has been primarily awarded to SOEs, why bond issuance is decided by government officials, rather than by the shareholders of the companies involved, and what the rationale behind the official approval/denial has been.

3 Improve managerial incentive structures

An effective incentive structure for SOEs' management should be established. The performance of a firm, either an SOE or a bank, depends on the effort and quality of its management. This is true no matter whether a firm's stock is listed or not. In order to establish an effective incentive structure to motivate the management to maximize the ROE, it is necessary to reward management for outperformance and hold the management accountable for underperformance and/or mismanagement (Zeng 1997a). As previously analysed, to reward an outperforming SOE manager by promoting her/him to a senior position within the political system is not an economically effective incentive structure and does not generate an appropriate interest alignment between the management and shareholders of a firm. Evidence in developed market economies has demonstrated that it is more effective to recognize, measure and financially reward the managerial expertise of managers. The scheme of awarding Executive Stock Options (ESO) is a useful tool for the establishment of an effective incentive structure for SOE management, and its structure, pitfalls and improvements were analysed by us (Goodhart, 1997).

4 Reinforce the corporate governance structure

'Corporate governance' generally refers to the system of checks and balances that ensures that corporate management, boards of directors, various board committees, executives, auditors and corporate advisers all carry out their fiduciary responsibilities owed to those they represent.

A paper examining how corporate governance is closely related to capital market development in particular and property rights infrastructure in general (Sheng *et al.*, 2003) suggests that good corporate governance relies heavily on an array of supporting institutions, or the property rights infrastructure (PRI). Sheng *et al*. argue that a major task in the transition from a planned economy to a market economy is to build a strong and well-functioning PRI. Good corporate governance and a competitive market economy can only be built upon a strong PRI.

As described in that paper, the essential elements of a modern PRI include the following institutions grouped in three broad categories:

1   Institutions for delineation of property rights

- A Central Registry of property right [e.g. land registry, share registry] to provide an official record of property rights. This is crucial for transparency of property rights and reducing the costs of enforcement.
- Accounting and legal processes to define property rights (annual audits and the right of lawsuit to protect property rights).

2   Institutions for the exchange of property rights

- Trading processes (such as a stock exchange trading platform to enable transparent trading of property rights, and public auctions).
- Clearing, settlement and payment infrastructure (clearing house and payment system operated by banking system to enable transfers to be cleared and settled in final form through delivery of property rights).
- Regulated intermediaries (intermediaries who participate in the transfer process should be sanctioned if they do not perform according to the rules of the game).

3   Institutions for enforcement and fine-tuning of property rights

- Rules of the Game: norms, standards, codes, regulations, and law that help protect the property rights of participants against abuses of the system.
- Enforcement infrastructure: there must exist regulators to enforce the rules but enforcement costs should not exceed benefits to markets.
- Independent and transparent judiciary to adjudicate disputes over property rights.
- Transparent media and disclosure regime to ensure that property rights can be independently verified and accountable (e.g. disclosure rules and mandatory publication of financial statements).

Sheng *et al*. believe that, in a well functioning market, the PRI essentially functions to vet the entry of market participants and ensure that they perform to market and ethical norms and those that damage public interest through inefficiency or misconduct (theft or fraud) exit the market. Each sector of the (financial) system will have a different PRI, such as the trading, clearing and settlement system for the securities market. If the PRI is defective, then the property rights are not protected, and indeed may well be expropriated by players that are inefficient, loss-making and in effect subsidized by the rest of the market.

Hernando De Soto (2000) has uncovered six hidden benefits of private property:

- enabling the economic potential of assets (efficient use of capital);
- integrating dispersed information into one system (economy of scale in PRI and standards and low transaction costs);
- making people accountable (private property as an ultimate guarantee on contract fulfilment or fulfilment of responsibility);
- making assets fungible (allowing convergence of risk-adjusted return on various assets);
- networking people (increasing the extent of the market and facilitating specialization);
- protecting transactions (low enforcement costs when private property can be used as collateral and reduce transaction costs).

Sheng *et al.* pointed out that the Latin American experience shows that weaknesses in the PRI give rise to a system that is not accountable, not fungible, with no network benefits and little trading. Consequently, there is no credit culture. Ultimately, the poor are disadvantaged because the costs of entry into business become overwhelmingly high for small enterprises and poor people, whereas large enterprises can engage in regulatory capture to protect their vested interests against competition. When PRI is defective, transactions costs are high because of high risks and/or rent-seeking activities.

We also agree with Sheng *et al.* that PRI is a public good that requires a large investment to establish, but it can generate sustained benefits in the form of drastically reduced transaction costs in the economy. This is why the government has a responsibility for building a well-functioning PRI as soon as possible if the society wants a modern market economy. It will be very difficult to revitalize the SOEs, and then the banking system in China, in the absence of a well defined and protected PRI.

To ensure the effectiveness of a capital market, China also needs to improve the enforcement of laws, rules and regulations. We observe that China has enacted more and more laws and regulations, but their enforcement is less satisfactory. In a market without discipline it is difficult to avoid problems like adverse selection.

Finally, we believe that it is important to clarify, standardize and quantify the issue of which social functions should remain with SOEs (and NSOEs), and which should be the responsibility of the government. The cost of transferring such functions to the state would be offset in part by higher profit taxes, which are explicit and transparent.

Even after being released from the need to provide some social functions, there would still be loss-making SOEs; perhaps in some cases because these were seen as strategic, and sometimes monopolistic, institutions whose prices remained subject to control. Railways and post offices have been common examples in Western market economies; no doubt there would be more in a socialist market economy. Nevertheless the questions remain: who should decide which loss-making SOEs should continue to be supported; on what principles or criteria should such decisions be made (e.g. cost/benefit); what is the likely net cost of such decisions; and, for the purpose of this chapter on the reform of the financial sector, who should bear that cost? The argument made out here is that the cost should *not* be shouldered in the form of a hidden subsidy from the banks to loss-making SOEs in the guise of rising NPLs. The need is to make the cost of SOE social provisions and the support of loss-making SOEs open and transparent, and justified on fiscal grounds.

What is the way forward for Chinese banks?

When the governments of many emerging market countries have not been able to find sufficient tax revenues to support those loss-making SOEs that they have wanted to maintain, they incline to use the banking system, banks and equity markets as a subsidiary source of funding for this purpose, thereby, as an unintended by-product, undermining the efficiency and profitability of the banking system.

If the main commercial banks continue to be used as supplementary fiscal piggy-banks, then it is doubtful whether any interim measures to inject capital and clean up the banks will succeed for long.

Even if such reforms could be enacted, and it would probably take quite a long time – a worthy objective for a five-year strategic plan? – the culture of the main commercial banks has, we believe, been, at least in part, that of a soft budget partner of the government and (loss-making) SOEs rather than an efficient profit-maximizing bank with effective risk management and internal control processes. In this latter respect the involvement of some of the best and most sophisticated Western banks in investment schemes with the main commercial banks seems, on this view, to be a major step in the right direction, as is the grant of more independence to the commercial banks to refuse (politically supported) potentially loss-making loans to SOEs. Indeed, the issue of how to handle the entry of, and competition from, foreign banks under the WTO seems to be being handled smoothly at present. That said, it may be premature to be pressing ahead with stock listing, and equity market introductions, of the Big Four commercial banks until the question of banks' involvement in the finance of loss-making SOEs is satisfactorily and finally resolved. Once the issue of the continuing flow of new NPLs from additional loans to loss-making SOEs is resolved, the question of how to handle the existing stock of NPLs is simple in principle, though their subsequent handling in AMCs, and the incentives for AMC managers, need further consideration.

So we believe that the reform of the banks depends on the reform of the SOEs, and the reform of capital markets depends in some large part on the reform of the banks. The small and medium enterprises (SMEs), especially NSOEs, should borrow from the banks, while the larger (profitable) enterprises, both SOEs and NSOEs, should finance themselves more in the capital markets (both equity and bond). But, as already noted, given the government's inclination to use banks to fund loss-making SOEs, macro monetary control is attempted via direct credit controls and interest rates are held low, as one of the implicit subsidies to such SOEs. So often there is no incentive for large enterprises to go to the capital market, whereas SMEs are usually unable to access either bank loans or the capital market.

If SOEs could be put on a hard budget basis, then interest rates could be freed up to act as a market mechanism. Given the spread that banks charge, that should act as an incentive for the better large-scale enterprises to go to capital markets for funding.

At the moment the financial regulators act not only as a regulator, but also as a manager of financial institutions and the controller (together with the political authorities) of new issues of IPOs and of corporate bonds. It is far from clear whether this is really effective or efficient. As argued before, we believe that financial regulators should focus on setting and enforcing the rules, identifying false disclosure, disciplining fraudulent practice by market participants, and nurturing a fair and orderly competition environment. Financial regulators should also encourage the development of market discipline and ethics among financial professionals. This brings us back to the need for the establishment of a property rights infrastructure to assist in the provision of fair disclosure and a financial professional system, which will help in the revision of the law to encourage enforcement and intermediation by giving creditors, including minority shareholders, bond holders and banks, stronger rights.

Also, a well-structured financial safety net, such as a deposit insurance scheme and small investor protection fund, is very important for the financial reform of China. Any whiff of doubt about the safety of deposits, especially in the Big Four commercial banks, could lead to total disaster. In view of the lessons related to the financial safety net in developed countries, China can consider adopting the following features for the deposit insurance scheme to make it more effective and incentive compatible (Zeng, 1997b):

1 to make the insurance deposit scheme explicit, not implicit;
2 to include all banks into the deposit insurance scheme and differentiate them by taking a risk-based premium schedule to distinguish strong banks from weak banks;
3 to reduce the moral hazard of depositors by adopting co-insurance and loss deduction;
4 to reduce the moral hazard of bank management by ordering more closure/ bankruptcy liquidation of insolvent banks and implementing more rigorous discipline against the management of failing banks;
5 to strengthen the information disclosure of banks and establish an early warning system for bank crises.

But the most urgent issues in China's financial reform is to end the financing of underperforming SOEs by banks, terminate intervention from governments in the management and operations of SOEs and banks, recruit and appoint the managements of banks and SOEs by market-based approaches, rationalize the incentive structure and improve the corporate governance of companies and banks, and establish a well-structured deposit insurance system. Unless these issues are solved, all else will be built on shifting sands.

Notes

1 This paper reflects entirely the authors' personal views and does not represent the views of any other entity or institution. The authors are grateful to Professor Mervyn K. Lewis for comments on this chapter and Mr Andrew Sheng for comments on part of this chapter. An earlier version was first published in the *Journal of Chinese Economic and Business Studies*, 4 (3), in November 2006. The editors and publisher of this volume wish to thank the CEA (UK) for permission to reproduce it in full.

References

De Soto, H. (2000) *The Mystery of Capital: Why Capitalism Triumphs in the West and Fails Everywhere Else*, New York: Basic Books.

Garg, S. and Zeng, X. (2005) 'China Banks: Bubble Trouble, Oh No, Not Another Bear,' *JP Morgan Asian Financial Weekly*, 9 September.

Goodhart, C. (1995) *The Central Bank and the Financial System*, London: Macmillan.

Goodhart, C. (1997) 'The Incentive Structure in Financial Regulation,' *Swiss Journal of Economics and Statistics*, 132, 637–648, republished (1997), *Financial Studies* (Chinese), Beijing.

Sheng, A., Geng X. and Wang, Y. (2003) 'Corporate Governance and Property Rights Infrastructure: The Experiences of Hong Kong and Lessons for China', in (eds), *Policy Reform and Chinese Markets: Progress and Challenges*, Stanford, CA: Stanford University Press.

Zeng, X. (1995) 'The Constraints and Solution in the Reform of State-owned Enterprises,' *Wuhan University Academic Journal* (Chinese), 10, 69–74.

Zeng, X. (1997a) 'On Information Disclosure and Financial Regulation,' *International Financial Studies* (Chinese), September.

Zeng, X. (1997b) 'Deposit Insurance System: Operations, Pitfalls, and Improvements,' *Securities Market Herald* (Chinese), September.

Zeng, X (1998) 'Executive Stock Option Scheme: Structure, Accounting Recognition, Pitfalls, and Improvements', *Securities Market Herald* (Chinese), April, 49–52

8 Ownership reform, foreign competition and efficiency of Chinese commercial banks

A non-parametric approach

Shujie Yao and Zhongwei Han

Introduction

State-owned commercial banks in China have been notorious for their low efficiency, mounting non-performing loans (NPLs) and loss-making. China's bank reforms have lagged far behind reforms in the real economic sectors for two reasons. First, the banking industry has been overwhelmingly dominated by state ownership and enjoyed immense monopolistic power. Second, state commercial banks have enjoyed a significant leverage of soft budget constraints because they are frequently entrusted or coerced by local authorities to provide policy lending or to help rescue insolvent state-owned industrial enterprises. Slow banking reform, however, has been a critical constraint on China in sustaining its economic growth. Gradually, the government has had to address this issue by launching a comprehensive reform programme to make the banking system competitive and efficient to support the fast development of the real economy, which has, for almost three decades now, been growing at nearly 10 per cent per year.

Aggressive banking reforms started in the late 1980s, initially to separate policy lending from commercial operations by establishing three state policy banks and then stripping off the NPLs from the largest state-owned commercial banks, including the Bank of China (BOC), China Construction Bank (CCB), the Industrial and Commercial Bank of China (ICBC), the Agricultural Bank of China (ABC) – the Big Four hereafter – using four newly created state asset management companies. The latest reforms since China joined the WTO in December 2001 have been pushed by both internal and external pressures. Internal pressure arises because of fierce competition from regional and private banking institutions, and external pressure comes from the free entry of foreign banks into the Chinese market.

But how have the state commercial banks reacted to these new pressures for reform? Answering this question requires a comprehensive analysis of the change of efficiency and productivity of these banks in recent years. There are potentially many ways to evaluate bank efficiency. Two most frequently used methodologies are the stochastic production function approach and the data envelopment analysis, or DEA, approach. As the former requires a specific functional form, it may not be suitable for the data period when the banking industry in China underwent dramatic changes. Hence, we use the latter approach, which is not subject to such a problem. This paper is probably the first attempt in the literature to evaluate the technical efficiency of the Chinese commercial banks using DEA to analyse the efficiency levels of these banks over the period 1998–2005, which covers both the pre-WTO and the first few years of the post-WTO era in China. In addition, a Malmquist index is calculated and decomposed to evaluate how the Chinese commercial banks have improved their productivity through reform and adoption of new technologies in order to face up to the immense competition ahead of them by 2006, the year when China finally had to open up its financial markets fully to foreign banks.

A common perception in both academic and policy circles is that Chinese state-owned commercial banks may face a complete meltdown once foreign banks are allowed to enter China without any restriction. The only reason why they may survive is because the government will bail them out through direct subsidies. This is true to a great extent because the government provided massive support to the Big Four by stripping off RMB2.57 trillion of NPLs to the state asset management companies and injected another US$72 billion of foreign exchanges to recapitalize CCB, BOC and ICBC before they were listed on the stock exchanges in 2005 and 2006 (Garcia-Herrero *et al.*, 2006; Shi, 2005). However, the government made it clear that state subsidies were one-off and could not be repeated if the banks failed to improve their performance and competitiveness after they became shareholding companies. Consequently, the ability of these banks to improve efficiency is critical for the success of bank reform in China as it would be impossible for the state to repeat another round of capital injection of such a phenomenal order to bail out the banks without rendering China into a serious financial crisis, or even the collapse of the entire economy.

This chapter will focus on the efficiency issue in order to evaluate whether the Chinese state commercial banks have reacted positively and successfully to the new reforms and challenges. It uses data from all the national commercial banks, state- and non-state-owned, domestic and foreign-invested, over the period 1998–2005. It employs the data envelopment analysis (DEA) approach to measure the efficiency scores of banks and then conducts a Malmquist index analysis to study the evolution of productivity changes. The DEA results show that the Big Four are not necessarily less efficient than their joint-equity counterparts. In fact, two state-owned banks, CCB and BOC, continuously outperform their state-owned peers and most joint-equity banks.[1] However, joint-equity banks have a significant advantage over state-owned banks in terms of asset quality. The Malmquist index analysis indicates that the average productivity of all the Chinese banks rose 5.6 per cent per annum over the data period. The productivity growth was almost equally explained by efficiency improvement and technological progress. Much of the productivity growth of the state-owned commercial banks was due to efficiency improvement and little due to technological progress. In contrast, much of the productivity growth of the joint-equity commercial banks was due to technological progress and little due to efficiency improvement. Such empirical results have interesting and important policy implications because they imply that government policies should be designed differently to improve the performance of different banks.

The reform of China's banking industry

Before economic reforms, China had only one large bank, the People's Bank of China (PBC), which had an absolute monopoly power in all banking activities. The reform of China's banking industry started from 1979. By 1992, four state-owned commercial banks and a number of joint-equity banks were established. This led the PBC to focus on its role as the central bank. In 1994, three policy banks were set up to take over policy banking activities, enabling the state-owned commercial banks to focus on commercial operations. The promulgation of the Central Bank Law and the Commercial Bank Law in 1995 and 1996 strengthened the authority of PBC and provided commercial banks a legal framework for operation. In 2003, the China Banking Regulatory Commission, CBRC, was established to take over the supervisory function from PBC. By 2004, apart from the Big Four, China had eleven national joint stock banks, 111 city commercial banks, three rural commercial banks, 35,544 rural credit cooperatives and 204 foreign bank subsidiaries.[2]

According to the *Almanac of China's Finance and Banking* (National Bureau of Statistics, 2005), the market shares of the Big Four account for 60 per cent of total deposits and 57 per cent of total loans. However, the average ratio of non-performing loans of the Big Four was over 30 per cent in the 1990s (Table 8.1). The mounting NPL implies that the Big Four are effectively insolvent and their continuing survival is supported by the state through soft budget constraints. The World Bank (2002) suggests that to restore the banking system into a financially healthy state the stock of government debt will have to increase from 20 per cent to 75 per cent of China's total GDP.

The high level of NPLs implied that various reforms implemented before 2001 failed to achieve their objectives. By 1999, NPLs amounted to about 30 per cent of China's gross domestic product (GDP) or 2.18 times China's total budgetary revenue (Shi, 2005).[3] The NPL/loans ratio was as high as 45 per cent for ABC and 23 per cent for CCB, with a total amount of RMB2.5 trillion for the Big Four (Table 8.1) and about RMB3.6 trillion for all the commercial banks in China.[4]

With its accession to the World Trade Organization (WTO) in December 2001, China had an obligation to fully open up the domestic market to foreign banks for competition. In order for the Chinese commercial banks to compete and survive in a liberalized environment, further reforms were imperative, but it appeared that the last hope of resolving the problem was ownership reform, which was not contemplated before 2001. A critical element of ownership reform was to restructure the Big Four as well as other commercial banks to enable them to be listed on China's stock exchanges, subjecting them to monitoring and control by shareholders rather than politicians.

One important condition for the state-owned commercial banks to be listed

Table 8.1 Non-performing loans and ratios of the Big Four, 1999–2004 (billion yuan and per cent)

Year	ICBC		BOC		ABC		CCB	
	NPL ratio (%)	Total NPL	NPL ratio (%)	Total NPL	NPL ratio (%)	Total NPL	NPL ratio (%)	Total NPL
1999	39.5	958.0	37.4	605.5	45.0	680.0	23.0	281.0
2000	34.4	831.0	27.2	409.6	33.2	493.4	15.7	218.2
2001	29.8	792.0	27.5	436.0	42.1	693.4	19.4	291.4
2002	25.7	759.9	22.5	408.5	36.7	701.1	15.2	268.0
2003	21.2	720.8	16.3	351.7	30.7	695.5	9.1	193.5
2004	19.0	703.6	5.1	109.9	26.7	692.3	3.9	87.3
2005	4.5	210.0	9.6	195.0	23.5	701.0	3.5	86.1

Sources: Shi (2005) for 1999–2004; Bankscope for 2005, with the absolute amounts of NPLs estimated by authors.
Note: Full names of banks are given in Appendix 8.1.

on the stock exchanges was a substantial reduction in the level of NPLs and a significant increase in working capital. This required huge state assistance to the Big Four. Starting from 1999, there have been three big waves of state support to strip off NPLs from the Big Four and inject new capital (Table 8.2). The first wave was in 1999 when four state asset management companies were set up to accommodate RMB1.4 trillion of NPLs, equivalent to almost 20 per cent of China's GDP in the same year. The second wave of support was in 2003 and 2004, when RMB475.6 billion of NPLs was stripped off from CCB and BOC. In the meantime, the government provided US$22.5 billion, taken from the country's huge foreign exchange reserves, to support each of these two banks. The final wave of support was in 2005, when RMB705 billion of NPLs was stripped off from ICBC, with an additional capital injection of US$15 billion and the issuance of US$12.1 billion in subordinated debt (Garcia-Herrero *et al.*, 2006).

The purpose of state support was to make the initial public offerings (IPOs) of CCB, BOC and ICBC attractive to investors. In the meantime, the Big Four introduced a strict monitoring mechanism to control non-performing loans and reduced their workforce by 250,000 (The Economist, 2006).

The first of the Big Four to be listed was CCB, whose IPO in Hong Kong in October 2005 raised US$8 billion. It was followed by BOC, which was listed in Hong Kong and Shanghai in May 2006, raising US$11.2 billion. The IPO of ICBC in October 2006 in Hong Kong and Shanghai raised US$21.9 billion, setting a new world record, surpassing the IPO record set by Japan's NTT Mobile Communications Network Inc., which raised US$18.4 billion in 1998 (Mitchell, 2006).

The initial public offering of ICBC was a milestone on the road to China's banking reform. ICBC is the largest state-owned commercial bank in China with the largest number of branches and customers throughout the country. In 2005, its total assets were RMB6.45 trillion, with 2.8 million clients and 150 million depositors with credit cards.[5] Its share price jumped by almost 15 per cent in Hong Kong and more than 5 per cent in Shanghai when its shares were first traded on 27 October 2006. The strong demand for ICBC's shares was partly driven by

Table 8.2 State assistance to strip off NPLs from the Big Four, 1999–2005

Year	Amount of support	Support mechanism
1999	RMB1.4 trillion to the Big Four	NPLs transferred to 4 state asset management companies
2003	RMB56.9 billion to CCB RMB140.0 billion to BOC	Write-off of NPLs
2004	RMB128.9 billion to CCB RMB149.8 billion to BOC	NPLs transferred to state asset management companies
2005	RMB705.0 billion to ICBC	NPL transferred to state asset management companies

Source: Shi (2005).
Note: Full names of banks are given in Appendix 8.1.

investors' positive expectation of China's future economic growth and partly due to the inherent strength of ICBC because of its sheer size and ability to reduce non-performing loans and to generate profits. The latest statistics show that the rate of NPLs was only 4.5 per cent in 2005 as compared with 40 per cent in 1999 and 19 per cent in 2004 (Table 8.2). Of course, the drastic reduction in NPLs was largely due to the huge injection of state capital and the stripping off of its NPLs during 1999–2005. A similar story can be told from the IPOs of CCB and BOC (Tables 8.2 and 8.3).

The most recent restructuring of the Big Four and other commercial banks shows the determination of the Chinese government to fundamentally reform the banking sector. Not only are the domestic banks being changed from state-owned to shareholding companies, foreign banks are also allowed to buy shares of these banks as well as setting up their branches in China.

Although China's banking sector was opened to foreign banks in 1981, foreign participation was extremely restrictive until December 2001, when China joined the WTO. Since 2001, the restriction has been gradually relaxed to allow full access by 11 December 2006. Foreign banks initially opened offices and branches; and more recently there have been a number of foreign equity capital investments as part of China's restructuring of its own banking system. Foreign banks, according to CBRC statistics, by October 2005, had 225 operating outlets and 240 representative offices and a market share of around 2 per cent. In October 2005, nineteen overseas financial institutions owned stakes in sixteen Chinese banks, having invested around US$16.5 billion (CBRC, 2006).

According to CBRC, the development of foreign banks in China has three features: they are radiating outwards from concentrations in the Yangtze, Pearl and Bohai Rim economic circles; they are expanding rapidly, increasing their market share; and they are providing more than 100 kinds of business services under twelve business categories. The most active foreign bank in China is HSBC, which has significant investments in the CBC (US$1.75 billion, or 19.9 per cent of the total equity) and some regional city commercial banks. The Royal Bank of Scotland has bought 4.37 per cent of the total share equity of BOC. Most other foreign investors, including the Asian Development Bank, International Financial Corporation, CitiBank, Hang Seng Bank, Newbridge Asia and Commonwealth Bank of Australia have focused their investments in the regional city commercial banks.

Privatization and foreign investments have provided significant impetus for the Chinese domestic commercial banks to improve their performance through restructuring, strict control and monitoring of lending activities and the reform of corporate governance. In 2006, foreign banks and their subsidiaries had all business and geographical restrictions on serving Chinese customers lifted. It is therefore urgent for domestic commercial banks to improve efficiency to survive in a more competitive market.

Table 8.3 Input and output variables of Chinese commercial banks: 2005 (billion RMB)

Bank	(1) Interest income	(2) Interest expense	(3) = (1)/(2)	(4) Non-interest income	(5) Non-interest expense	(6) = (4)/(5)	(7) NPLs/gross loans (%)
ICBC	224.5	86.6	2.59	13.2	57.9	0.23	4.5
ABC	128.4	61.4	2.09	8.6	53.2	0.16	23.5
CCB	173.6	57.1	3.04	11.7	49.4	0.24	3.9
BOC	167.9	66.9	2.51	21.3	49.3	0.43	9.6
CBC	49.7	18.1	2.75	7.8	14.7	0.53	2.4
CMB	26.0	9.3	2.80	1.2	7.1	0.17	2.5
CITIC	22.0	9.6	2.29	0.7	5.9	0.12	5.6
CEB*	16.1	8.1	1.99	0.5	5.0	0.10	5.0
PDB	22.3	8.7	2.56	0.6	5.5	0.11	2.2
CMSB	23.6	11.0	2.15	0.5	5.9	0.08	1.4
GDB*	13.2	7.8	1.69	0.6	4.7	0.13	12.5
FIB	17.2	7.9	2.18	0.3	3.8	0.08	2.2
HXB	13.3	6.0	2.22	0.3	3.4	0.09	3.0
BOS	8.2	3.1	2.65	0.6	2.1	0.29	2.5
SDB	9.1	3.8	2.39	0.4	2.5	0.16	10.6
Average	61.0	24.4	2.50	4.6	18.0	0.25	6.1

Source: Bankscope.

Notes:

Full bank names and further explanations are given in Appendix 8.1.

* Numbers are estimated. NPLs = non-performing loans, or impaired loans.

Banking efficiency literature and DEA methodology

Over the past two decades, numerous studies have focused on measuring the efficiency of commercial banks. Berger and Humphrey (1997) document 130 studies on financial institutions efficiency, using data from twenty-one countries, from various types of institutions including banks, bank branches, savings and loans companies, credit unions and insurance companies. Richard *et al.* (2002) use a constrained multiplier, input-oriented, DEA model to evaluate the production efficiency of the US commercial banks during 1984–98. They find strong and consistent relationships between efficiency and independent measures of performance. Pastor (1999) proposed a new sequential DEA procedure for Spanish banks to break down the main indicators of banking risk provision for loan losses into internal and external components. Girardone and Casu (2004) investigated the main determinants of Italian banks' cost efficiency over the period 1993–96. They found that X-inefficiencies tend to decline over time for all bank sizes. The inclusion of risk and output quality variables in the cost function reduces the significance of the scale economy estimates.

The efficiency of banks in Taiwan and Hong Kong has also attracted strong academic interest. Chen and Yeh (2000) adopted the intermediation approach in the DEA model according to which deposits are treated as an input since a bank's main business is to borrow funds from depositors and then lend to others. The approach specifies three outputs – the provision of loan services, portfolio investment and non-interest income – and three inputs – bank staff, assets and deposits. They also noted that the increase of staff salary and market competition may result in difficulties in improving technical efficiency. Drake *et al.* (2003) used the Hong Kong banking data to examine the macroeconomic and regulatory factors on bank efficiency. In the Tobit regression, external factors such as GDP and government expenditures are tested instead of firm characteristics.

Few studies have been found to address the efficiency issues of China's banking industry in the English language literature. Fu and Heffernan (2005) have measured concentration, market share, X-efficiency and scale efficiency of Chinese banks to test both the market-power and the efficient structure hypotheses. Their results show that during the first phase of reform large state banks exercised market power as major loan providers were subsidized by the government. During the second phase of reform, state bank subsidies were cut, allowing the relatively more X-efficient joint stock banks to earn higher profits although they were less scale-efficient. Chen *et al.* (2005) examined the cost, technical and allocative efficiency of forty-three Chinese banks during 1993–2000. The results show that large state-owned banks and small banks were more efficient than medium-sized banks. The financial deregulation in 1995 was found to have improved both technical and allocative efficiency. There is also evidence of continuous dominance of technical efficiency over allocative efficiency, implying that Chinese banks need to improve their ability to minimize cost through input combinations. Yao *et al.* (2006) have employed a stochastic production frontier function to investigate the effects of ownership structure and hard budget constraint on technical efficiency of Chinese domestic banks. They found that non-state banks are 8–18 per cent more efficient than state banks, and that banks facing a harder budget tend to perform better than those heavily capitalized by the state or regional governments.

Technical efficiency measures how well inputs are converted into outputs during a specific production process. It is defined as 'the ratio of weighted sum of outputs to weighted sum of inputs'. It becomes a relative efficiency measure if the ratio is restricted to a value less than or equal to 1. DEA was originally developed for efficiency measurement in an input–output setting based on the concept of the Pareto optimum (Charnes *et al.*, 1978). The relative technical efficiency of a decision-making unit is defined as the ratio of the sum of the weighted outputs to the sum of its weighted inputs, the weights having been determined in order to show the unit at maximum relative efficiency. What is produced is an 'efficiency frontier' made up of those DMUs (decision-making units) that are efficient relative to the other units under evaluation. The frontier consists of the 'best' units in the evaluation set and represents a linear combination of empirically derived maximum output per given input. Each DMU is assigned an efficiency rating based on its position relative to the frontier. The efficient units, those making best use of resources, are rated as being 100 per cent efficient whereas the inefficient ones obtain lower scores.

This chapter uses a production boundary based linear programming model which is referred to as envelopment model 1. Mathematical proof of equivalence of efficiency rating to the Pareto Efficiency concept can be found in Thanassoulis (2001). The technical input efficiency of DMU k (decision making unit k, or bank k in our case) is a solution to the following problem:

$$\min E_k - \varepsilon \left[\sum_{i=1}^{p} s_j^- + \sum_{i=1}^{q} s_j^+ \right] \tag{8.1}$$

$$\text{subject to } \sum_{k=1}^{n} \lambda_k x_{ik} = E_k x_{ik} - S_i^- \text{ and } \sum_{k=1}^{n} \lambda_k x_{jk} = S_j^+ + y_{jk}$$

$$\lambda_k, , j = 1, 2, \ldots q, i = 1, 2, \ldots p$$

x_{ik} and y_{jk} denote the level of the ith input and jth output observed at DMU k. Any feasible set of λ values in model 8.1 identifies a point within the production possibility set which can be constructed from DMU k ($k=1, 2, \ldots, n$). S^- is defined as the input excesses and S^+ the output excesses. ε is a non-archimedean infinitesimal. The optimal solution to model 8.1, E_k^*, means that the corresponding input or output of DMU k can improve further, after its input levels have been pulled to the proportion E_k^*. After E_k has been minimized, the model seeks the maximum sum of the slack values of S_i^- and S_j^+. DMU k is technically efficient if and only if $E_k^* = 1$, $S_i^- = 0$ and S_j^+. The envelopment model is a more straightforward linear programming and λ values provide information about efficient peers in the reference sets.

In this chapter, we will measure three types of efficiency scores: constant return to scale (CRS), variable return to scale (VRS) and scale efficiency. The CRS efficiency score draws from the assumption of constant returns to scale and represents technical efficiency, which measures inefficiencies due to the input/output configuration as well as the size of operation. The VRS efficiency score is based on the assumption of variable returns to scale and represents pure technical efficiency. Scale efficiency can be calculated by dividing pure technical efficiency into technical efficiency. To assess the input efficiency under VRS, we can still use model 8.1 but include only the so-called convexity constraint:

$$\sum_{k=1}^{n} \lambda_k = 1$$

In the following section, we first use a CRS input-oriented envelopment model to assess the technical efficiency of Chinese national commercial banks and then construct an output-oriented Malmquist index to examine the productivity growth in China's banking industry.

Efficiency analysis of the Chinese commercial banks

1 Efficiency scores and ranks

Interest income and non-interest income have been widely recognized as outputs of commercial banks. However, there is a debate on whether deposits should be treated as an input or output. We do not agree that banks use deposits to produce loans. Deposits are intermediate substances which help banks achieve interest income and non-interest income through banking services. The input is not the deposit itself but the resources that are used to generate the deposit, e.g. the interest expenses and labour cost. As such, the inputs should contain interest expenses and non-interest expenses such as salary costs. During the process of transferring deposits to loans, banks will inevitably incur some impaired loans. Banking in this sense is a sort of risk business. Impaired loans are a cost that banks have to bear and can be dealt with as a resource to gain interest yields from gross loans. The ratio of impaired loans, or non-performing loans, to gross loans is included in this study as the third input variable, taking the asset quality into account. Obviously, given the output levels, the lower the ratio, the higher is the efficiency of banks.

Table 8.3 describes the input and output levels of the fifteen largest Chinese national commercial banks in 2005. The data for efficiency analysis consist of all the fifteen banks over 1998–2005. The data are extracted from Bankscope. The first column lists banks' name abbreviations (the full names are given in Appendix 8.1) followed by columns containing the information about interest incomes, interest expenses, non-interest incomes, non-interest expenses and the ratio of NPLs to gross loans for each bank. Only the Big Four achieve interest incomes greater than RMB100 billion. In terms of interest incomes, the biggest state bank is ICBC and the biggest joint-equity bank is CBC. The interest income gap between them is RMB174.5 billion. However, when interest expenses are considered, the Big Four do not seem to perform much better than joint-equity banks. CCB has the highest ratio of interest incomes to interest expenses, at 3.04, and the runner-up is CMB with a ratio of 2.80. With respect to the ratio of non-interest incomes to non-interest expenses, state-owned banks outperform joint-equity banks. Three of the Big Four, BOC, CCB and ICBC, have a ratio greater than 0.2, and only two of the joint-equity banks, CBC and BOS, have a ratio above 0.2. Without reference to asset quality, state-owned banks are not poor performers at all, contrary to a common perception on the Chinese banking industry. The overall performance of the Big Four is greatly undermined by their mounting NPLs before 2004. However, with the massive state support in 2004 and 2005, ICBC, CCB and BOC were able to reduce the NPL ratio to less than 10 per cent, although the NPL ratio of ABC was still above 20 per cent in 2005 (last column, Table 8.3). Because different indicators provide mixed information, it is important to use a 'compound' single index to fully evaluate bank performance. The best candidate for the compound single index is efficiency scores.

Table 8.4 presents the estimated CRS input-oriented efficiency scores for the fifteen commercial banks in 1998–2005. The software is DEA Excel Solver, developed by Joe Zhu (2003). The average efficiency score of Chinese state-owned commercial banks over the data period is 0.85. It demonstrates that many banks are producing close to the frontier, which is led by BOC and CCB. In other words, the efficiency levels of the sample banks are very close to each other. There are two possible explanations for the results. First, the data include only the national banks, which have similar characteristics in terms of inputs and outputs. Second, in the data period, the banking system was highly competitive as inefficient banks have to emulate efficient banks quickly in order to avoid being taken over or forced out of business.

For whatever explanation, the relatively high level of average efficiency scores implies that Chinese banks were trying to improve their competitiveness prior to and after WTO accession. This is reflected by the small but obvious improvement on the average efficiency scores over the data period. The industrial average efficiency scores rose from 0.78 in 1999 to 0.91 by 2005 (Figure 8.1).

Three banks, CCB, BOC and CBC, are identified as the most technically efficient as their average efficiency scores are equal or close to unity. Of the Big Four, CCB, BOC and ICBC are among the most efficient banks but ABC is the second most inefficient in the sample. This explains why the government has allowed the former three to be listed on the stock markets but kept ABC in its present form.

The finding that CCB, BOC and ICBC are among the most efficient commercial banks in China contradicts a common perception and results of some previous studies. The relative understatement of the state-owned commercial banks in China by some other studies may have been due to their modeling methods. If deposits are included as inputs, the stock of deposits in the Big Four is much bigger than those in the joint-equity banks, leading to a low efficiency rating of the Big Four. However, the expenses of maintaining the deposits by the Big Four are low. If deposits are excluded from the model as is done in this paper, the efficiency rating of the Big Four is improved, although ABC is still highly inefficient.

The most inefficient joint-equity bank is GDB, justifying why the government

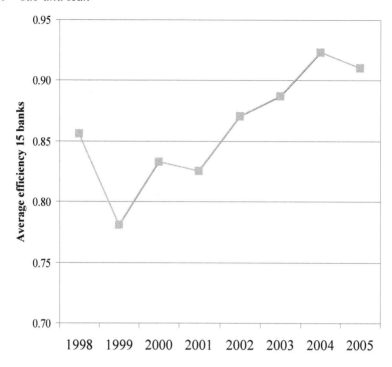

Figure 8.1 Average efficiency scores of 15 Chinese commercial banks, 1998–2005 (source: Table 8.4).

has been negotiating with Citigroup and Société Générale to buy 85 per cent of GDB's share capital. China has been reluctant to allow any foreign bank to have a controlling stake in any Chinese bank. However, there are exceptional cases if foreign participation can fundamentally transform the performance of a local bank and provide valuable experiences for the reforms of others by introducing the best foreign managerial practices and corporate governance. One such exceptional case was the San Francisco-based capital fund, Newbridge, which was allowed to become the largest and controlling shareholder of SDB through the procurement of a 17.8 per cent stake worth $145 million from its four government shareholders in May 2004 (Dong, 2005).

2 Slacks and targets

As for input-efficiency, an efficiency score equal to 1 means that efficient banks lie on the boundary and their input levels cannot be radically reduced for a given output level. DEA results not only help managers to identify the best practice in the sector, but also point to the direction and magnitude that inefficient banks can improve. In 2005, for example, CEB had an efficiency score of 0.79, which means that the maximum radial contraction (0.21) is possible to the input level without reducing its output. According to the DEA model, the input and output slacks

Table 8.4 Efficiency scores and ranking of Chinese commercial banks: 1998–2005

Bank	1998	1999	2000	2001	2002	2003	2004	2005	Average	Rank
ICBC	1.00	0.98	0.92	0.83	0.84	0.91	0.98	1.00	0.93	3
ABC	0.74	0.68	0.67	0.68	0.75	0.77	0.77	0.73	0.72	14
CCB	0.95	0.87	0.79	0.84	0.99	0.99	1.00	1.00	0.93	4
BOC	1.00	0.78	1.00	1.00	0.91	1.00	1.00	1.00	0.96	1
CBC	0.61	0.78	0.82	0.80	0.87	0.93	1.00	0.98	0.85	10
CMB	0.84	0.81	0.80	0.87	0.97	0.99	1.00	0.99	0.91	5
CITIC	1.00	0.57	0.81	0.79	0.85	0.87	0.91	0.91	0.84	11
CEB	1.00	0.75	0.78	0.71	0.77	0.82	0.81	0.79	0.81	13
PDB	0.76	0.78	0.78	0.79	0.96	0.99	1.00	0.99	0.88	9
CMB	0.81	0.85	0.85	0.89	0.85	0.97	1.00	0.97	0.90	6
GDB	0.59	0.61	0.64	0.68	0.67	0.64	0.64	0.66	0.64	15
FIB	0.79	0.87	0.86	0.88	0.93	0.83	0.96	0.97	0.89	7
HXB	0.82	0.81	0.92	0.86	0.87	0.92	0.92	0.93	0.88	8
BOS	0.93	0.84	1.00	0.93	1.00	0.89	0.99	0.92	0.94	2
SDB	1.00	0.74	0.86	0.82	0.84	0.78	0.84	0.82	0.84	12
Average	0.86	0.78	0.83	0.82	0.87	0.89	0.92	0.91	0.85	

Source: Bankscope.
Note: Full names of banks are given in Appendix 8.1.

must be taken into account. As a result, the target for efficiency improvement will be the sum of the radial reduction and the existing slack. Take CEB as an example, the target ratio of NPLs/gross loans will be $(0.05 * 0.79) - 0.028 = 0.011$.

After knowing the targets for efficiency improvement, inefficient banks need to find out the most feasible way to catch up. It is crucial that the process of efficiency improvement should be made in a short time period. In the long term, inefficient companies will have already been forced to leave the market. The efficiency theory suggests that it is always good to learn from efficient peers with the same or similar input–output mix. The reference set offers inefficient banks a feasible means to emulate their efficient peers by learning from their practice.

Taking CEB in 2005 as an example, CMB and PDB are identified as its efficient peers as their corresponding $\lambda = 0.296$ and $\lambda = 0.498$ are the only positive values at the optimal solution to the envelopment model. Compared with CEB, PDB has less non-interest expenses and a lower NPL/gross loan ratio but more interest and non-interest incomes (*Table* 8.5). Although PDB has 3 per cent more interest expenses than CEB, the former earns 17.5 per cent more interest income than the latter. It is clear, even without comparing their efficiency scores derived from DEA, that PDB is more efficient than CEB. If we scale down PDB and CMB by 0.498 and 0.296 respectively and compare them with CEB, the results are shown in Table 8.5.

The combination of scaled down input levels of PDB and CMB offers the same interest income as CEB could deliver but it uses only 87 per cent of the inputs used by CEB. This underlies the Pareto-efficiency rating of CEB at 0.87. PDB and CMB are thus regarded as the efficient benchmarks for CEB in 2005. It requires high managerial skills for inefficient banks to study their efficient peers' practice and set up the targets in relation to the combination of input and output levels of their efficient benchmarks.

Table 8.6 presents the frequencies of efficient banks in the reference sets. Among the state banks, CCB and BOC are most frequently referenced. Another

Table 8.5 Input–output comparison between CEB and its efficient peers, 2005 (billion RMB)

	Interest expense	Non-interest expense	Impaired/gross loan ratio (%)	Interest income	Non-interest income
PDB	8.70	5.50	2.20	22.30	0.60
PDB × 0.498	4.33	2.74	1.10	11.11	0.30
CMB	9.30	7.10	2.50	26.00	1.20
CMB × 0.296	2.75	2.10	0.74	7.70	0.36
CEB	8.10	5.00	5.00	16.10	0.50
(PDB × 0.498 + CMB × 0.296)/CEB	0.87	0.97	0.37	1.17	1.31

Source: Data are derived from Bankscope.
Note: Full names of banks are in Appendix 8.1.

Table 8.6 Frequencies of efficient banks quoted in the reference sets

Bank	1998	1999	2000	2001	2002	2003	2004	2005
ICBC								
ABC								
CCB	1	1	1	1	6	3	2	5
BOC			1	1	5	6	3	3
CBC	3		1	1				
CMB	5	1				5	3	2
CITIC				1				
CEB	2							
PDB		2			1	8	6	7
CMB				2		3	1	2
GDB								
FIB		4	2				1	
HXB			6	3				
BOS	1	4	4	4	6		3	4
SDB	4							

Note: Full names of banks are in Appendix 1.

efficient state bank, ICBC, has never been referenced. In this sense, CCB and BOC should be regarded as the efficient benchmarks for the inefficient state bank ABC. The empirical results provide a strong theoretical backing for the government's decision on the priority order of restructuring CCB, BOC and ICBC of the Big Four.

PDB and BOS are often quoted in the reference sets of joint-equity banks although their average efficiency scores are not the highest among the joint-equity banks. One possible explanation for their frequent appearance in the reference sets is that their operating practices and environment match more closely with the less efficient joint-equity banks than the other more efficient counterparts. In particular, PDB is dominant among joint-equity banks after China's accession to the WTO in 2001. As the banking market becomes more competitive, joint-equity banks tend to perform better than their state-owned counterparts as the former are less burdened with NPLs than the latter.

3 Scale type and scale efficiency

In theory, an efficient bank must produce at constant returns to scale. At a production point with increasing return to scale (IRS), the firm raising its input levels by a small percentage will lead to an expansion of its output by a higher percentage. At a point of decreasing returns to scale (DRS), a small expansion of output requires a larger percentage increase in inputs. Obviously, when IRS holds, a bank should increase its scale size. Similarly, when DRS holds, a bank should reduce its operation. The ideal scale size is where CRS holds. Table 8.7 shows the types of scale for the fifteen banks in a dynamic context.

Table 8.7 Identification of returns to scale of Chinese national commercial banks

Bank	1998	1999	2000	2001	2002	2003	2004	2005
ICBC	CRS	CRS	CRS	DRS	DRS	DRS	DRS	DRS
ABC	DRS	DRS	DRS	DRS	DRS	IRS	DRS	DRS
CCB	CRS	CRS	CRS	CRS	CRS	CRS	CRS	CRS
BOC	CRS	CRS	CRS	CRS	CRS	CRS	CRS	CRS
CBC	CRS	CRS	CRS	CRS	CRS	IRS	CRS	CRS
CMB	CRS	CRS	DRS	CRS	IRS	CRS	CRS	CRS
CITIC	CRS	DRS	CRS	DRS	DRS	IRS	IRS	IRS
CEB	CRS	CRS	DRS	DRS	DRS	IRS	IRS	IRS
PDB	IRS	CRS	DRS	DRS	CRS	CRS	CRS	CRS
CMB	IRS	IRS	IRS	CRS	CRS	CRS	CRS	IRS
GDB	DRS	DRS	DRS	DRS	IRS	IRS	IRS	IRS
FIB	IRS	CRS	CRS	CRS	CRS	IRS	CRS	CRS
HXB	IRS	CRS	CRS	CRS	IRS	IRS	IRS	IRS
BOS	CRS	CRS	CRS	CRS	CRS	IRS	CRS	CRS
SDB	CRS	IRS	IRS	DRS	IRS	IRS	IRS	IRS

Sources: Bankscope.

Notes: Full names of banks are in Appendix 1.
CRS = constant return to scale, DRS = decreasing return to scale, IRS = increasing return to scale.

It is striking to note that inefficient state banks in most years exhibit DRS whereas inefficient joint-equity banks show IRS. The empirical results in Table 8.7 provide valuable information for policymakers to justify their capital injection initiatives and business expansion regulations. It is interesting to deduce that the reason non-state ownership in joint-equity banks has not brought about superior performance over their state-owned and bigger counterparts is clearly the lack of scale economies. To improve the overall performance of the Chinese banking industry will require not only ownership reform but also a consolidation of operation to exploit the economies of scale in the non-state sector.

If banks are at an inefficient scale, it will be in their interests to know the magnitude of inefficiency caused by scale size. Scale efficiency measures the impact of scale size on the technical efficiency of a bank. In the input-oriented model, scale efficiency is defined as $SE_j = CRS_j/VRS_j$, where SE_j denotes scale input efficiency of bank j, CRS_j and VRS_j represent the technical input efficiency score and pure technical input efficiency score of bank j. As VRS_j is always greater than CRS_j, scale efficiency scores will never exceed 1. Unlike the CRS efficiency rating, the VRS efficiency rating is obtained when scale size is controlled for so that the divergence in the efficiency measurements captures the impact of scale size on technical efficiency (Thanassoulis, 2001).

By controlling for the scale effect, joint-equity banks become relatively more efficient than their state-owned counterparts. In particular, CMB, HXB and BOS improve their efficiency and ranking dramatically, implying that joint-equity banks should be encouraged to expand their branch networks in order to improve their competitiveness and the overall efficiency level of the entire banking industry in China. Scale inefficiency is the biggest source of the overall technical inefficiency of joint-equity banks.[6]

4 Correlation between firm size, efficiency ranking and profitability ranking

It is interesting to investigate the relationship between efficiency and profitability rankings of commercial banks. Studies such as Berger and Humphrey (1997) find that firm size is a possible factor that influences efficiency and profitability of commercial banks. Table 8.8 presents the summary statistics of profitability and firm size of the Chinese commercial banks and their estimated efficiency scores in 2005. The rankings of fifteen banks are compared, based on different financial indicators. The ratio of return on asset is used to present profitability, which is measured as the ratio of pre-tax profit over total assets.

There is no evidence of any strong correlation between the rankings of efficiency scores, profitability and firm size, implying that firm size is not an important factor in efficiency and profitability. Because profitability is measured as the ratio of pre-tax profit to total assets, it effectively measures the accumulated historical performance of banks instead of their current operating performance. In this sense, the DEA efficiency score is a better measurement of firm performance than profitability.

Table 8.8 Efficiency, profitability and firm size: 2005

Company	Efficiency Score	Ranking	Profitability ROA%	Ranking	Asset (billion yuan)	Ranking
ICBC	1.00	3	0.20	15	6454.1	1
ABC	0.73	14	0.40	11	4771.0	2
CCB	1.00	2	1.50	1	4585.7	3
BOC	1.00	1	1.00	4	4740.0	4
CBC	0.98	6	0.90	5	1423.4	5
CMB	0.99	4	1.10	2	734.6	6
CITIC	0.91	11	0.40	11	611.9	7
CEB	0.79	13	0.40	11	528.3	8
PDB	0.99	5	0.90	5	573.1	9
CMB	0.97	8	0.90	5	557.4	10
GDB	0.66	15	0.40	11	477.3	11
FIB	0.97	7	0.90	5	474.0	12
HXB	0.93	9	0.80	9	356.1	13
BOS	0.92	10	1.02	3	239.4	14
SDB	0.82	12	0.50	10	222.4	15

Sources: Bankscope. Efficiency scores and their rankings are from Table 8.4.
Note: Full names of banks are in Appendix 8.1.

There is also no evidence that joint-equity banks outperform the state-owned banks. CCB and BOC enjoy high ranking based on both efficiency and profitability indices. Similar results are obtained in other years. Our finding is in accordance with the conclusions ascertained in recent research by Bonin, Hasan and Wachtel (2005) but contradicts some other studies that are based on a different research methodology (Yao *et al.*, 2006). With respect to the impact of ownership, privatization or joint-equity arrangement is not a sufficient condition to increase bank efficiency, as state-owned banks are not appreciably less efficient than private or joint-equity banks as far as our sample is concerned. However, it is found that the more efficient commercial banks, whether they are state-owned or of joint-equity, happened to be those that have been listed in the stock markets recently whereas the inefficient banks have not been allowed to be listed.

The Malmquist index

The Malmquist index has been frequently used to measure productivity changes of various industries. The advantage of the Malmquist index as opposed to other alternative measurements is that productivity change can be decomposed into efficiency improvements and technological progress. The first empirical study related to the Malmquist index in a DEA context is Färe *et al.* (1989). The Malmquist index captures productivity change in terms of quantities without reference to input prices or output values. As the Malmquist index is always computed maintaining a constant returns to scale assumption, its value is the same whether it is computed in an input or output orientation (Thanassoulis, 2001). Hence, the output orientation efficiency scores are used to conduct the Malmquist index to fit the interpretation of productivity change. The Malmquist index of DMU k in the output orientation is defined in equation (8.2).

$$MI_k = \left(\frac{E_{T_t}^{D_t} E_{T_{t+1}}^{D_{t+1}}}{E_{T_t}^{D_t} E_{T_{t+1}}^{D_t}} \right)^{1/2}$$

(8.2)

where $E_{T_t}^{D_t}$ is the technical output efficiency of DMU k computed in period t (D_t), relative to the efficient boundary of the same period (T_t). Equation (8.2) can be decomposed in equation (8.3).

$$MI_k = \left(\frac{E_{T_{t+1}}^{D_{t+1}}}{E_{T_t}^{D_t}} \right) \left[\left(\frac{E_{T_t}^{D_{t+1}}}{E_{T_{t+1}}^{D_{t+1}}} \right) \left(\frac{E_{T_t}^{D_t}}{E_{T_{t+1}}^{D_t}} \right) \right]^{1/2}$$

(8.3)

The first term in equation (8.3) compares the closeness of DMU k in each period to the period's efficiency boundary. This is called the catch-up term. A value of 1 for this term would mean that DMU k has the same distance from the respective boundaries in periods t and $t+1$. The second term in equation (8.3) is called the boundary shift term, representing a productivity gain (loss) by computing the geometric mean of outputs in periods t and $t+1$ with respect to the respective efficient boundaries, controlling for input levels.

Calculation of the Malmquist index and its decomposition can be done on an annual basis for individual banks or for a given data period. To save space, the detailed calculations on annual, or period, basis are not presented here. Table 8.9 presents the geometric average annual growth rates of total factor productivity, measured by the Malquist index in column 1, the geometric average annual growth rates of technical efficiency in column 2 and the geometric average annual growth rates of technological progress in column 3.

Except for CITIC, CEB and SDB, all the banks achieved significant total factor productivity growth over the data period. The star performer was CCB, becoming the benchmark for other state banks. Over the data period, CCB achieves an average annual growth of more than 15 per cent in total factor productivity. Among the joint-equity banks, CBC, CMB and PDB outperform their peers. They achieve an annual productivity growth of 7.5 per cent or more. In contrast, CITIC, CEB and SDB experience serious deterioration in their productivity, with a negative growth rate of nearly 4 per cent per annum.

On average, the Chinese national commercial banks achieved a remarkable growth in total factor productivity. The average growth is 5.6 per cent per annum pulling fifteen banks together over the entire data period. The average growth rate after China's accession to the WTO in 2001 was more than 10 per cent per year, much higher than the average growth prior to the WTO accession. This implies

Table 8.9 Decomposition of productivity, geometric average annual growth, 1998–2005

Banks	Malmquist index (%)	Efficiency growth (%)	Technical change (%)
ICBC	4.20	1.83	2.33
ABC	7.10	5.96	1.07
CCB	15.70	15.51	0.15
BOC	10.50	10.50	0.00
CBC	11.20	11.12	0.07
CMB	5.50	3.78	1.65
CITIC	−4.10	−5.54	1.52
CEB	−5.10	−7.89	3.03
PDB	7.60	3.10	4.37
CMSB	8.60	5.20	3.23
GDB	0.30	−4.63	5.17
FIB	4.60	0.49	4.09
HXB	2.60	−3.46	6.28
BOS	0.40	−3.55	4.09
SDB	−3.20	−4.41	1.27
Mean	5.60	2.88	2.64

Sources: Bankscope.
Note: Malmquist index indicates geometric average annual growth of total factor productivity, which is decomposed into efficiency growth and technological change, i.e. Malmquist index = efficiency growth × technical change.

that WTO accession has been a powerful impetus to reforms in China to improve bank efficiency.

The Malmquist index can be decomposed into efficiency changes and technological progress, or frontier shift. As shown in column 3 of Table 8.9, the average industrial technical efficiency change is 2.88 per cent per annum, which accounts for more than half of the total factor productivity growth. CCB and BOC are the best performers in terms of efficiency growth, as both achieve double-digit annual growth in the data period. In contrast, some joint-equity banks, such as CITIC, CEB, GDB, SDB and BOS, suffered a significant loss in total factor productivity. The contribution of technological progress to total factor productivity is presented in the last column in Table 8.9. The average annual growth is 2.64 per cent for all the banks over the whole data period. It is striking to find that all the banks achieve positive technological growth, and the best performers are not the Big Four state-owned banks but the joint-equity banks, such as HXB, BOS, PDB and CEB.

The decomposition results in Table 8.9 have important policy implications. First, the Chinese banking industry has become considerably more competitive in recent years, especially after the WTO accession, although state-owned banks still enjoy some encapsulated market power and government protection and financial support. Second, the growth of total factor productivity is almost equally explained by its two components: efficiency improvement and technological progress. Third, large state-owned banks make more progress in improving their technical efficiency than their joint-equity counterparts, but the latter achieve more technological progress than the former. Possible explanations for the significant improvement of total factor productivity growth, especially for CCB and BOC, include their efforts to retrench employment, to implement a stricter monitoring and control mechanism on lending and to improve management and corporate governance.

Conclusion

This chapter uses the latest banking data to assess the efficiency of Chinese national commercial banks. It is the first attempt to use the resource approach to identify inputs and outputs in the banking context with reference to asset quality. One key finding is that Chinese national commercial banks do not have substantial differences in technical efficiencies as the average scores of efficiency are high and the aggregate gaps in technical efficiency are low at only 15 per cent. Another important finding is that the total factor productivity of the sample banks rose significantly at 5.6 per cent per annum over the data period. These empirical results show clear evidence that Chinese national commercial banks have reacted positively and aggressively to ownership reform and foreign competition.

Three large state-owned banks, CCB, BOC and ICBC dominate the market as they have high technical efficiency and profitability, explaining why their IPOs in 2005 and 2006 were so heavily demanded by investors. Despite the improvements in efficiency and productivity and the success of transformation into share-holding companies, it has to be pointed out that the achievements of bank reform in China in the last few years may have been artificially created, or at least supported, by the government. The direct capital injection to, as well as the NPLs stripped off from, the Big Four during the data period amounted to some 3 trillion RMB, which was more than 35 per cent of China's GDP in 1999. Such a colossal amount of state support would have led to a huge financial crisis had China not been able to maintain a two digit annual growth in its GDP over the last eight years.

On the other hand, the empirical results in this chapter provide some useful additional insights on the Chinese commercial banking industry. They contradict a perceived conception that Chinese state-owned banks cannot withstand the onslaught of foreign banks entering into China after WTO accession. There is also a popular view that state subsidies to the Big Four were wasteful as more subsidies would only induce more inefficiency and loss-making in the industry. It is true that the government has been bailing out the Big Four since the beginning of banking reform in the early 1980s, rising to a peak prior to and after China's accession to the WTO. In some senses, the large state-owned commercial banks seem to be the largest black holes in the state budget and there is no hope of filling these holes in a given time horizon. However, the government has made it clear that no more state assistance will be given to the three listed banks, CCB, BOC and ICBC.

The successful IPOs of CCB, BOC and ICBC indicate that the government has achieved its first goal of ownership reform with foreign competition after WTO accession, which is to transfer the Big Four from state-owned banks into shareholding companies. From now on, the listed banks will have to learn how to survive in a liberalized environment without additional state assistance. However, it remains to be tested over time whether these banks will eventually become as competitive as their foreign counterparts.

Anecdotal evidence and observation in the past two years show that the Chinese commercial banks have made significant progress in improving their efficiency and corporate governance. Apart from reducing the number of employees, the Big Four have improved their lending strategies and tried to steer away from intervention by local governments. Some commercial banks have tried to form strategic alliances with foreign commercial banks by accepting their investments in an effort to learn from their advanced managerial and organizational experiences.

This chapter shows some strong and unambiguous results that CCB and BOC have emerged as China's best performing commercial banks, better, even, than many of the joint-equity banks. Although it is too early to predict whether the Big Four will compete successfully with foreign banks and establish themselves as world-class commercial financial institutions, the fact that the Chinese commercial banks in general and the CCB, BOC and ICBC in particular, have achieved admirable productivity growth implies that the most recent banking reforms in China have produced some encouraging results.

The empirical results in this paper also indicate that the Big Four, except for ABC, were able to improve total factor productivity mainly through improving technical efficiency rather than technological progress. In contrast, the joint-equity banks have improved their productivity mainly through technological progress rather than efficiency improvement. In addition, they appear to have suffered from the lack of scale economies because they do not have a large network of branches as do their larger state-owned counterparts. In other words, the joint-equity banks have not been able to exploit their ownership advantage over the Big Four because they are not big enough. They were initially established by regional governments with a clear objective of serving the local market. Although they have expanded their services throughout the country, they are still locally controlled and do not have the ability to become really national, let alone international, by exploiting economies of scale and scope. Consequently, the future bank reforms in China will have to continue in the following directions. First, the Big Four must change their ownership structure to become truly large commercial banks with minimum intervention from central and regional governments. Bank directors should be appointed based on professional qualifications and managerial ability rather than party seniority. Second, the reforms applied in the state sector should also be similarly applied in the joint-equity sector, but mergers and acquisitions should be encouraged to enable them to exploit any available economies of scale and scope.

Appendix 8.1: Names and abbreviations of national commercial banks in China

Abbreviations	Full names of banks
ICBC	Industry and Commercial Bank of China
ABC	Agricultural Bank of China
CCB	China Construction Bank
BOC	Bank of China
CBC	China Bank of Communications
CMB	China Merchant Bank
CITIC	China Investments and Trust Bank
CEB	China Everbright Bank
PDB	Pudong Development Bank
CMSB	China Mingsheng Bank
GDB	Guangdong Development Bank
FIB	Fujian Investment Bank
HXB	Huaxia Bank
BOS	Bank of Shanghai
SDB	Shenzhen Development Bank

Notes:
All banks listed in this table are national commercial banks, meaning that they can provide banking services throughout the country without any geographical restriction. The state-owned commercial banks are the Big Four, ICBC, ABC, CCB and BOC. The others are joint-equity banks. These fifteen banks account for over 80 per cent of China's total commercial lending activities and deposits. There are many other commercial banks, credit unions and foreign bank subsidiaries in China but, unlike the national commercial banks listed in this table, they can only operate in a particular location or economic sector.

Notes

1 Throughout this paper, only the abbreviations of the full names of banks will be used for simplicity of presentation. The full names of these abbreviations are provided in Appendix 8.1.
2 In this paper, we only consider the Big Four state-owned commercial banks and the eleven national joint-equity banks. The city commercial banks, rural commercial banks, rural credit cooperatives and foreign bank subsidiaries are not included because they are either too small, or do not have consistent data for analysis. The fifteen national commercial banks included in this paper, however, accounted for more than 80 per cent of China's commercial lending activities and deposits.
3 China's GDP in 1999 was RMB8.2 trillion, and the state budgetary revenue was RMB1.14 trillion at current prices (National Bureau of Statistics, 2002, pp. 281, 55).
4 The world's top 100 commercial banks had an average NPL ratio less than 2.5 per cent in 1999 (Shi, 2005).
5 In 2005, ICBC had total assets of RMB6.45 trillion, ABC RMB4.77 trillion, CCB RMB4.59 trillion and BOC RMB4.74 trillion. China's fifth largest commercial bank, CBC, had total assets of RMB1.4 trillion in the same year. CBC was the first Chinese bank to be listed in the stock exchanges.
6 To save space the detailed decomposed results relating to the economies of scale are not reported here but are available on request.

References

Berger, Allen N. and Humphrey, David B. (1997) 'Efficiency of Financial Institutions: International Survey and Directions for future Research,' *European Journal of Operational Research*, 98, 175–213.

Bonin, John P., Hasan, Iftekhar and Wachtel, Paul (2005) 'Bank Performance, Efficiency and Ownership in Transition Countries,' *Journal of Banking and Finance*, 29, 31–53.

Charnes, Abraham, Cooper, Williams W. and Rhodes, E. (1978) 'Measuring the Efficiency of Decision Making Units,' *European Journal of Operational Research*, 2, 429–444.

Chen, Tser-Yieth and Yeh, Tsai-Lien (2000) 'A Measurement of Bank Efficiency, Ownership, and Productivity Changes in Taiwan,' *The Service Industries Journal*, 20 (1), 95–109.

Chen, Xiaogang, Skully, Michael T. and Brown, Kym (2005) 'Banking Efficiency in China: Application of DEA to Pre- and Post-Deregulation Eras: 1993–2000,' *China Economic Review*, 16: 229–245.

Chinese Banking Regulatory Commission (CBRC) (2006) Internal monitoring report on Chinese commercial banks, CBRC, Beijing.

Dong, Xiaochang (2005) 'New Banking Industry: Shenzhen Development Bank's Great Step Forward,' *China Internet Weekly*, 1 November, Online. Available <www.ciweekly.com/article/2005/0111/A20050111380937.html>.

Drake, Leigh M., Hall, Maximillian J.B. and Simper, Richard (2003) 'The Impact of Macroeconomic and Regulatory Factors on Bank Efficiency: A Non-Parametric Analysis of Hong Kong's Financial Services Sector,' Nottingham University Working Paper.

The Economist (2006) *A Survey of China*, 25 March, 3–20.

Färe, Rolf, Grosskopf, Shawna, Lindgren, B. and Roos, P. (1989) 'Productivity Developments in Swedish Hospitals: A Malmquist Output Index Approach,' Discussion Paper No. 89-3, Carbondale, IL: Southern Illinois University.

Fu, Xiaoqing and Heffernan, Shelagh (2005) 'China: The Effects of Bank Reform on Structure and Performance,' Cass Faculty of Finance Working Paper WP-FF-19-2005.

Garcia-Herrero, Alicia, Gavila, Sergio and Santabarbara, Daniel (2006) 'China's Banking Reform: An Assessment of its Evolution and Possible Impact,' *CESifo Economic Studies*, 52 (2), 304–369.

Girardone, C and Casu, B. (2004) 'Large Banks' Efficiency in the Single European Market', *Services Industrial Journal*, 24 (6), 129–142.

Mitchell, Tom (2006) 'Report of IPO of ICBC,' *Financial Times*, 24 October.

National Bureau of Statistics (2002) *China Statistical Yearbook*, Beijing: China Statistical Press.

National Bureau of Statistics (2005) *Almanac of China's Finance and Banking 2005*, Beijing: Cjina Statistical Press.

Pastor, Jose M. (1999) 'Efficiency and Risk Management in Spanish Banking: A Method to Decompose Risks,' *Applied Financial Economics*, (9), 371–384.

Richard, Barr S., Kory, Killgo A., Thomas, Siems F. and Sheri, Zimmel (2002) 'Evaluating the Productive Efficiency and Performance of U.S. Commercial Banks,' *Managerial Finance*, 28 (8), 3–22.

Shi, Huaqiang (2005) 'State-Owned Commercial Banks' Non-Performing Loans on their Balance Sheets, Adjustment Factors and Seriousness: 1994–2004,' *Finance Research* (Chinese), 12, 10–15.

Thanassoulis, Emmanuel (2001) 'Introduction to the Theory and Application of Data Envelopment Analysis,' Massachusetts: Kluwer Academic Publishers.

World Bank (2002) *Transition: The First Ten Years*, Washington: The World Bank.

Yao, Shujie, Jiang, Chunxia, Feng, Gengfu and Willenbockel, Dirk (2006) 'WTO Challenges and Efficiency of Chinese Banks,' *Applied Economics*, 39(5), 629–643.

Zhu, Joe (2003) *Quantitative Models for Performance Evaluation and Benchmarking Data Envelopment Analysis with Spreadsheets and DEA Excel Solver*, Massachusetts: Kluwer Academic Publishers.

9 Local states and the building of a regulatory state

Implementing reforms in China's cotton sector[1]

Björn Alpermann

Introduction

For almost three decades of reforms the Communist Party-led government of China has presided over extraordinary economic growth and has directed the shift from a planned to a 'socialist market economy'. This transformation also entailed profound changes in the functions performed by the state and in its relationship vis-à-vis the economy. A number of competing conceptions of the Chinese state's character and functions are currently discussed in the pertinent literature. The following chapter will discuss their relevance regarding one sector in the economy which has until now remained relatively under-researched, namely the cotton processing industry. It will also explicitly take into account the different levels of the state engaged in economic policymaking and implementation.

Western studies of China's political economy during the reform era have long recognized the crucial role of local states for economic (under)development.[2] There is an abundance of 'models' to depict the patterns of local state–economy relations. Local states have been variously described as 'developmental', i.e. assisting economic growth (especially of private businesses) by indirect means, or 'entrepreneurial', in cases in which they engage in business themselves via local state-owned or collective companies (see Blecher, 1991; Blecher and Shue, 1996, 2001). Some authors have likened their role in the economy to that of a board of directors, as in Oi's model of 'local state corporatism' (see Oi, 1992, 1996, 1999; Walder, 1995), whereas others have pointed to the "predatory" nature of local governments, expounding their rent-seeking activities (see Lü Xiaobo, 2000). There has been much discussion about the merits and demerits of these and other labels on offer for local governmental activity in China's economy (see Tsai, 2002, pp. 256–257; Wang 2005). Certainly, there is no one model to fit all the existing patterns of local state–economy relations in China. Yet there is general agreement that these characterizations tentatively describe very real differences of local developmental experiences in rural China. Since in reality these patterns may change over time or may even coexist, it is suggested here that these models are best thought of as ideal-types to which existing local states may bear more or less resemblance. In this sense, these models can be used as heuristic devices to systematize empirical findings. They are applied here to denote a certain characteristic pattern of local state–economy interaction, not as an essentialist notion of the local states' 'nature'.

More recently, other scholars have hinted at the possibility of China's Communist Party-dominated polity turning itself into a 'regulatory state' while adapting to a market economy (see Pearson, 2005). In their view, the state increasingly confines itself to a more limited, yet at the same time more effective, role vis-à-vis the economy and substitutes a rule-bound approach to economic governance for the old-fashioned administrative interventionism. The most comprehensive argument in this vein has been advanced by Dali Yang, who has claimed that the Chinese state had transformed itself through a host of reform steps so that a new 'philosophy of relative regulatory neutrality' had been extended to an array of industries (Yang, 2004, p. 59). Among other things, he based his claim on the study of several regulatory enforcement agencies with economy-wide responsibilities such as the State Administration for Industry and Commerce (SAIC) or the Quality Technology Supervision Bureaucracy (QTSB) (see ibid., pp. 94–98). In a similar vein, Mertha argued that Beijing applied a strategy of ' "soft" centralization' to strengthen administrative oversight in selected agencies, including SAIC and QTSB (see Mertha, 2005, pp. 794–795). Other authors have more specifically analysed changes in one particular industry, such as finance or coal mining.[3] Yet none of these studies has so far discussed how the new regulatory role the central state designs for itself relates to the above-mentioned types of local states. Therefore, this chapter sets out to examine regulatory change in one sector of the economy – the cotton processing industry – with a special focus on the changing functions performed by the state on different levels and the characteristics of local states.

The chapter proceeds as follows. First, regulatory changes at the national level are discussed: the following section investigates the governance structure that emerged in recent years as the monopsony formerly held by supply and marketing cooperatives was dissolved and a host of new competitors entered cotton procurement.[4] It will be demonstrated that policymakers still regard cotton as a strategic product and that the state therefore attempts to retain a strong position in the partially liberalized cotton market. Cotton policy aims at two goals: (i) the state attempts to reduce its *direct* involvement in the market and in particular to get rid of its loss-making cotton companies; (ii) the state is also committed to enhancing industry-wide cooperation by concentrating processing in vertically integrated conglomerates. This should serve to improve quality management and thus the international competitive position of Chinese cotton and cotton textiles. Such an approach confirms observations by Waldron, Brown and Longworth (2006) on the Chinese state's role in promoting agricultural development. It is also consistent with what Pearson called the 'Chinese leadership's "metavision" for the country's industrial future' (2005, p. 313). Yet these policy goals – with their clear developmental thrust – also belie the notion of regulatory neutrality.

Second, provincial regulations on the cotton sector are briefly analysed, followed third by two case studies on implementation in county-level localities in

Shandong and Hubei. These provinces were selected to represent the two traditional cotton growing regions of the North China Plain and the Middle and Lower Yangtze-Region respectively. The localities studied are Xiajin County, Shandong, and Tianmen city, a county-level city directly administered by Hubei province.[5] The two case studies suggest that trends at the regional and local level significantly dilute the central state's ability to steer the envisaged changes in the industry. The central state's efforts to redefine its role as that of a regulator encounters numerous problems once the regional and local levels are taken into account.

Developments at the national level

Emerging governance structures in China's cotton sector

The Chinese cotton sector entered the reform period with its planned economy structure largely intact. State-dominated supply and marketing cooperatives (SMCs, *gongxiao hezuoshe*) and their subordinate cotton and fibre companies (CFCs, *mianma gongsi*) were the sole legal agents to purchase and process seed cotton. However, under increasing pressure as government outlays for cotton procurement exploded, the state twice attempted to liberalize the sector during the mid-1980s and early 1990s. As these reforms and their failures are discussed in detail elsewhere, we will here focus on the third and ultimate reform attempt starting in 1999 (see Sicular, 1996; Ma Kai, 1997; Wedeman 2003, chapter 4; Alpermann 2006, chapter 3). Suffice it so say that the two rounds of deregulation and recentralization left the SMC cotton monopsony intact, at least formally. As a monopsonist the state was still able to dictate prices but not output levels, which fluctuated widely over the 1980s and 1990s.

Recentralization proved imperfect, however, as state-set official prices were undermined by two developments. First, the monopsony could not be enforced absolutely and small-scale private cotton trading, although illicit, continued throughout the 1990s. Second, and more importantly, recentralization only localized monopsonist powers and vested them in SMCs at the county level, which in turn competed for the cotton harvest. This competition between local SMCs gave rise to a quasi-market mechanism, which adjusted black-market prices to supply and demand. Moreover, local SMCs worked the system to the detriment of the central state. In years when demand exceeded supply of cotton, local SMCs could leverage their position to force farmers within their jurisdiction to sell cotton at low state-set prices and resell the processed cotton on a lively black market at much higher prices. Profits were retained at the local state level, while the responsibility for losses incurred by local SMCs was transferred to the central state. These were particularly high in years when supply exceeded demand, and SMCs, as the sole legitimate purchasing agent, were legally bound to procure all of it, even as prices for processed cotton plummeted. Although no officially published data are available for these losses, a researcher at the State Council's Development Research Centre gave them as RMB20.7 billion accumulated from the latter half of 1995 through 1998.[6] Mostly on account of these huge internal imbalances of the cotton industry – but also spurred on by the imminent agreement with the United States of America on China's WTO accession – the Chinese government began to conceive of a third reform in late 1998.

A first step of reform, taking effect in the cotton season of 1999, allowed existing state farms and seed and textile companies to establish forward and backward linkages with the cotton sector. Preferably, they were to enter into long-term purchasing agreements with existing CFCs to realize economies of scale. Furthermore, state-set fixed prices were abolished in favour of non-binding guidance prices. Thus, administrative price-setting was officially put to an end and supply and demand were to freely influence cotton prices.[7] The state retained newly created instruments for macro-control, attempting to avoid wide swings in prices and output levels. These instruments were the state cotton reserve system and state control of cotton imports and exports as well as quality control through administrative departments.

The second and decisive step came with central-level documents issued from July to September 2001. Taken together these regulations instituted a new governance structure for the cotton sector that could be termed a 'managed market'. Enterprises applying for a license to purchase and/or process cotton had to fulfil certain set requirements including most notably a specific size and amount of fixed and circulating capital as well as machinery and technicians trained to produce up-to-standard lint cotton.[8] A business license would be granted at the provincial level, but not automatically. Instead, new registrations had to accord to a general provincial plan for cotton processing facilities to be decided upon and administered by provincial-level Economic and Trade Commissions (*jingji maoyi weiyuanhui*). To strengthen quality control, respective administrative responsibility was relocated away from the SMCs to state administration, namely the QTSB. From this it can be inferred that the two major concerns of the state in this new market structure were overcapacity and quality issues.

To reduce the state's involvement in the sector the central government in 2001 mandated a separation of the SMCs and CFCs, which was fleshed out in further regulations over the following years with the eventual goal of establishing CFCs as independent market actors. The provincial-level administrations were ordered to help healthy CFCs with their operations and with establishing bigger cotton conglomerates with interregional reach. Cotton companies with mediocre performance were to be restructured through mergers and acquisitions and hopelessly loss-making CFCs allowed to go bankrupt.[9] As a further indication of the state's diminished role in the sector, central documents stipulated a gradual decrease of policy loans issued through the Agricultural Development Bank of China (ADBC) and a corresponding commercialization of loans for cotton procurement. In sum, all this hints at a neutral role for the state, shedding its role as a market actor in favour of that of a regulator.

On the other hand, the central state clearly goes beyond a mere regulatory role in that it also tries to steer the sector towards industrial upgrading, to develop large and vertically integrated conglomerates and to balance overall demand and supply. First, this becomes visible in its efforts to improve quality standards by gradually raising demands on machines for cotton processing enterprises as well as in its preference for big and presumably more efficient conglomerates, which ideally should evolve out of CFCs. Second, the state's strategy of macro-control over the cotton sector through its reserves system and through remaining controls over import and export adds another aspect to its steering of sectoral development. Generally speaking, a mechanism of market prices under state macro-control, thus aiming at a combination of flexibility and a general balance between supply and demand, is a principle enshrined for agricultural marketing of all products in the agriculture law and other relevant documents.[10] However, specific regulations vary considerably for different commodities as will be shown below. In May 2002 the State Council permitted the establishment of the China National Cotton Reserves Company (CNCRC), now under the administration of the National Development and Reform Commission (NDRC). CNCRC was formed from the pre-existing reserve system to manage cotton stocks more efficiently. Henceforth, CNCRC was charged with holding government stocks, which should be turned over every two to three years via open bidding at the China National Cotton Exchange (see State Council, 2002, pp. 14–15; CNCE, 2004). Although this is ostensibly in line with a market-based approach to economic governance, CNCRC is also a prime instrument of the central state to influence prices in the domestic market and to push for higher quality standards (see NDRC, 2004b).

Furthermore, despite the constraints imposed on the central state under the WTO accession agreements with regard to interfering in international cotton trade, in cases of excess domestic demand the Chinese state still retains considerable leverage on trade flows. The state is free to voluntarily issue higher quotas to importers to satisfy domestic demand – an option which has been used in all recent years. Whereas the TRQ of 4.5 million bales agreed for the time after China's WTO accession, constituting 2.6 times China's average imports over the last ten years, seemed enormous at the time, it has since been dwarfed by the fast growth of actual imports to 19 million bales in 2005/06 (Meyer *et al.*, 2007). Moreover, the distribution system for tariff rate quotas is tuned to favour sizeable conglomerates, a fact which is supposed to have ramifications for consolidating the upstream cotton sector as well.[11] Thus, so far, the WTO-induced cotton trade regime has been used by the state to steer sectoral development.

Third, in spite of the gradual reduction of policy loans, discretionary credit allocation is still consciously employed by the central state as an instrument for sectoral development. For instance, the NDRC continues to direct policy loans through ADBC according to the current market situation. When granting these loans ADBC is expected to take other policy aims into account, for example favouring enterprises with more advanced machinery. What is more, even commercial banks are still directed by administrative documents to either restrict or expand lending to the cotton sector. At times of restriction, as in 2003, all financial institutions are exhorted to strictly adhere to commercial considerations in making lending decisions. At times of oversupply, however, as in the procurement season of 2004, these institutions are encouraged to lend 'enthusiastically' to cotton enterprises, and local governments are even directed to take on the financial risks in cases where local cotton enterprises lack creditworthiness (see NDRC *et al.*, 2003a,b, 2004). The emergence of big market actors is further supported through an array of financial measures (see State Council Office, 2002, pp. 12–13; and more generally Gale and Collender, 2006).

In sum, industrial upgrading is fostered by a number of instruments ranging from regulating market access to positive incentives such as preferential procurement for state reserves, allocation of credit or import quotas. The state can still be said to retain a strong position in the cotton market. In short, this new model of governance structures in the cotton sector aims at establishing what can be tentatively termed a managed market in which the state assumes a regulatory as well a developmental role.[12] In other words, if the two models of regulatory and developmental state are thought of as two extremes in a theoretical continuum, as suggested by Pearson (2005, p. 297), it would be misleading to stress only one of these aspects. The strategic importance attached to cotton is highlighted by the fact that market access is much more tightly controlled than, for instance, in the wool or grain sectors. In the cotton industry the central state still shields CFCs from competition that is deemed 'excessive' in order to foster the development of big and healthy conglomerates based on formerly state-controlled cotton enterprises, whereas in neither of the other commodities sectors does this developmental aspect receive such an emphasis in policy documents.[13] This approach is, however, premised on implementation by regional and local state actors, to which we turn below.

Provincial regulations on the cotton sector

Whereas central regulations on the cotton sector established the principles of a managed market and defined the requirements for gaining market access in the new licence system (*mianhua shougou jiagong zige rending zhidu*), most of the regulatory work was delegated to provincial administrations. Specifically, central regulations stipulated that enterprises wanting to engage in cotton procurement and/or processing needed adequate finances (registered capital as well as circulating funds), physical capital (machines, factory and storage space) and human resources (technicians with specialized training) so that such companies would be able to fulfil national cotton quality standards. Most items were left to be further detailed in provincial regulations, but minimum standards for machines were established nationwide. Provincial governments were called upon to establish a licensing system in which the provincial level itself would be the gatekeeper for the cotton market. The administrative agencies charged with the task included Provincial Development and Reform Commissions (PDRC), Industrial and Commercial Bureaux (ICB, i.e. the regional and local departments of SAIC) and provincial QTSB, i.e. exactly those agencies used by Yang as prominent examples of the building of a regulatory state in China.

Provincial authorities apparently used this leeway when formulating their own regulations according to regional conditions. Although respective documents could not be obtained from every provincial-level unit, even an incomplete comparison suffices to indicate the range of differences.[14] Henan, Hubei and Jiangxi, which already suffered from serious overcapacity in cotton processing, reacted to the first liberalizing step in 1999 with a rather restrictive approach. While Jiangxi deliberately set the minimum requirement for circulating funds at a high RMB6 million, Henan and Hubei flatly forbade any new enterprises in the sector (see Jiangxi, 1999; Henan, 1999; Hubei, 1999b). Other provinces, such as Gansu (1999), did not include such restrictive stipulations at this point. Two years later, with the second step of liberalization introduced by central leaders, Henan allowed new companies with a minimum of RMB1 million registered capital (as did Guangdong), and Jiangxi lowered the previously high threshold to RMB500,000 in circulating funds.[15] Obviously, these sums are not directly comparable as they pertain to different forms of capital. But as a baseline for comparison they show that Shandong's regulations were clearly more stringent. Shandong distinguished between different enterprise activities (see Shandong, 2001a). Those engaging only in seed cotton procurement were required to prove RMB1 million in registered capital, of which at least RMB500,000 had to be circulating funds, and to possess a total business space of at least 1,000 square metres. The respective minimum requirements for processing companies were RMB3 million (RMB1 million of which in circulating funds) and 5,000 square metres, and even higher for combined procurement and processing enterprises at RMB3.5 million (RMB1.5 million; 6,000 square metres).

Yet other provinces had a less straightforward approach: Hunan, Shanxi and Zhejiang did not bother to stipulate minimum sums for certain capital forms; but the first two referred to a 'reasonable local distribution' of cotton-processing companies (as did the central-level regulations), ostensibly leaving much leeway for case-by-case decisions (see Hunan, 2002; Shanxi, 2002; Zhejiang, 2001). Hubei's approach differed somewhat: although formally stipulations similar to those in Hunan and Shanxi applied, i.e. no set minimum capital was required, the Hubei provincial government also ordered stricter controls of cotton companies and a reduction of (outdated) processing capacity. Furthermore, it explicitly prohibited local SMCs from extending registrations to private cotton companies.[16] From this brief overview we can conclude that Shandong's approach to regulate access to the cotton market was comparatively strict, yet based on clear guidelines, whereas Hubei's stipulations were less explicit and left substantial leeway to be interpreted by lower-level administrations.

In 2003 central policy guidelines tightened again. The proliferation of mostly small-scale, private cotton companies in recent years had created serious overcapacity and raised the spectre of market chaos. Therefore, NDRC promulgated a notice that (again referring to 'reasonable local planning') prohibited any further establishment and registration of cotton-processing enterprises (NDRC *et al.*, 2003a). Instead overcapacity should be gradually reduced. Hubei tried to comply with these new regulations and Gui Lixin, an official at the provincial ICB, claimed that registrations had been stopped. According to Gui (2004) there was a total of 891 licensed enterprises in 2003, namely 288 private, 157 state-owned and 466 belonging to the SMC network. Obviously, there was some confusion in this data even at the aggregate level since the actual sum should rather have been 911. More seriously, enterprise numbers given in another source point to the fact that even officially licensed companies continued to grow in double digits despite the ban, to 1,043 in 2004. In addition, some 500 unlicensed companies were said to be active in Hubei's cotton sector (see Zhang Jie, 2004).

An even more glaring gap between official provincial figures and reality was evident in Shandong. A policy document issued in 2005 by Shandong PDRC claimed that three batches of companies had so far received official licences for cotton processing. Of this total of 475 companies, 302 belonged to the CFC system, 46 were textile companies, 17 were part of the agricultural system (such as seed companies run by local agricultural bureaux) and the remaining 110 fell in the 'other' category. A fourth batch of another 200 firms was currently awaiting the provincial government's final permission to enter the market in 2005 – in obvious violation of the NDRC's ban on new licences (see Shandong, 2005a). However, even when these are added, a total of 675 cotton companies for the whole of Shandong, with only a minor part being independent private firms, appears far removed from reality. As will be detailed below, Xiajin county alone had some 350 cotton processing enterprises in 2005 (see Ma Junkai, 2005, p. 44). In fact, the same provincial document admitted having failed to implement the licensing system in some parts of the province. In view of that, in November 2005 Shandong PDRC promulgated a plan to upgrade cotton processing capacity during the five years 2005–9. This document implemented a province-wide ban on newly established cotton companies, as NDRC had requested two years earlier (see Shandong, 2005b). A *People's Daily* report on Shandong's new policy acknowledged the fact that the province possessed some 2,000 cotton processing enterprises of which only 801 (sic) had a proper license. According to that report the total provincial processing capacity of 4 million metric tons was scheduled to be halved by 2009, mostly through mergers made feasible by policy loans to stronger companies (see People's Daily, 2005).

In sum, in Hubei as well as in Shandong, the number of actually operating cotton firms was considerably in excess of officially licensed figures. Moreover, there is ample evidence to suggest that the same situation pertained elsewhere too (see for instance Ma Daolin, 2006, p. 12; Su Xuhong, 2006, p. 5; Wang Jinbo *et al.*, 2006, p. 26). In view of the above-mentioned provincial data the SAIC's national figure of 8,458 licensed cotton processing companies in 2005 looks highly dubious (see SAIC, 2006). The question that needs to be addressed is how central and provincial licensing institutions could fail so clearly.

Local management of the cotton sector

The local setting

The two localities chosen as case studies represent different patterns of local state–economy relations and serve to illustrate diverging trends in the implementation of cotton sector reforms. Xiajin county in Shandong province has a record as a pioneer in cotton reforms since it abolished the link between the local SMC and the CFC in 1984, bringing the latter under direct county control. As mentioned above, this separation became national policy only in 2001. More importantly, county leaders directed the CFC in establishing a cotton trading centre under whose cover private cotton companies could enter procurement and processing in 1999, i.e. two years prior to the legalization of private cotton businesses.[17] This move was legalized only retroactively as an experiment in cotton reform. Following the 2001 national liberalization, control of the growth of the private cotton business was greatly relaxed and these companies mushroomed in the county. The Xiajin county leadership currently fosters the development of larger corporate structures spanning the production, procurement and processing of cotton as well as the further processing into yarn. It is even contemplating the expansion of the local value chain into cloth-making. To this end it has selected a number of 'home-grown' private enterprises as local industry champions to receive preferential treatment and attracted a large-scale investment by a private textile group from Zhejiang. The local CFC on the other hand was finally dissolved in 2003 after a series of reform measures proved unsuccessful. Thus, shortly after liberalization Xiajin's cotton sector thrived on a combination of private business dynamic and developmental initiatives on the part of the local state which brings it close to the type of 'local developmental state' described by Blecher and Shue. Following this recipe, Xiajin has by now come close to realizing the central state's goal of establishing larger and vertically integrated cotton and textile conglomerates if, however, at the cost of undermining the central and provincial policies on market access and licensing.

Tianmen city in Hubei province provides a counter-example of unsuccessful state meddling in the cotton sector. Tianmen's flagship cotton enterprise, Jintian, was salvaged from bankruptcy in 1992 by a private Shenzhen investor. After a period of rapid growth and breakneck expansion it ran into political trouble in 1999: the new Tianmen party secretary attempted to reverse the outward investments undertaken by Jintian to keep the financial resources under local control. But his motives apparently were more 'predatory' than 'entrepreneurial'. A breathtaking saga of corruption and predation evolved, which landed first Jintian's innocent general manager and finally the (former) party secretary in jail (see Li Yuanyou and Ye Fei 2003; Zheng Biao 2004; Cao Kanglin 2004). In the end, with Jintian's demise not only had Tianmen lost its most profitable enterprise and biggest taxpayer, but the city's high-flying hopes of establishing an integrated cotton and textile conglomerate had also been dashed. At the time of fieldwork in 2004 the two formerly state-owned cotton-spinning companies had been sold off cheaply (Jintian among them). The new owners were no longer contemplating integrating spinning with production and processing of cotton, but were content to purchase lint cotton on the free market. The biggest cotton enterprise in Tianmen was the local state-owned CFC, which remained in an unreformed and uncompetitive state. But still it was propped up by cheap policy loans to the tune of RMB100 million in 2003 and continued to dominate the local cotton sector, claiming some

50 per cent of the harvest while at the same time incurring losses of some RMB 20 million.[18]

Implementation of cotton reforms

These different patterns of local state–economy relations not only had a bearing on the economic fortunes of these two localities, but also impacted directly on the regulatory regime in the cotton sector. In terms of restricting small-scale private enterprise proliferation, Tianmen proved much more effective than Xiajin. An internal report to the Xiajin county government put the figure of private cotton enterprises at 210 for 2003 and a published account claimed 350 such companies existed in 2005 (see Xiajin county, 2003, p. 4; Ma Junkai, 2005, p. 44). In contrast, Tianmen city professed only seventy-nine licensed cotton enterprises in August 2004 (including illegally operating ones, the number was being given as more than 100). Cotton production in the two localities is of comparable dimensions. To understand the differences in implementation outcomes at the local level we need to look at regional cotton policies as well as their local implementation.

In general, it can be said that Shandong provides a more positive attitude on private sector growth than Hubei (see Yang Xiaochuan and Xu Hanchu, 2003, pp. 211–2), which is also reflected in their ways of implementing reforms in the cotton sector. In comparison, documents on cotton sector reforms issued by Hubei provincial authorities are much more ambiguous about the future role of CFCs after opening up the market to other actors, including private enterprises. A case in point is the document promulgated in March 1999 by Hubei's government: on the one hand it demanded a separation of management between CFC and SMC to enhance efficiency, but at the same time it decreed that CFCs should remain the main economic force in the cotton sector and that no new capacity for cotton processing should be added (see Hubei, 1999a,b). In 2001 Hubei's government simply reiterated its insistence on restricting cotton market access for private enterprises. In contrast to that, authorities in Shandong were urged to relax market access to ensure that the bumper harvest could be regularly purchased and farmers would not be unable to sell their cotton (see Hubei, 2001; Shandong, 2001c). More tangibly, CFCs in Hubei still received considerable policy loans for cotton procurement when in Shandong these were almost eliminated. This is the reason why Tianmen's CFC could still count on ADBC loans for cotton procurement in 2003.[19] Thus, to some degree the differences found between Tianmen and Xiajin are explicable in terms of diverging provincial policies.

Nevertheless, other key factors for differing implementation outcomes appear to rest with the county level and in particular the local leadership's attitude towards private businesses. As shown above, Xiajin founded its own cotton trading centre with the county government's help. The centre now attracts huge amounts of seed cotton from other counties and even provinces, which is then being processed within the county.[20] The mushrooming of small-scale private cotton enterprises alluded to above was made possible by the county ICB's benign neglect of the

fact that companies registered only for trading in cotton also engaged in processing. Minimum capital requirements were circumvented with the simple ruse of
several smallish firms registering as one sufficiently big limited liability company,
a method known as 'one licence, many firms' (*yi zheng duo chang*) and expressly
prohibited in central and provincial regulations. On the other hand, state-set
requirements regarding quality issues – pertaining to machines and technical
training – are being implemented reasonably well in Xiajin's private cotton enterprises and the county has established a good reputation by now. Moreover, the
county leadership attempts to raise quality levels by providing financial incentives
for upgrading machinery. Thus, despite its lax implementation of the licensing
system, Xiajin county's pro-private business attitude was instrumental in creating
a vibrant local cotton sector. What is more, Xiajin also came closer to realizing the
state-set goal of building several vertically integrated cotton and textile conglomerates. This is in fact the more crucial part of the story as a strategy of regulatory
relaxation is easily copied elsewhere and competition by other localities mounts
quickly.[21] Thus, only by moving up the value chain – integrating cotton processing, yarn spinning and possibly cloth fabrication – can Xiajin's cotton industry
hope to stay ahead of the competition.

In contrast, Tianmen's approach to the cotton sector remains clumsy. Instead
of providing financial incentives for the development of selected private cotton enterprises, all these companies are illegally charged a fee of RMB10,000
a year by ICB. More importantly, a new and controversial policy planned for
the cotton harvest of 2004 aimed at considerably reducing the number of private
enterprises in the sector. Ostensibly, the main goal was to raise product quality
through tightened requirements regarding processing machines. However, the
major thrust in Tianmen appeared to be squeezing unwelcome private competitors out of the market. According to the 'local industry plan' under deliberation,
capacity requirements for cotton baling machines, for instance, would have been
raised to double that of national standards. Such a move can only be characterized
as arbitrary since local leaders were well aware that (i) many private enterprises
had just upgraded to the national norm, most of these struggling to do so with tight
finances, and (ii) none of the enterprises in Tianmen, including the CFC, had a
baling machine matching the new standard. The declared purpose of this measure
was to foster industry concentration on some ten enterprises within three to five
years. To pool capital smaller companies would be 'persuaded' to merge or close
down. The role of mediator in this process of industrial restructuring was to be
played by a Cotton Sector Association. This organ, which was officially founded
in 2003 by the CFC in reaction to a provincial policy, was, however, defunct by
the time of fieldwork in 2004 (see Hubei, 2003). Unsurprisingly, the one company
which was to be strengthened above all others as a 'dragon head enterprise' (*long-
tou qiye*) was the CFC itself.[22]

Although this plan was not yet finalized at the time of fieldwork some observations can be made. First, the general direction of the policy was in line with a
developmental approach to economic governance, and in fact it predated similar
moves in Shandong in 2005 and nationally in 2006 (see People's Daily, 2005;

NDRC *et al.*, 2006). Yet the timing was bad. For a regulation to take effect for the 2004 cotton year it was already too late: by September, the new cotton harvest was beginning to enter the market and all new machines had already been bought and installed. Second, the new rules, if enforced, would result in extraordinary waste of funds as they would obliterate all investment by private enterprises in equipment matching national requirements. However, relevant officials in the city government were unfazed. How these enterprises should be made to 'pool their capital' remained an unresolved issue. This indifference underscores the third observation that the whole plan was tuned to discriminate against (smaller) private enterprises to the advantage of the CFC. In spite of its continued bad management and mounting losses Tianmen's political leadership still felt obliged to prop up remnants from the planned economy era.

However, it needs to be stressed that, although Tianmen's leaders were probably extreme in their attitudes towards private companies in the cotton sector, this was reinforced by the general political climate in Hubei. A policy document issued by Hubei PDRC and other administrative organs at the provincial level in October 2004 has a thrust very similar to the local policy under discussion in Tianmen a month earlier. It ambiguously states that 'excessive competition' for cotton resources should be avoided by limiting the number of cotton enterprises to one for each 7,000 tons to 10,000 tons of cotton harvested. This feat should be achieved through merging or restructuring cotton enterprises 'according to market principles' (see Hubei 2004). Yet what this means is left unspecified and it is hard to see such a concentration happening without considerable administrative intervention. In fact, this approach seems to clearly contravene current central regulations, which stipulate that no local administration or bureau may restrict the procurement area of licensed cotton companies. It is very likely that discussions on a new cotton sector strategy in Tianmen during my fieldwork were only mirroring a similar debate going on at the provincial level, which finally produced the document cited. In any case, the provincial regulations leave so much leeway for local governments that even drastic measures against (private) enterprises would be justifiable. In other words, administrative interventions in the cotton sector, as the measures being discussed in Tianmen, arise from a combination of provincial and local factors.

In sum, in both localities the two policy goals set by the central state were only partially achieved. Although Tianmen was more successful in reining in overcapacity in the cotton sector, it proved largely ineffectual in fostering the growth of a vertically integrated and competitive cotton and textile conglomerate and it failed to revitalize its CFC. Xiajin came closer to the ideal of forging conglomerates, but only after letting private enterprises develop freely, selecting the stronger ones from among them for further promotion while dismantling its CFC. In other words, the central policy of introducing a managed market for cotton enabled local state agents to selectively implement those parts of the new governance structure which fitted well with their particular attitude towards the private economy and to disregard other policy goals. Thus, Tianmen emphasized the 'regulatory' tasks, whereas Xiajin favoured 'developmental' goals over proper licensing procedures.

The administrative restructuring described by Mertha as ' "soft" centralization' has so far failed to show effects in the cotton sectors of these two localities. This is more clearly the case in controlling overall processing capacity than regarding quality: state standards pertaining to machinery and technical training of staff are reasonably well enforced in both localities, although quality supervision of proc-essed cotton is conducted only sporadically in both cases. Insufficient control of lint cotton is mostly due to a lack of manpower and technical expertise within the relevant administration, since QTSBs possess specialized departments for fibre quality only down to the district level. Regular supervision at the county level is therefore not feasible and QTSB mostly confines itself to check infrastructural conditions like machinery and technical training of the staff.

Conclusion

The analysis of central level regulations has demonstrated that the paradigmatic shift from plan to (managed) market has been effected in China's cotton industry. The central state instituted a governance structure for the cotton sector in which provincial administrations are supposed to function as gatekeepers for market access. Following the abolition of state-set prices and the introduction of pri-vate competitors the character of the sector has changed tremendously. However, the farther-reaching goals of central cotton policy – restraining overcapacity and building vertically integrated cotton and textile conglomerates to raise quality and efficiency – proved more elusive. Although no comprehensive national data is available, excessive processing capacity remains a key concern in many cotton producing provinces. In spite of the changes introduced in regulatory agencies such as the Administration for Industry and Commerce and the Quality Technol-ogy Supervision Bureaucracy to enhance their vertical accountability, the licens-ing system proved ineffective in limiting the number of market participants. In the case of the Administration for Industry and Commerce, the blame seems to rest with local state interventions, whereas in quality supervision lack of technical and personal resources appears to be the main problem. So far, the reforms of the administrative structure of the Chinese economy analysed by Yang and Mertha have failed to have a positive impact on the cotton sector.

The mechanisms at work in Xiajin and Tianmen are certainly rather common in rural China. Facing the widespread failure of the licensing system – admitted even by the National Bureau for Fibre Inspection of QTSB (see *Zhongguo xian-wei jianyan ju mianhua zhiliang jianduchu*, 2006, p. 16) – the central government changed tack and issued a new set of regulations in July and October 2006 (see State Council, 2006; NDRC *et al.*, 2006). The revised licensing system pertains only to cotton processing whereas the market for seed cotton procurement is liberated from any special restrictions. Starting with the 2006 harvest season, pro-curement companies need only a valid business registration with the local ICB, which is issued without any further preconditions. In other words, higher levels of administration are freed from the task of controlling a multitude of small cotton traders, which may have been unrealistic in the first place. At the same time, SAIC started a two-month campaign to strictly check these business registrations.[23] Experience with similar campaigns in the past suggests caution regarding its prospects of success. On the other hand, the threshold for entering cotton processing is deliberately being raised.[24] First, generally no new licences will be granted for the time being. Significantly, the final decision on allowing new actors market access is recentralized from provincial administrations to NDRC. Second, after a transitional period (so far left unspecified) all processing enterprises will have to fulfil higher standards for their machinery. These are identical with the ones being considered in Tianmen during the time of fieldwork and later adopted in Hubei. However, a crucial difference rests with the fact that the central state does not require properly licensed enterprises to meet these new standards immediately, but gives them time to adapt. The central thrust of the new regulations is clearly – yet again – towards a simultaneous reduction in processing capacity and raising of quality levels applying the principles of a managed market.

The new regulations wrest some regulatory authority away from provincial administrations and recentralize it to NDRC. They are obviously devised to govern the cotton sector for a considerable period (hence the provisions on relicensing after five years). But it is too early to speculate if they will stand the test of time. Since the central state continues to depend on its regional and local agents to implement its vision of a managed market, the recentralization of licensing decisions is unlikely to have a large impact. Local states can be expected to maintain their particular influence on policy implementation and thus limit the possibilities of the centre to reinvent the Chinese administration as a regulatory state. As long as this perennial problem of central–local relations remains unresolved, discussions of an emerging regulatory state in China seem premature.

With regard to the usefulness of different models of the Chinese state a balanced assessment seems in order: on the one hand, it has been demonstrated that the regulatory state approach risks obscuring crucial development-oriented goals in China's economic policy. As observed by Margaret Pearson (2005, p. 297), the Chinese state fully adheres neither to the regulatory nor to the developmental model but comes in somewhere between these poles of a theoretical continuum. In fact, it appears to be misleading to take China's progress towards either the developmental state or the regulatory state model as a yardstick, as arguably aspects of both are integral components of the central state's strategy to achieve what I suggest calling a managed market. On the other hand, it is equally true that employing various models of local state behaviour without paying due regard to regional, most importantly provincial, trends will provide a lopsided image of policy implementation. Therefore, a combination of these approaches appears to be the most promising avenue for a multilevel study of the outcomes of China's economic policy.

China's cotton policy analysed above has evolved in the context of a booming textiles industry, which benefited tremendously from WTO accession at the end of 2001 and the lifting of quota restrictions on textile exports on 1 January 2005. The total industrial output value of China's textile sector has increased 2.3 times over the period 2000 to 2005, and its export value doubled (see *Zhongguo fangzhi gongye xiehui*, 2001/2006). To sustain this growth of the downstream textiles industry and to help the cotton sector develop simultaneously, a policy of forging intersectoral linkages and raising quality standards is certainly recommendable. Yet, instead of doling out policy loans to state-owned companies such as the CFCs, a better way to achieve these would probably be a strengthening of the state's regulatory capacity while leaving investment decisions to private businesses. A related matter is the alignment of agricultural producers' and manufacturers' interests. The state has consistently failed to entice farmers to enter into long-term contractual arrangements with big textile companies, which would help guarantee a more uniform product quality. Most likely, this has to do with the peasants' residual fear of collectivization. Maybe if these integrated cotton and textile companies had less obvious links with the state the Chinese farmers' reluctance to join long-term procurement contracts could be overcome.

Appendix 9.1: Legal and policy documents quoted in the text

1 Central-level documents

Cited as	Date	Full title	Source
CNCE, 2004	August 2004	Quanguo mianhua jiaoyi shichang: Quanguo mianhua jiaoyi shichang chubeimian jingjia caigou banfa (CNCE: CNCE measures for competitive procurement of reserve cotton)	www.hubcotton. gov.cn (29 March 2005)
NDRC, 2003	September 2003	Guojia fazhan he gaige weiyuanhui: 2004 nian liangshi, mianhua jinkou guanshui pei'e shuliang, shenqing tiaojian he fenpei yuanze (NDRC: Principles governing size, application conditions and distribution of import TRQ for grain and cotton in 2004)	www.sdpc.gov. cn (5 December 2003)
NDRC, 2004a	November 2004	Guojia fazhan he gaige weiyuanhui: Mianhua chubei tongzhi (NDRC: notice on cotton reserves)	www.hubcotton. gov.cn (29 March 2005)
NDRC, 2004b	October 2004	Guojia fazhan he gaige weiyuanhui: 2005 nian liangshi, mianhua jinkou guanshui pei'e shuliang, shenqing tiaojian he fenpei yuanze (NDRC: Principles governing size, application conditions and distribution of import TRQ for grain and cotton in 2005)	www.china.org.cn (13 March 2005)
NDRC *et al.*, 2003a	December 2003	Guojia fazhan he gaige weiyuanhui *et al.*: Guanyu jiaqiang mianhua shichang he zhiliang guanli de tongzhi (NDRC: Notice on strengthening the administration of the cotton market and quality)	www.sdpc.gov. cn (5 December 2003)
NDRC *et al.*, 2003b	December 2003	Guojia fazhan he gaige weiyuanhui *et al.*: Guanyu yinfa mianhua zhiliang jianyan tizhi gaige fang'an de tongzhi (NDRC *et al.*: Notice on printing the blueprint for reform of the cotton quality control system)	www.hubcotton. gov.cn (29 March 2005)
NDRC *et al.*, 2004	September 2004	Guojia fazhan gaige weiyuanhui deng: Guanyu zuo hao 2004 niandu mianhua shougou gongzuo de tongzhi (NDRC *et al.*: Notice on carrying out the task of cotton procurement in 2004)	www.hubcotton. gov.cn (29 March 2005)

Cited as	Date	Full title	Source
NDRC et al., 2006	October 2006	Guojia fazhan he gaige weiyuanhui, guojia gongshang xingzheng guanli zongju, guojia zhiliang jiandu jianyi jianyi zongju: Mianhua jiagong zige rending he shichang guanli zanxing banfa (NDRC, SAIC, QTSB: Provisional measures on certifying qualification for cotton processing and on market administration)	www.gov.cn (3 November 06)
NPC, 2002	December 2002	Quanguo renmin daibiao dahui: Zhonghua renmin gongheguo nongyefa (NPC: PRC agriculture law)	GWGB 2003/2, 10–18
SAIC, 2006	April 2006	Guojia gongshang xingzheng guanli zongju: 2005 nian quanguo shichang jiandu guanli jiben qingkuang (SAIC: Basic national situation of market supervision and administration in 2005)	www.saic.gov.cn (4 November 2006)
SDPC, 2002a	February 2002	Guojia fazhan jihua weiyuanhui: 2002 nian zhongdian nongchanpin jinkou guanshui pei'e shuliang, shenqing tiaojian he fenpei yuanze (SDPC: Principles governing size, application conditions and distribution of import TRQ for key agricultural products)	www.sdpc.gov. cn (5 December 2003)
SDPC, 2002b	August 2002	Guojia fazhan jihua weiyuanhui: Guanyu 2002 nian zhongyao nongchanpin jinkou guanshui pei'e zaifenpei de gonggao (SDPC: Public notice on redistribution of import TRQ for key agricultural products in 2002)	www.sdpc.gov. cn (5 December 2003)
SETC, 2002	November 2002	Guojia jingmaowei: Guanyu zuo hao gongxiaoshe yu mianhua qiye fenkai youguan gongzuo de tongzhi (SETC: Notice on some problems regarding the separation of SMCs and cotton companies)	www.hubcotton. gov.cn (29 March 2005)
SETC et al., 2002	August 2002	Guojia jingmaowei deng: Guanyu gongxiaoshe yu mianhua qiye fenkai de shishi yijian [SETC et al.: Opinions on implementing the separation of SMCs and CFCs]	GWGB 2002/31, 17–19
State Council, 1998a	June 1998	Guowuyuan: Liangshi shougou tiaoli (State Council: Regulations on grain procurement and trade)	GWGB 1998/15, 611–615

Cited as	Date	Full title	Source
State Council, 1998b	October 1998	Guowuyuan: Guanyu qieshi zuo hao 1998 niandu mianhua gongzuo de tongzhi (State Council: Notice on resolutely carrying out work related to cotton in 1998)	*Jiangxi Zhengbao* 1998/22, 15–17
State Council, 2001	August 2001	Guowuyuan: Mianhua zhiliang jiandu guanli tiaoli (Regulations on the administration of cotton quality supervision)	*Shandong Zhengbao* 2001/17, 3–6
State Council, 2002	May 2002	Guowuyuan: Guanyu zujian Zhongguo chubeimian guanli zonggongsi you guan wenti de pifu (State Council: Reply on questions regarding the establishment of CNCRC)	*GWGB* 2002/18, 14–15
State Council, 2004a	May 2004	Guowuyuan: Liangshi liutong tiaoli (State Council: Regulations on grain circulation)	*GWGB* 2004/21, 7–12
State Council, 2004b	May 2004	Guowuyuan: Guanyu jin yi bu shenhua liangshi liutong tizhi gaige de yijian (State Council: Opinions on progressively deepening reform of the grain circulation system)	*GWGB* 2004/21, 17–23
State Council, 2006	July 2006	Guowuyuan: Mianhua zhiliang jiandu guanli tiaoli (xiugai) (Regulations on the administration of cotton quality supervision (revised))	www.gov.cn (3 November 2006)
State Council Office, 2001a	September 2001	Guowuyuan bangongting: Mianhua shougou jiagong yu shichang guanli zanxing banfa (State Council Office: Provisional rules on cotton procurement, trade and market administration)	*Shandong Zhengbao* 2001/19, 8–11
State Council Office, 2001b	September 2001	Guowuyuan bangongting: Guanyu zuo hao 2001 niandu mianhua gongzuo you guan wenti de tongzhi (State Council Office: Notice on several problems regarding work related to cotton in 2001)	*Shandong Zhengbao* 2001/19, 11–12
State Council Office, 2002	March 2002	Guowuyuan bangongting: Guanyu luoshi zhonggong zhongyang, guowuyuan zuo hao 2002 nian nongye he nongcun gongzuo yijian you guan zhengce wenti de tongzhi (State Council Office: Notice on policy problems related to executing CCP Central and State Council opinions on carrying out agricultural and rural work in 2002)	*GWGB* 2002/12, 12–13

2 Provincial-level documents

Cited as	Date	Full title	Source
Gansu, 1999	September 1999	Gansu sheng renmin zhengfu bangongting: Gansu sheng mianhua shougou jiagong jingying zige rending banfa (Gansu Province People's Government Office: Gansu province measures regarding the confirmation of qualification for cotton procurement, processing and trade)	www.law-lib. com (16 December 2005)
Guangdong, 2002	2002	Guangdong sheng Mianhua shougou jiagong qiye zige rending shishi xize (zanxing) (Guangdong province detailed implementation regulations regarding confirmation of qualification for cotton procurement and processing enterprises (provisional))	*Guangdong Zhengbao* 2002/5, 91–96
Henan, 1999	August 1999	Henan sheng renmin zhengfu: Guanyu jin yi bu shenhua wosheng mianhua liutong tizhi gaige qieshi zuo hao 1999 niandu mianhua gongzuo de tongzhi (Henan Province People's Government: Notice on gradually deepening Henan's cotton circulation system reforms and resolutely carrying out work related to cotton in 1999)	*Henan Zhengbao* 1999/10, 17–19
Henan, 2001	September 2001	Henan sheng renmin zhengfu bangongting: Henan sheng mianhua shougou jiagong zige rending zanxing banfa (Henan Province People's Government Office: Henan province provisional measures regarding the confirmation of qualification for cotton procurement and processing)	*Henan Zhengbao* 2001/10, 55–57
Hubei, 1999a	August 1999	Hubei sheng renmin zhengfu: Guanyu zuo hao 1999 niandu mianhua gongzuo you guan wenti de tongzhi (Hubei Province People's Government: Notice on some problems concerning the carrying out of work related to cotton in 1999)	*Hubei Zhengbao* 1999/9, 33–35
Hubei, 1999b	March 1999	Hubei sheng renmin zhengfu: Hubei sheng mianhua liutong tizhi gaige shishi yijian (Hubei Province People's Government: Hubei province opinions on carrying out reforms of the cotton circulation system)	*Hubei Zhengbao* 1999/4, 43–44

Cited as	Date	Full title	Source
Hubei, 2001	April 2001	Hubei sheng renmin zhengfu bangongting: Guanyu jiaqiang mianhua zhiliang he shichang guanli gongzuo de tongzhi (Hubei Province People's Government Office: Notice on strengthening work relating to cotton quality and market administration)	*Hubei Zhengbao* 2001/8, 54
Hubei, 2003	January 2003	Zhonggong Hubei shengwei, Hubei sheng renmin zhengfu: Guanyu jiakuai nongye nongcun jingji fazhan de jueding (Hubei Province CCP Committee/ Hubei Province People's Government: Decision on quickening agricultural and rural economic development)	*Hubei Zhengbao* 2003/3, 13–17
Hubei, 2004	October 2004	Hubei sheng fazhan he gaige weiyuanhui deng: Guanyu zuo hao 2004 niandu mianhua shougou gongzuo de tongzhi (Hubei PDRC *et al.*: Notice on resolutely carrying out work related to cotton procurement in 2004)	www. hubcotton.gov. cn (29 March 2005)
Hunan, 2002	April 2002	Hunan sheng renmin zhengfu bangongting: Hunan sheng mianhua shougou jiagong qiye zige rending shishi xize (Hunan Province People's Government Office: Hunan province detailed implementation regulations regarding confirmation of qualification for cotton procurement and processing enterprises)	www.law-lib. com (16 December 2005)
Jiangxi, 1999	May 1999	Jiangxi sheng gongshangju: Mianhua shougou jiagong qiye zige rending zanxing banfa (Jiangxi Province ICB: Provisional measures regarding confirmation of qualification for cotton procurement and processing enterprises)	*Jiangxi Zhengbao* 1999/13, 16
Jiangxi, 2001	March 2001	Jiangxi sheng renmin zhengfu bangongting: Guanyu mianhua zhiliang he shichang guanli jiancha qingkuang de tongbao (Jiangxi Province People's Government Office: Inspection report on the situation of cotton quality and market administration)	*Jiangxi Zhengbao* 2001/6, 24–26
Shandong, 2001a	October 2001	Shandong sheng renmin zhengfu: Shandong sheng mianhua shougou yu jiagong zige rending guanli zanxing banfa (Shandong Province People's Government: Shandong province provisional regulations regarding confirmation of qualification for cotton procurement and processing enterprises)	www.law999. net (16 December 2005)

Cited as	Date	Full title	Source
Shandong, 2001b	September 2001	Shandong sheng renmin zhengfu: Guanyu jin yi bu shenhua mianhua liutong tizhi gaige he zuo hao 2001 niandu mianhua gongzuo de tongzhi (Shandong Province People's Government: Notice on gradually deepening cotton circulation system reform and carrying out work related to cotton in 2001)	*Shandong Zhengbao* 2001/20, 22–24
Shandong, 2005a	2005	Shandong sheng fazhan he gaige weiyuanhui: Fangzhi mianhua jiagong nengli guosheng cujin qiye guifan youxu jingzheng (Shandong PDRC: Preventing overcapacity in cotton processing, promoting standardized and orderly competition)	www.sdjw.gov. cn (15 December 2005)
Shandong, 2005b	2005	Shandong sheng fazhan he gaige weiyuanhui: Shandong sheng mianhua jiagongye shengchan shebei gengxin gaizao guihua yijian (Shandong PDRC: Opinions on the plan for updating cotton processing machinery in Shandong province)	www.sdjw.gov. cn (15 December 2005)
Shanxi, 2002	March 2002	Shanxi sheng renmin zhengfu bangongting: Shanxi sheng mianhua shougou jiagong qiye zige rending banfa (Shanxi Province People's Government: Shanxi province regulations regarding confirmation of qualification for cotton procurement and processing enterprises)	www.law-lib. com (16 December 2005)
Xinjiang, 2005	May 2005	Xinjiang weiwuerzu zizhiqu gongshang xingzheng guanliju: Guanyu mianhua shougou, jiagong zige rending shixiang gongshi (Xinjiang UAR ICB: Notice implementing the confirmation of qualification for cotton procurement and processing enterprises)	www.xjaic. gov.cn (16 December 2005)
Zhejiang, 2001	September 2001	Zhejiang sheng renmin zhengfu bangongting: Zhejiang sheng mianhua shougou jiagong qiye zige rending shishi xize (Zhejiang Province People's Government Office: Zhejiang province detailed implementation regulations regarding confirmation of qualification for cotton procurement and processing enterprises)	www.zjda.gov. cn (16 December 2005)

Notes

1 Fieldwork for this research project was facilitated by a DAAD scholarship, and the final version of this chapter was written during a stay as visiting scholar at the Center for Chinese Studies, UC Berkeley, financed by the Fritz Thyssen Foundation. Both sources of funding are gratefully acknowledged.

2 Here 'local state' refers to the township and in particular the county level, which can be said to be the lowest tier of full-blown state administration. For provincial and district levels the term 'regional' will be employed.

3 See Heilmann (2005); Wang Shaoguang (2006). Pearson's cases include the financial and energy sectors as well as telecommunications and civil aviation; see Pearson (2005).

4 A monopsony is a market form with many suppliers but only one actor on the demand side.

5 A total of eight months of fieldwork was conducted by the author in 2002 and 2004; for detailed discussion see Alpermann (2006), Appendix A.

6 See Xu Xiaoqing (2001, p. 515). More recently Zhang Quanxin (2003, p. 26), quotes insiders as estimating the total of SMC cotton debts as RMB50.15 billion.

7 See State Council (1998a); all legal and policy documents cited in the text are listed in a separate appendix. Also see Song Hongyuan *et al.* (2002, pp. 111–115).

8 See State Council Office (2001a,b); State Council (2001). Quality problems arise from accidentally or intentionally mixing plastic and other fibres into cotton bales during the processing and packaging, which causes great financial damage to textile mills; see Xu Wenying (2002, p. 155).

9 See SETC *et al.* (2002, pp. 17–19). These points were reiterated in November 2002; see SETC (2002).

10 See chapter 4 of the revised agriculture law (NPC, 2002, pp. 12–13). This is in turn the concretization of the economic principle enshrined in the constitution (article 15), which provides for a combination of markets and state macro-management; see Heuser (2006, p. 24).

11 See SDPC (2002a,b); NDRC (2003, 2004b). The distribution system deliberately favours applicants that have received import rights previously. Thus, it exerts a 'lock-in' effect and restrains competition; see Colby and Antoshak (2001, p. 30).

12 The term 'managed market' is here used as shorthand for the governance model detailed above. It should also serve to clearly distinguish this market model, since some observers erroneously claim that China has committed itself to work toward a 'free-market economy' in agricultural marketing; see Han Donglin (2005, p. 932).

13 On grain see State Council (1998b, 2004a,b); on wool see Brown *et al.* (2005, 160–163).

14 Although at least all cotton-producing provinces can be expected to have promulgated their own regulations, scanning provincial government bulletins as well as the internet delivered only a limited number of examples. A list of relevant legal and policy documents is included in the appendix.

15 See Henan (2001), Guangdong (2002) and Jiangxi (2001). In Xinjiang (2005) the minimum for circulation funds was set at RMB1 million.

16 See Hubei (2001). An official website lists the requirements for registration see www. whbts.gov.cn/showbszn.asp?colid=299 (*Wuhan zhiliang jishu jiandu wang*/Wuhan quality and technology control net) (accessed on 16 December 2005).

17 Previously, attempts at establishing a cotton trading centre had been undertaken in the latter half of the 1980s and again in the early 1990s, but twice the markets had been ordered closed by higher-level administration (author's interviews; also see Wedeman, 2003, p. 97; Ma Kai *et al.* 1997, p. 333).

18 Author's interviews (August and September 2004).

19 Author's interviews (August 2004).

20 The amount of cotton traded given on the Cotton Trading Centre's own webpage is 150,000 metric tons for 2003, or three times the local production; see 'Xiajin mianhua jiaoyi zhongxin yunying qingkuang jianjie' (Short introduction to the operation of Xiajin county cotton trading centre), www.xiajinny.gov.cn/ltqy-mhjyzhx.htm (accessed on 13 May 2005).
21 See author's discussions with county officials and entrepreneurs during follow-up visit (August 2006).
22 Author's interviews (September 2004).
23 See 'Guojia gongshang zongju fachu tongzhi yaoqiu renzhen kaizhan mianhua shichang zhuanxiang zhengzhi' (SAIC issues a notice requesting to thoroughly carry out special reordering of the cotton market), 24 October 2006, www.saic.gov.cn/ggl/zwgg_detail.asp?newsid=460 (accessed on 4 November 2006).
24 Also see 'Mianhua jiagong zige rending he shichang guanli zanxing banfa chutai. Fangkai mianhua shougou, tigao jiagong menkan' [Provisional rules on certifying qualification for cotton processing and on market administration issued. Cotton procurement opened up, threshold on processing raised], 31 October 2006, www.saic.gov.cn/hdxw/news.asp?newsid=1142 (accessed on 4 November 2006).

References

Alpermann, Björn (2006) *Economic Transition and State Capacity: The Case of the Chinese Cotton Sector*, unpublished PhD thesis, Cologne: University of Cologne.
Blecher, Marc (1991) 'Developmental State, Entrepreneurial State: The Political Economy of Socialist Reform in Xinji Municipality and Guanghan County,' in Gordon White (ed.), *The Chinese State in the Era of Reform: The Road to Crisis*, Houndmills: Macmillan, 265–291.
Blecher, Marc and Shue, Vivienne (1996) *Tethered Deer: Government and Economy in a Chinese County*, Stanford, CA: Stanford University Press.
Blecher, Marc and Shue, Vivienne (2001) 'Into Leather: State-Led Development and the Private Sector in Xinji,' *China Quarterly*, 166 (July), 368–393.
Brown, Colin G., Waldron, Scott A. and Longworth, John W. (2005) *Modernizing China's Industries: Lessons from Wool and Wool Textiles*, Cheltenham: Edward Elgar.
Cao Kanglin (2004) '*Chen Yuanhao, beiqing gaobie "fangzhi diguo". Zhang Erjiang gei yi ge zhiye jingliren zhizao de kuangshi qiyu*' (Chen Yuanhao's sad goodbye to his "textiles empire". Incomprehensible injustice inflicted by Zhang Erjiang upon a professional manager), *Jingji Guanlizhe* [Economic Manager], 5, 32–38.
Colby, Hunter and Antoshak, Robert (2001) 'China's WTO Accession: Impact on Cotton and Textile Sectors,' in Bureau of Cotton and Jute/Research Centre for Rural Economy (eds), *2001 China International Cotton Conference 'Prospects of the World Cotton Market and the Chinese Cotton Industry in the New Millenium'*, Guilin 27–29 June 2001, 26–35.
Gale, Fred and Collender, Robert (2006) 'New Directions in China's Agricultural Lending,' *Electronic Outlook Report from the Economic Research Service*, Washington, DC: USDA, Economic Research Service. Online. Available <www.ers.usda.gov/Publications/WRS0601> (assessed on 10 January 2006).
Gui Lixin (2004) '*Zai Hubei sheng mianhua xiehui chengli dahui ji mianhua xingshi fenxihui huiyi shang de fayan*' (Talk given at the founding congress of Hubei Province Cotton Association and conference to analyse the cotton situation), 9 September 2004. Online. Available <www.hubcotton.gov.cn/mhxh_16.htm> (assessed on 15 December 2005).

Han Donglin (2005) 'Why has China's Agriculture Survived WTO Accession?,' *Asian Survey*, 45 (6) (November/December), 931–948.

Heilmann, Sebastian (2005) 'Regulatory Innovation by Leninist Means: Communist Party Supervision in China's Financial Industry,' *China Quarterly*, 181 (March), 1–21.

Heuser, Robert (2006) *Grundriss des chinesischen Wirtschaftsrechts* (An Outline of China's Commercial Law), Hamburg: Institute of Asian Affairs.

Li Yuanyou and Ye Fei (2003) *'Tianmen shi youxiu qiyejia Chen Yuanhao bei pohai an diaocha'* (Investigation of the case of Chen Yuanhao, an excellent entrepreneur being destroyed in Tianmen City), *Zhongguo Minying Keji Yu Jingji* (China Non-governmental Technology and Economy), 12, 42–46.

Lü Xiaobo (2000) 'Booty Socialism, Bureau-preneurs, and the State in Transition. Organizational Corruption in China,' *Comparative Politics*, 32 (2) (April), 273–294.

Ma Daolin (2006) *'Dui "liang xiao yi tu" feifa shougou jiagong mianhua you guan wenti de qingkuang fenxi'* (Situation analysis of problems related to illegal cotton procurement and processing with "two small and one local" machines), *Zhongguo Xianjian* (China Fibre Inspection), 10, 12–18.

Ma Junkai (2005) 'Shandong Xiajin xian shishi san bu kuayue. Nuli dazao mianfangzhi jidi xian' (Shandong's Xiajin county carries out three steps to transformation. Energetically laying the basis for a cotton textile base county), *Zhongguo Mianhua* (China Cotton), 5, 44.

Ma Kai (1997) (ed.) *Zhongguo mianhua tizhi gaige yanjiu* (Study on China's Cotton System Reform), Beijing: Zhongguo wujia chubanshe.

Ma Kai, Sun Zhixin, Liang Tao and Ye Zhimin (1997) *'Dui 1994 niandu mianhua zhengce de ji dian sikao – Shandong diaocha huilai'* (Some thoughts on cotton policy for 1994 – upon returning from a study-trip to Shandong), in Ma Kai (ed.) *Zhongguo mianhua tizhi gaige yanjiu* (Study on China's Cotton System Reform), Beijing: Zhongguo wujia chubanshe, 331–342.

Mertha, Andrew C. (2005) 'China's "Soft" Centralization: Shifting *Tiao/Kuai* Authority Relations,' *China Quarterly*, 184 (December), 791–810.

Meyer, Leslie, MacDonald, Stephan and Foreman, Linda, 'Cotton Backgrounder,' *Electronic Outlook Report from the Economic Research Service*, Washington, CD: USDA, Economic Research Service. Online. Available <www.ers.usda.gov/publications/CWS/2007/03Mar/CWS07B01/cws07B01.pdf> (accessed on 30 March 2007).

Oi, Jean C. (1992) 'Fiscal Reform and the Foundation of Local State Corporatism in China,' *World Politics*, 45 (1) (October), 99–126.

Oi, Jean C. (1996) 'The Role of the Local State in China's Transitional Economy,' in Andrew G. Walder (ed.), *China's Transitional Economy*, Oxford: Oxford University Press, 170–187.

Oi, Jean C. (1999) *Rural China Takes Off: Institutional Foundations of Economic Reform*, Berkeley, CA: University of California Press.

Pearson, Margaret M. (2005) 'The Business of Governing Business in China: Institutions and Norms of the Emerging Regulatory State,' *World Politics*, 57 (January), 296–322.

People's Daily (2005) *'Shandong yasuo mianhua jiagong nengli. 5 nian nei bu zai shenpi xin jiagong qiye'* (Shandong reduces cotton processing capacity. No approvals for new processing companies for five years), originally published in *Renmin Ribao*, 1 December 2005, reproduced in www.gov.cn/gzdt/2005-12/01/content_114115.htm (accessed on 4 November 06).

Sicular, Terry (1996) 'Redefining State, Plan and Market: China's Reforms in Agricultural Commerce,' in Andrew G. Walder (ed.), *China's Transitional Economy*, Oxford: Oxford University Press, 58–84.

Song Hongyuan (2002) *Jiu wu shiqi de nongye he nongcun jingji zhengce* (Agricultural and rural economic policies during the Ninth Five-Year Plan), Beijing: Zhongguo nongye chubanshe.

Su Xuhong (2006) '*Mianhua shichang huigu yu zhanwang*' (Cotton market review and perpectives), *Zhongguo Minahua Jiagong* (China Cotton Processing), 3, 5–6.

Tsai, Kellee S. (2002) *Back-Alley Banking: Private Entrepreneurs in China*, Ithaca, NY: Cornell University Press.

Walder, Andrew G. (1995) 'Local Governments as Industrial Firms: An Organizational Analysis of China's Transitional Economy,' *American Journal of Sociology*, 101 (2) (September), 263–301.

Waldron, Scott, Brown, Colin and Longworth, John (2006) 'State Sector Reform and Agriculture in China,' *China Quarterly*, 186 (June), 277–294.

Wang Jinbo, Song Xiaohong, Wu Xianghua and Li Qing (2006) '*Dangqian mianhua wenti de zhengji ji duice*' (The crux of current cotton problems and counter-measures), *Jiangxi Mianhua* (Jiangxi Cotton), 10, 25–26.

Wang Juan (2005) 'Going Beyond Township and Village Enterprises in Rural China,' *Journal of Contemporary China*, 14 (42) (February), 177–187.

Wang Shaoguang (2006) 'Regulating Deaths at Coalmines: Changing Mode of Governance in China,' *Journal of Contemporary China*, 15 (46) (February), 1–30.

Wedeman, Andrew H. (2003) *From Mao to Market: Rent Seeking, Local Protectionism, and Marketization in China*, Cambridge: Cambridge University Press.

Xiajin county (2003) '*Guanyu Xiajin mianhua shichang guifan fazhan de qingkuang huibao*' (Situation report on the progress in standardized development of Xiajin's cotton market), county government internal document (dated 16 October).

Xu Wenying (2002) '*WTO yu Zhongguo fangzhi hangye de jishu jinbu he chanye shengji*' (WTO and technological development in China's textile industry and industrial upgrading), in Mao Shuchun and Yu Shuxun (eds), *WTO yu Zhongguo mianhua* (WTO and Chinese cotton), Beijing: Zhongguo nongye chubanshe, 132–156.

Xu Xiaoqing (2001) '*Mianhua liutong tizhi yanjiu*' (Study on the reform of the cotton circulation system), in Ma Hong and Wang Mengkui (eds), *Zhongguo fazhan yanjiu 2001. Guowuyuan yanjiu zhongxin yanjiu baogaoxuan* (China development studies 2001: The selected research reports of the Development Research Centre of the State Council), Beijing: Zhongguo fazhan chubanshe, 510–523.

Yang, Dali L. (2004) *Remaking the Chinese Leviathan: Market Transition and the Politics of Governance in China*, Stanford, CA: Stanford University Press.

Yang Xiaochuan and Xu Hanchu (2003) '*Hubei de geti siying jingji*' (Hubei's individual and private economy), in Zhang Houyi, Ming Lizhi and Liang Chuanyun (eds), *Zhongguo siying qiye fazhan baogao No.4 (2002)* (Development report of China's private enterprises no. 4 (2002)), Beijing: Zhongguo shehui kexue wenxian chubanshe, 205–217.

Zhang Jie (2004) '*Guanyu Hubei sheng mianhua liutong hangye guanli xiehui gengming wei "Hubei sheng mianhua xiehui" you guan qingkuang de shuoming*' (Explanation of several circumstances relating to the change of names from Hubei Province Cotton Circulation Sector Administration Association to 'Hubei Cotton Association'), 9 September 2004. Online. Available <www.hubcotton.gov.cn/mhxh_16.htm> (accessed on 15 December 2005).

Zhang Quanxin (2003) '*Mianhua xuyao huan yi zhong siwei, huan yi zhong caozuo fangshi*' (In cotton there is a need to change thinking and methods), *Zhongguo Nongcun Jingji* (Chinese Rural Economy), 8, 24–29.

Zheng Biao (2004) '*Chen Yuanhao mengyuan shimo*' (The whole story of framing Chen Yuanhao), *Qiye Guanli* (Enterprise Management), 1, 18–21.

Zhongguo xianwei jianyanju mianhua zhiliang jianduchu (China Bureau for Fibre Inspection, Department for Cotton Quality) (2006) '*Guanche shishi "Mianhua jiagong zige rending he shichang guanli zanxing banfa" yi fa jiaqiang mianhua zhiliang jiandu*' (Implementing the 'Provisional Measures on Certifying Qualification for Cotton Processing and on Market Administration' and strengthening cotton quality supervision based on the law), *Zhongguo Xianjian* (China Fibre Inspection), 11, 15–16.

Zhongguo fangzhi gongye xiehui (China National Textile and Apparel Council) (ed.) (2001/2006) *Zhongguo fangzhi gongye fazhan baogao* (Development report on China's textiles industry), Beijing: Zhongguo fangzhi chubanshe.

10 The dynamics of industrial clusters in China

The case of the Ningbo clothing cluster[1]

Wang Jinmin, Yang Chen and Richard Sanders

Introduction

Since the mid-1990s, the textile and clothing clusters of the Yangtze River Delta (consisting of Shanghai city, Zhejiang province and Jiangsu province, eastern China) and the Pearl River Delta (mainly in Guangdong province, southern China) have developed to such an extent that, only five years after joining the World Trade Organization at the end of 2001, China has become the largest producer and exporter of textile and clothing products in the world. It is the aim of this chapter to examine the institutional dynamics of this change.

With the termination of ATC (the Agreement on Textiles and Clothing) on 1 January 2005, China's share in global textiles and clothing trade had increased, reaching a new peak level of 24 per cent in 2005 if EU (25) intra-trade is included and 31 per cent if EU (25) intra-trade is excluded. The new quotas introduced in 2005 have capped the expansion of Chinese textiles sales to the US and EU markets in 2006 and 2007. However, the annual growth rates of these quotas are well above past import demand trends, so China's share of imports in these two markets can be expected to increase over the next few years (WTO, 2006). The rapid expansion of China's exports of textiles and clothing has been closely linked to the phenomenon of industrial clustering of textiles and clothing firms at the Yangtze River Delta and the Pearl River Delta, which has important economic and social implications with the creation of a large number of enterprises, entrepreneurs and employment.

In the course of Chinese private economic development, the most impressive models of development have been the 'Wenzhou model' (in Zhejiang province, eastern China), the 'Sunan model' (in Jiangsu province, eastern China) and the 'Pearl River Delta Model' (in Guangdong province, southern China).[2] In Zhejiang province, there are about sixty specialized markets with the annual sales volume exceeding RMB1 billion. The market network has promoted the rapid development of industrial districts. Shaoxing is one of the largest textile cities in China, with over 2,500 key textile enterprises. It is also the synthetic fibre base in Zhejiang province, with an annual output of 2.7 billion metres of all types of fabrics. Ningbo is one of the most important apparel manufacturing cities in China with about 2,000 apparel enterprises, accounting for about 5 per cent of the national total. In Wenzhou, there are over thirty specialized towns or counties with the output exceeding RMB1 billion among a combined total of 143 such towns and counties. There are over 5,000 shoe enterprises, accounting for a 20 per cent share of the national market, over 500 manufacturers of spectacles that have exported 90 per cent of their products to the overseas market and over 260 cigarette lighter enterprises whose output accounts for up to 70 per cent of the world market. In addition, many other industrial clusters such as the stocking industry in Yiwu, the tie industry in Shengzhou and the leather industry in Haining have made great achievements.

In the light of such achievements, many scholars both in China and abroad have argued that it has been the very existence of private firms in the industry that has been the greatest dynamic for development of the industry, that private firms have exerted the strongest force and been the primary catalysts for institutional change with the government making purely passive institutional adjustments (see, for example, Shi, 2004; Barbara *et al.*, 2004). As a result, they argue, privatization should be further encouraged and reinforced. In this chapter, however, we argue that such scholars' interpretation of China's rapid industrial cluster development is a misreading of events and that, although private firms have frequently taken the lead in such development, it has been within a framework established by the state, particularly at local level, which has given private firms the wherewithal to flourish and become internationally competitive, providing them not only with an appropriate business, legal and ideological framework but also crucial services without which they would have struggled to do so. And contrary to the views of those scholars, we argue that it is important to see the public sector as a crucial component of any future industrial cluster development.

'There is no one best model for organizing an industrial district or cluster. A diversity of institutional arrangements is possible and each has proved successful in different circumstances' (Carlo, 2004). At present, the Chinese economy is, indeed, characterized by a growing private sector with the state having significantly reduced its overarching role in many parts of the economy. The growth and upgrading of industrial clusters in China has been closely linked with shifts in the nature of the public–private interface, which has been evolving alongside ideological change and economic transition. This research, using the Ningbo clothing cluster in Yangtze River Delta as a case study, is thus designed to offer a better understanding of the interplay between institutional change and the rapid development of industrial clusters in China than has been previously argued, giving due weight to the role of the public sector in such development.

Key features of industrial clusters

Up to now, the definition of industrial clusters still varies greatly in academic circles. There are, however, some commonly accepted features of industrial clusters in the literature which include the following:

1 *A predominance of small and medium enterprises (SMEs):* This does not mean that large firms and transnational corporations are absent nor that some SMEs will not become large-scale companies or even transnational corporations. Indeed, successful economic performance of an industrial cluster will boost its status in the global value chain, allowing the cluster to become the superior location should large companies outside the district and overseas transnational corporations try to expand their business there. However, the predominance of SMEs will not be changed fundamentally. The existence and development of large-scale enterprises depend on foundations provided by SMEs.

2 *A local network based on specialization and cooperation:* Specialization not only reduces the average labour cost of production but also improves the capacity to acquire and accumulate wider social knowledge, and the deliberate cooperation of firms can generate collective efficiency which the simple agglomeration of firms can hardly achieve. This specialization and cooperation increases firms' interdependence and the stability of local networks.

3 *Common social and cultural backgrounds:* Embeddedness means that all kinds of networks and firms' operations are based on a common social structure. The depth of embeddedness is closely related to the stability and sustainable development of industrial clusters. With regard to many export processing zones in China, the production networks have been established by enterprises from the same areas or foreign countries but they have relatively weak embeddedness because they do not have the characteristics of common local social and cultural structures. The local network is very sensitive to political and social changes at home and abroad, allowing the cluster to survive periodic instability and trade fluctuations.

4 *Organization of linkages among business and non-business actors in formal and informal networks:* Industrial clusters usually include an agglomeration of vertically and/or horizontally linked firms operating in the same line of business in conjunction with supporting institutions including business associations and universities.

Industrial clusters in developing countries

Cluster theory has developed predominantly on the basis of the successful experiences of developed countries, particularly in Italy. Since most developed countries have a sound industrial base, advanced technology and strong innovative capability, researchers and policymakers have focused on how industrial clusters improve national and regional competitiveness as specific regional, social, cultural and economic systems. In fact, the background of industrial clusters in developing countries is different from that in developed countries.

The capacity of clustered firms to be economically viable and grow larger has attracted a great deal of interest in development studies. In developing countries, industrial clusters are popular in Asia and South America as an important part of small-scale industrial organization. Some industrial clusters have grown out of urbanization whereas others are the outcome of rural industrialization; some have been formed spontaneously while others are promoted by industrial policy. Clustering may be considered as a major facilitating factor for a number of subsequent developments: division and specialization of labour, the emergence of a wide network of suppliers, the appearance of agents who sell to distant national and international markets, the emergence of specialized producer services, the materialization of a pool of specialized and skilled workers, and the formation of business associations.

During the 1970s and 1980s, developing countries with cost advantages obtained a greater market share of some labour-intensive products than developed countries. Subsequently, many export-oriented industrial clusters came into being in these countries. However, most of these industrial clusters in developing countries had comparative advantage only in terms of low price and were hardly in a position to enter mainstream international markets. In contrast, the industrial clusters in developed countries maintained competitive advantages in terms of quality, pace of innovation, design capacity and speed of response to market changes.

It has become increasingly popular in recent studies to pursue the cluster approach in relation to global value chains (GVC) and their role in clusters' upgrading processes (Schmitz, 2004; Giuliani *et al.*, 2005a,b). Exporting firms in developing countries that are integrated within a global value chain are commonly controlled by foreign firms. They are linked into the chain – sometimes simply through outsourcing – mainly because of their low labour cost advantage and their flexibility in entering into chain arrangements, perhaps combined with the advantage of natural resource endowments. From the local firms' points of view, the global value chain is seen, first of all, as a means of obtaining access to export markets and second as a potential source of upgrading and value-added expansion opportunities.

Export-oriented industrial clusters can scarcely achieve success unless they are integrated into global value chains (Gereffi, 1999). The export promotion policies adopted by developing countries in the course of industrialization have stimulated the rapid development of domestic export processing industries and the spatial transition of labour-intensive industry from developed to developing countries, strengthening the dependency of the latter on international markets. On the other hand, the demand for high-quality commodities by developed countries has promoted technology linkages between domestic producers and overseas clients. The upgrading of export-oriented industrial clusters and regional development thus ultimately depends on the degree to which clustered enterprises are integrated within global value chains.

The opportunities for SME upgrading and competitiveness enhancement in developing countries depend on the type of relations in which they are involved and the possibilities available to them to move from one level of relations to another. Business upgrading can affect process, product, functional or intersectoral capacities or some combination of these: process upgrading results in increased production efficiency arising from the use of new technology or the improved management of existing technology; product upgrading occurs as a result of moving into higher value products or services than previously supplied; functional upgrading refers to the redistribution of activity so that the overall skill content of activities increases; inter-sectoral upgrading occurs when firms apply the knowledge acquired in one area of activity to move into a separate activity, such as when skills acquired assembling television sets are applied to the assembly of computer equipment (Humphrey and Humphrey, 2002).

In what ways are SMEs in developing countries integrated in global value chains or foreign business cooperation when they first enjoy such integration? What are the possibilities for the clustered firms not to end in an immersizing[3] growth process but to upgrade and enhance their activities? With regard to the leading or governing firm in the chain, it is assumed that this will be a large transnational corporation with resources to and experience of operating in international markets. Indeed, one of the major hypotheses of the global commodity chain approach is that development requires linking up with the most significant 'lead firm' in an industry (Gereffi, 2003). However, besides 'lead firms', there are many other types of international relations to consider. Second, only a limited number of firms in developing countries can be accommodated in global chains governed by the large leading multinationals. This raises the question of whether the lead firm in, say, a textile chain needs to be a company like Zara, Gap or H&M, i.e. an international brand leader. In reality, it can be expected that many internationalized SMEs located in developed countries have links to firms in developing countries. The advantage of internationalized SMEs lies in their intelligence of the global economy where factors of production are moving freely (Audretsch, 2003). Located in high wage areas, SMEs in developed countries may well be interested in downsizing employment and avoiding large investment commitments by outsourcing activities, preferring value chains with partners located in proximity to the SME with the ability to control production and save scarce management resources.

The organization of value chains typically takes one of four forms: (i) arm's-length market relations that do not lead to the development of close ties between buyer and supplier; (ii) networks involving firms interacting with each other and jointly determining the allocation of competencies between them; (iii) a quasi-hierarchy in which one firm exercises control over other firms in the chain, for example, specifying the characteristics of the product to be produced and the processes to be followed; or (iv) a clear hierarchy in which a lead firm takes direct ownership of some operations in the chain. Upgrading prospects of clusters differ according to the type of value chain to which they connect. Insertion in quasi-hierarchy offers favourable conditions for fast process and product upgrading but hinders functional upgrading. With arm's-length market relations, process and product upgrading is slow but the route can open for functional upgrading. Networks offer the most ideal upgrading conditions but are least likely to exist for clusters in low-income countries (Humphrey, 2002).

Giuliani, Pietrobelli and Rabellotti have focused on the analysis of relationships existing between clustering, global value chains, upgrading and sectoral patterns of innovation in Latin America. They find that sectoral specificities matter and influence the mode and the extent of upgrading in clusters integrated in global value chains. For example, in traditional manufacturing sectors such as textiles, clothing and footwear, technology has important tacit and idiosyncratic elements and therefore upgrading depends strongly on the intensity of technological externalities and cooperation among local actors (e.g. firms, research centres, technology and quality diffusion centres). Moreover, global buyers may be more involved and interested in their providers' upgrading if the technology required is mainly tacit and requires intense interaction. In other sectors, such as natural resource-based industries, technology is more codified and access to external sources of knowledge, such as transnational corporations or research laboratories located in developed countries, becomes more critical for upgrading. Meanwhile, global buyers are less keen to get directly involved in the upgrading process while imposing compliance to strict quality standards (Giuliani, *et al.* 2005a). In the study on the Sinos Valley footwear cluster in Brazil, quasi-hierarchical value chains led by US buyers obstruct the development of local skills in design and marketing, their key competencies. Only standards such as the quality process standard and the prohibition of child labour, which matter for global buyers, are promoted. Other standards, such as environmental standards or core labour standards, have to be enforced by other type of agencies outside value chains (Navas-Aleman and Bazan, 2005).

Recent research indicates that external linkages are vital to establish and maintain a local network of relationships for both emerging and established clusters (O'Riain, 2004; Saxenian and Hsu, 2001). External links allow access to knowledge, skills, contacts, capital and information about new technological opportunities and new markets. These relationships allow upgrading of the industrial base and reduction of the risk of lock-in by keeping the clusters open to new ideas and technologies from outside. The analysis of two successful clusters in Chile (one in agri-business and the other in salmon aquaculture) highlights interactions between the state, local firms and multinationals, and the conditions enhancing collective firm learning. The argument is that the emergence of dynamic clusters depends on building institutions that enable coordinated learning among firms to improve capabilities, processes and products (Perez-Aleman, 2005).

The industrial clusters in developing countries are confronting new challenges in the face of globalization. The competition has become fiercer and world markets demand quick responses from firms and high-quality products in small quantities. Moreover, developing countries have to give up all kinds of export subsidies as a result of trade liberalization. The above factors have weakened the comparative advantages of clustered firms in developing countries. External linkages may, indeed, play a crucial role in increasing clusters' and firms' competitiveness, but they are not the panacea (Giuliani, 2005b). There is a great deal of heterogeneity in terms of patterns of governance of value chains, of sectoral specificity of the upgrading and learning processes, of firms' absorptive capacity and of the role played by policy.

There are also a number of studies on industrial clusters in China. An emerging citywide information and communication technology (ICT) cluster in Nanjing, involving various software parks and universities as well as a huge concentration of computer shops, was studied by Dijk and Wang (2005) at a time when ICT clusters were first evolving. Meanwhile, subsidiaries of multinational corporations have played an important role in the formation of manufacturing clusters in Guangdong province, southern China. The relevant data indicate that there is an agglomeration of firms in the clothing, leather and related products and furniture manufacturing industries. Chinese investors looking for low-cost investment locations near their hometowns have contributed to form some of the strongest localized clusters in Guangdong. This, in turn, has led to the bunching of more investments in these labour-intensive sectors, explaining their continued success (Beule *et al.*, 2005).

A stylized account of developing country clusters has gaps but two points of contrast with the corresponding account of clusters in high-income countries are relatively well supported: agglomeration economies provide limited capacity to manage changes in a cluster's market or product characteristics, and deliberate joint action is needed to make successful adjustments to external challenges. Such joint action is associated with enterprise growth but ultimately may become a constraint on the ability of the cluster to retain a common purpose. Without common objectives, the capacity to withstand intensified competition is put in doubt (Perry, 2005).

Industrial clusters and globally dispersed production systems are in constant tension. How this tension is played out has an important but contentious implications for local development. In Piore and Sabel's (1984) view, flexible specialized industrial clusters are a desirable form of development, being democratic, progressive and oriented to continual improvement in working conditions as well as profitability. Others reject this view. An important question is the direction in which the industrial district is moving: whether towards greater use of low-cost low-skilled labour or of higher-cost higher-skilled labour. The latter may require greater investment and ingenuity but is socially more sustaining (Christopherson, 1989).

Institutional change and growth of the Ningbo clothing cluster

The clothing industry in Ningbo has witnessed a long history and its development has gone beyond the administrative region of the city. The sewing workers from Cixi, Ningbo, known as *Zhecibang*, were famous for making traditional Chinese clothes and monopolized the clothing industry in Beijing between the 1680s and 1930s. However, those from Yinxiang and Fenghua, Ningbo, the *Hongbang*, did not enter Shanghai until the end of the eighteenth century. They grasped the skills of making Western-style suits as a result of communicating with foreigners living in the foreign concessions of Shanghai. The two schools of sewing workers operated outside Ningbo imparting their skills and clothing culture around Ningbo through their social networks.

The cooperatives initially created by villages and towns after the founding of the People's Republic of China in 1949 were turned into clothing factories in the 1950s. They made military uniforms and embroidered dresses in the 1960s and suits in the 1970s. The township and village enterprises (TVEs) developed very fast after China adopted the open-door policy in 1978 and their output rose by 30 per cent annually before 1983. Ningbo became the processing base for companies both in Shanghai and overseas, relying on its location advantage and good social relations. They were initially engaged in processing for the clothing factories in Shanghai and a number of Shanghai-affiliated factories emerged later as a result. Some garment industrial companies were established to manage the state-owned, large collective clothing enterprises in the mid-1980s while others created their own brands, winning awards for their products from ministry-level and provincial governments.

The transformation of the system took place after Deng Xiaoping's southern tour speech in 1992. Shanshan Enterprise achieved great success in establishing its own brand and many other local clothing firms followed suit. Other leading firms moved towards the establishment of world famous brands. Subsequently, the Shanshan Group and the Youngor Group were listed on the Shanghai Stock Exchange in 1996 and 1998 respectively. Private enterprises mushroomed in Ningbo after 1999 when the status of the private sector was officially recognized in the Chinese constitution.

The fever of establishing joint-venture clothing firms emerged in the new millennium. In the last few years, Ningbo has become an original equipment manufacture (OEM) production centre in China, emphasizing design, efficiency, cost, technology and diversification with a high degree of specialization and a relatively complete industrial chain.

The role of entrepreneurs

The Western concept of entrepreneurship is focused on the ability of the individual to identify profitable opportunities (Kirzner, 1973). But, in China, the key factor in successful entrepreneurship is the ability to form an alliance with those economic agents who possess or control financial assets, physical assets or specific human capital needed for brokering market entry, that is for starting production, securing supply and gaining access to distribution channels (Nee, 1989).

The institutional innovation of entrepreneurs and cluster development in Ningbo

Constant institutional innovation of entrepreneurs has invigorated enterprises and promoted the reform of the Chinese enterprise system. The institutional innovation of enterprises at the end of 1980s led to the rapid development of clothing firms. There were two types of clothing firms at that time: TVEs and family firms. Because of government intervention and inflexible operational systems, TVEs found it difficult to respond to the market sufficiently quickly and a number even went bankrupt. Meanwhile, family firms were confronted with potential crises due to the poor performance of managers, an inefficient management system and conflicts of interests among family members. The institutional innovation of Ningbo Yong Gang Clothing Factory (Shanshan Group) opened up the new space for TVEs. Zhen Yonggan, a factory director appointed by the government, argued that the responsible local government must reduce its direct interference in the management of clothing factory. The director of the factory became responsible for the strategy of the enterprise, which, itself, became a separate legal entity with operational and management autonomy. In 1992, he took the lead in completing the reform of the shareholding system with the support of the local government. Shanshan Group separated government functions from enterprise management and assumed sole responsibility for its profits and losses. In 1996, the company was listed on the Shanghai Stock Exchange and became the first listed clothing company in China, providing the enterprise with sufficient capital to establish a modern enterprise system.

The institutional innovation of Shanshan Group improved its performance rapidly, which, in turn, had enormous impacts on the growth of the clothing cluster in Ningbo. Other TVEs and private enterprises in Ningbo also undertook similar enterprise reform. Many family firms introduced a shareholding system and clarified property rights in order to pave the way for future enterprise growth. However, these institutional innovations, initially inspired by entrepreneurship, would, according to our research, have been impossible without the firm support of local government.

Entrepreneurship and diversified business of clustered firms

Although none of the clustered firms interviewed intended to leave the textile and clothing industry, more and more clustered firms in Ningbo have developed into large-scale business groups centred on a holding company with diversified business including finance, real estate and public health, all previously monopolized by the public sector. The Shanshan and Youngor groups are typical and significant examples of this process.

(a) The Shanshan Group began to undertake diversified business after being listed on the Shanghai Stock Exchange in 1997. Clothes, high-technology, non-ferrous metal and high-tech investment are the main sectors in which they are engaged at present. The group also set up Shanshan Ningbo Scientific Park in the district. In the first half of 2006, the sales of lithium battery materials reached RMB30 million, making Shanshan the leading supplier of such materials in China. In the future, the group aims to become the *world's* largest-scale supplier of comprehensive lithium battery materials. Its international partners include leading global firms including Sony Corporation, LG Chemical and VISTA. However, the group does not intend to exit the textile and clothing sector, which will still be expected to account for one-third of its total turnover by 2010.

In September, 2000, Changchun High-tech Industrial Group Co., Ltd, transferred its shares to Shanshan Group, which itself became the second largest shareholder of China Kinwa (600110), another listed company on the Shanghai

Stock Exchange. In April, 2002, Shanshan Group became the largest shareholder of China Kinwa after acquiring shares owned by Changchun Applied Chemistry Research Institute (Jilin province, northern China), affiliated with the Chinese Academy of Science.

In 2004, Shanshan Group entered into the oil business through China Kinwa's subsidiary Chanchun Zhong Ke Kinwa Scientific Development Co., Ltd, acquiring 95 per cent of the shares of Song Yuan Jin Hai, which, in turn, holds 50 per cent of the Jing Yuan Oil Corporation, jointly founded by COPC (China Oil and Petrochemical Corporation) and Song Huan Jin Hai Industrial Corporation. The company also purchased the remaining 5 per cent of the shares from another shareholder (Chong Qing Guan Hui Corporation). In addition, Shanshan Group took over Haerbin Song Jiang Copper Group, the biggest state-owned non-ferrous metals company (Heilongjiang province, northeast China) on 16 March 2005.

On 20 August 2006, Ningbo Shanshan Shareholding Co., Ltd, (Shanshan Gu Fen, registered in Ningbo in 1996) and Shanshan Investment Holding Company (Shanshan Kong Gu, registered at Zhangjiang High-tech Industrial Park, Shanghai on 30 August 2004) founded Zhong Ke Lang Fang Scientific Valley Co., Ltd, with Lan Fang State Holding Company in Hebei province through China Kinwa (see Figure 10.1). The registered capital reached RMB200 million. The ratios of registered capital by Shanshan Gu Fen and Shanshan Kong Gu accounted for 75 per cent and 10 per cent respectively.

(b) The Youngor Group has been seeking to become one of the largest clothing firms in the world. The company has been sticking to its own brand strategy while developing high value-added products to meet the increasing demands of the domestic market. While maintaining its market share of mens' suits, it has

Figure 10.1 Shanshan Group's involvement in the oil business. Source: Annual Reports of Shanshan Group Co., Ltd (2001–2005).

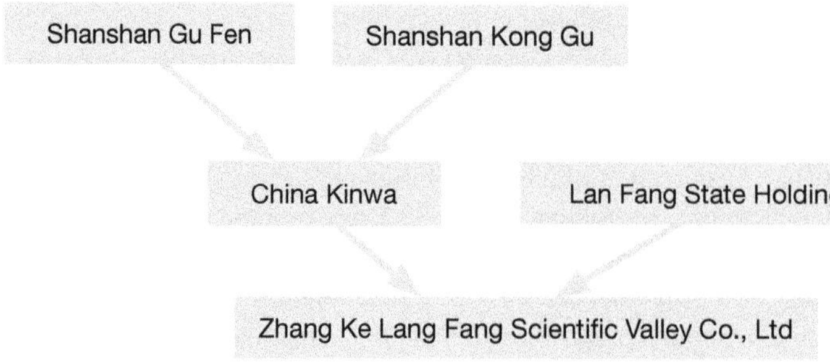

Shanshan Gu Fen   Shanshan Kong Gu

China Kinwa   Lan Fang State Holding Company

Zhang Ke Lang Fang Scientific Valley Co., Ltd

Figure 10.2 Shanshan Group's partnership with the state sector. Source: Annual Reports of
Shanshan Group Co., Ltd (2001–2005).

also entered into leisurewear, endeavouring to expand its international market
and exporting clothes with its own brand instead of conducting OEM for overseas
clients.

To realize a strategy of vertical integration, a 'Textile Town' was constructed
by Youngor Group with several leading Japanese *keiretsu*[4] together, with the
Youngor Group accounting for 70 per cent ownership and the *keiretsu* 30 per cent,
engaging in a range of processes from cotton spinning, mainly for shirt fabrics,
to printing, dyeing and finishing, wool spinning and synthetic fibre programmes.
More and more international giants are linking with the Youngor Group to procure high-quality fabrics. Meanwhile, with the rapid development of the clothing
industry in China generally, the domestic demand for high-quality fabrics continues to rise fast. There is still ample room for developing high-quality fabrics in
the near future and the group intends to take advantage of its vertical integration
strategy to improve its competitiveness.

In addition, Youngor Group has been engaged in the development of high-
quality residential apartments and the provision of supporting services with the
advantages of large land reserves and capital since 1992. The gross profits of
this real estate development business rose steadily from 2001 to 2005 (see Table
10.1). The total assets of Youngor Real Estate Development Corporation exceeded
RMB2.3 billion in 2005, by which time its net profits had reached the same level
as Youngor's mainstream clothing business. While maintaining its leading position in Ningbo, Youngor is making efforts to become one of the leading real estate
developers in China.

Table 10.1   The gross profits of clothing and real estate business in Youngor Group Co.,
Ltd, 2001–2005/(RMB100 million*)*

	2001	*2002*	*2003*	*2004*	*2005*
Clothing	7.25	8.32	6.91	7.87	9.29
Real estate	–	1.83	2.49	5.54	5.69

Source: Annual Reports of Youngor Group Co., Ltd (2001–2005)

More and more clustered firms including the Peacebird Group, the Louse Group and the Progen Group in Ningbo are also adopting diversification strategies as they develop. Sectoral specialization is likely to move increasingly away from the mono-sectoral pattern of specialization towards more diversified models of production.

Entrepreneurship and the public–private interface

Despite the growing significance of the private sector in the Ningbo clothing and textile cluster, it is clear from our research that the social connections between entrepreneurs and local government officials are indispensable to the successful implementation of any diversification strategy by the clustered firms. In the particular institutional environment of contemporary China, the political status and prestige of entrepreneurs have created ample room for their firms to make more profits. Many entrepreneurs actively try to strengthen the social relationship with local government officials. In addition, entrepreneurs of large-scale clustered firms have been taking an active part in political activities and improving their local political influence in order to gain advantages in market competition with their particular political identities.

The role of local government

During the development of the clothing cluster in Ningbo, the role of local government has continued to change. At the beginning in the early 1980s, the local government established collective clothing factories in order to develop the local economy, directly providing managers to operate these enterprises.

Since the mid-1980s, the local government has reduced its direct intervention with clustered firms, coordinated with local entrepreneurs to undertake shareholding system reform, established a modern enterprise system, strengthened the modes of macro-economic planning and regulation, improved the environment of industrial development and taken an active part in regional marketing.

In recent years, the local government has strengthened its functions of service and coordination, cultivated cultural connotations within the clothing cluster, improved the local investment environment and coordinated the competition and cooperation with neighbouring clusters with the aim of strengthening the cluster's locational advantages and improving its international competitiveness. The main functions of local government in the Ningbo clothing cluster include: (a) the formulation and implementation of industrial planning, (b) the creation of a sound industrial, investment and trade environment, (c) the provision of help to clustered firms to cope with trade frictions and the appreciation of the RMB and (d) the development of the peripheral industries.

Thus, with regard to industrial planning, the Ningbo municipal government has been involved in changing the previously weak cohesion and excessive competition of clustered firms by formulating and implementing mid- and long-term planning of the clothing industry to make full use of regional resources and improve the image of the clothing cluster. At the same time, the government has constructed industrial parks where clothing firms agglomerate to improve collective efficiency. The municipal government has also been playing an important role in creating a sound industrial investment environment and these measures can be regarded as important institutional innovations. The functions of government have been integrated in order to improve the quality of government service, the approval system has been simplified and government efficiency has been improved.

With regard to the trading environment, in order to keep the clothing cluster *au fait* with the rapid development of international markets and improve the competitive advantages of local brands, the municipal government has begun to make use of e-commerce to help firms to expand their business. An e-commerce platform has been created to diffuse information and facilitate transactions. Most of the clustered firms have joined the platform. Since 1997, the local government has held the Ningbo International Fashion Festival annually, which has helped to improve the cultural connotations and collective image of the clothing cluster. The China International Fashion Trading Fair (originally Ningbo International Fashion Fair) is one of the top five fashion fairs in China. The tenth fair, in 2006, attracted more than 600 clothing firms, 100 international fashion brands and over 5,000 overseas buyers from home and abroad, thereby promoting the internationalization of the clothing cluster in Ningbo. Moreover, the Ningbo municipal government has established clothing associations to promote the development of the clothing cluster. These associations play an important role in coordinating cooperation and exchange among clustered firms and in strengthening the collective efficiency of the clothing cluster.

With the implementation of a brand strategy by large-scale clustered firms, the demand for imported fabrics has increased considerably and testing fabrics has become essential. For those clustered firms engaged in the export and import business but with insufficient capacity to set up their own testing departments, the Ningbo Quality Supervision Bureau has established the Ningbo Fibre Inspection Institute to do the job. Whereas fabrics are upgraded rapidly and new products are launched into the market on a constant basis, the national testing system continues to lag behind. In recent years, the Ningbo Fibre Inspection Institute centre has cooperated with universities and research institutions to improve testing methods, thereby to offer better services to clustered firms. The municipal government has also created foreign trade development funds to help clustered firms establish overseas marketing centres, providing them with guaranteed credit security facilities.

Currently China is one of the major clothing exporters in the world and is the largest supplier to the United States, the European Union and Japan. Although the ATC came to an end on 1 January 2005, China's Ministry of Commerce signed a Memorandum of Understanding (MOU) with the European Union and the United States. The new quotas will apply until the end of 2007 for the EU and until the end of 2008 for the United States. In addition, the peg of the Chinese currency to the United States dollar was replaced by a peg to a basket of currencies, leading to a moderate appreciation of the RMB by 6 per cent by the end of May 2007. The RMB is expected to appreciate more in the near future. Almost all the clustered firms interviewed agreed that the appreciation of RMB has led directly to a loss of profits. Small and medium-sized clustered firms, those mainly undertaking labour-intensive and low value-added products, have been affected greatly. The trading companies in the cluster targeting American and European markets are under great pressure since the financial tools to avoid foreign exchange risks at local banks remain limited.

Facing the new restrictions on Chinese clothing exports, both central and local governments have taken series of measures to promote the structural adjustment of clustered firms, to strengthen the competitive advantage of original brands and to improve the collective efficiency of the clothing cluster. The export duties on seventy-nine textiles and clothing products were abolished on 30 May 2005 and the export taxes on seventeen textiles and clothing products, which were subject to quantitative restrictions based on the MOU with the EU Commission, were removed on 25 July 2005. In addition, the Ministry of Finance in China suspended all export taxes on textiles products on 1 January 2006.

The local government has helped the SMEs in the cluster to expand their potential markets in India, Russia, ASEAN countries, Africa and South America. Early warning information has been sent to firms to avoid anti-dumping and anti-subsidy allegations, including any information on provisional safeguard measures taken by importing countries. Above all, favourable policies have been formulated to encourage processing trade and the upgrade of the processing capacities in the cluster.

With regard to the development of peripheral industries, according to the interviewed enterprises in Ningbo, connections with large enterprises in regard to sourcing products locally are remarkably weak. Even their clothing accessories may be purchased outside Ningbo, the local clothing accessories market serving mainly small-scale garment factories. This phenomenon is mainly for the following reasons. First, because the style of menswear changes slowly (Ningbo being famous for menswear), scale economies of large-scale mechanized production are significant. Once enterprises have made use of modern clothing-making equipment, the production capacity can basically satisfy market demand and outsourcing is unnecessary. Second, there are currently three tiers in the Ningbo clothing industry. The Youngor and Shanshan Groups make up the first tier, the Peacebird Group and Progen Group the second, the rest the third. The groups in the first and second tiers attach more importance to building their own brands, making efforts to display the cultural content and specialty of their enterprises. However, subcontracting to the small-scale enterprises makes it difficult to control the quality of garments and increases the risk and cost, so the latter may have to make their own garments or subcontract with qualified producers outside the region. Moreover, there are also some enterprises making dresses and sophisticated leisure wear. As dresses needs more individualization and higher design capability, the risk and costs of subcontracting are relatively high.

However, the interactions among clustered firms in the region have been strengthened with deepening globalization. The clothing industry is labour-intensive and the technological content is not high. The majority of clustered firms are undertaking OEM business and it is often impossible for a single firm to complete one large order within limited time. Under these circumstances, several clustered firms usually cooperate to make deliveries on time, with local inter-firm alliances driven by the strength of demand. Different segments exist within the same industry and cooperation among firms at different positions in the value chain has taken place naturally.

An industrial cluster has the feature of flexible specialization, small and medium-sized enterprises being able to respond to the market very quickly. As competition becomes fiercer, local inter-firm alliances strengthen, allowing firms to face difficulties arising from, say, a shortage of rural labour or constant appreciation of RMB more easily. Distribution channels and logistics are attached more importance by the clustered firms as a result.

Concluding remarks

Our empirical research in the Ningbo clothing cluster in China shows that the development of the private economic sector has depended critically upon the work of the public sector in the past twenty-five years and continues to do so. The growth and upgrading of clothing clusters in China has been closely linked with shifts in the nature of the public–private interface, which has evolved alongside ideological change and economic transition.

The clothing cluster in Ningbo has developed on the basis of specific, *local*, social and economic conditions. Informal, formal and global institutions are closely related to the growth and upgrading of the cluster. In the initial period of development, some community members with entrepreneurship and market consciousness took advantage of their social network, gained advanced clothing-making skills and grasped market opportunities from their fellow villagers in Shanghai. With the support of local government, they established collective clothing firms. The achievements of entrepreneurs encouraged local people to set up more clothing firms, which led to the formation of the clothing cluster in the 1990s. The capital accumulation and technological achievements of TVEs and SOEs in the 1980s and early 1990s laid a solid foundation for the formation of the Ningbo clothing cluster and the growth of firms in the cluster.

Meanwhile, entrepreneurs accelerated institutional innovation and technological innovation with the help of local government. The implementation of brand strategy has improved the competitiveness of industrial cluster. The public–private interface still matters when the clustered firm is undertaking its diversification strategy.

The *government-as-leader* strategy of the 1980s has been gradually transformed into a *government-as-provider* strategy since the late 1990s: local government has changed its function from directly managing enterprises towards coordinating industrial development and regulation of the market generally in order to improve the collective efficiency of the clothing cluster. But local government continues to be the provider of the framework in which the clustered firms in Ningbo operate and the supplier of services to them. With increasing trade frictions and the constant appreciation of RMB, it adjusts its policies to improve the competitive advantage of the whole cluster.

Thus, although the Chinese economy is increasingly characterized by private rather than state-owned enterprises, our research into the Ningbo clothing cluster suggests that the public sector must continue to play its crucial role in the expansion of clustered firms and the upgrading of industrial clusters, leading to continued fast *and* sustainable growth of the Chinese economy in the coming decades.

Notes

1 Most clothing firms in Ningbo are located in Duantan town, Yinzhou district, and Jiangkou town, Fenghua city, covering an area of fifteen square kilometres. We conducted semi-structured in-depth interviews with CEOs and managers of fifteen clustered firms in Ningbo on their histories, businesses, competition, innovations, corporate strategies, inter-firm alliances, local–global linkages and viewpoints on the role, functions and impacts of local and central government in the summers of 2006 and 2007.
2 The 'Wenzhou model' is a typical private economic developmental model in China initiated by local entrepreneurs' induced institutional innovation. The 'Sunan model' involves economic development based on extant small SOEs and collective enterprises whereas the 'Pearl River Delta model' promotes local economic development mainly through foreign direct investment.
3 'Immersizing' growth, i.e. negative growth, occurs when, as a developing country increases its export volume, the prices of its exports fall, leading to deterioration in its terms of trade, making the country worse off.
4 A *keiretsu* is a set of companies with interlocking business relationships and shareholding. It is a type of business conglomerate.

References

Audretsch, D.B. (2003) *SMEs in the Age of Globalization*, Cheltenham: Edward Elgar.
Barbara, K. and Polos, L. (2004) 'Emerging Markets, Entrepreneurship and Uncertainty: The Emergence of a Private Sector in China,' in B. Krug (ed.), *China's Rational Entrepreneurs: The Development of the New Private Business Sector*, London: Routledge.
Beule, F., Bulcke D. and Xu L. (2005) 'Multinational Subsidiaries and Manufacturing Clusters in Guangdong, China,' in E. Giuliani, R. Rabellotti and M. Dijk (ed.) *Clusters Facing Competition: the Importance of External Linkages*, Aldershot: Ashgate.
Carlo, P. (2004) 'Upgrading and Technological Regions in Industrial Clusters in Italy and Taiwan,' in P. Carlo and A. Sverrisson (eds), *Linking Local and Global Economies: the Ties that Bind*, London: Routledge.
Christopherson, S. and Storper, M. (1989) 'The Effects of Flexible Specialization on Industry Politics and the labour Market: The Motion Picture Industry,' *Industrial and Labour Relations Review*, 42, 331–47.
Dijk, M. and Wang, Q. (2005) 'Cluster Governanace in an Emerging City-Wide ICT Cluster in Nanjing China, in E. Giuliani, R. Rabellotti and M. Dijk (eds), *Clusters Facing Competition: the Importance of External Linkages*, Aldershot: Ashgate.

Gereffi, G. (1999) 'International Trade and Industrial Upgrading in the Apparel Commodity Chain,' *Journal of International Economics*, 48, 37–70.

Gereffi, G. (2003) 'The International Competitiveness of Asian Economies in the Global Apparel Commodity Chain,' *International Journal of Business and Society*, 4, 71–110.

Giuliani, E., Pietrobelli, C. and Rabellotti, R. (2005a) 'Upgrading in Global Value Chains: Lessons from Latin America Clusters,' *World Development*, 33, 549–573.

Giuliani, E., Rabellotti, R. and Dijk, M. (2005b) *Clusters Facing Competition: The Importance of External Linkages*, Aldershot: Ashgate.

Humphrey, J. and Humphrey, S. (2002) 'How Does Insertion in Global Value Chains Affect Upgrading in Industrial Clusters?' *Regional Studies*, 36, 1017–1027.

Jinchuan, S., Xiangrong, J., Weidong, L. and Wei, Z. (2004) *Institutional Change and Economic Development: A Study on Wenzhou Model*, Hangzhou: Zhejiang University Press.

Kirzner, I.M. (1973) *Competition and Entrepreneurship*, Chicago: University of Chicago Press.

Navas-Aleman, L. and Bazan, L. (2005) *Making Value Chain Governance Work for the Implementation of Quality, Labor and Environmental Standards: Upgrading Challenges in the Footwear Industry*, Aldershot: Ashgate.

Nee, V. (1989) 'Peasant Entrepreneurship and the Politics of Regulation in China,' in V. Nee and D. Stark (eds) *Remaking the Economic Institutions of Capitalism*, Stanford, CA: Stanford University Press.

O'Riain, S. (2004) *The Politics of High-Tech Growth: Developmental Network States in the Global Economy*, Cambridge: Cambridge University Press.

Perez-Aleman, P. (2005) 'Cluster Formation, Institutions and Learning: The Emergence of Clusters and Development in Chile,' *Industrial and Corporate Change*, 14, 651–677.

Perry, M. (2005) *Business Clusters: An International Perspective*, Abingdon: Routledge.

Saxenian, A. and Hsu, J. (2001) 'The Silicon Valley–Hsinchu Connection: Technical Communities and Industrial Upgrading,' *Industrial and Corporate Change*, 10, 893–920.

Schmitz, H. (2004) *Local Enterprises in the Global Economy: Issues of Governance and Upgrading*, Cheltenham: Edward Elgar.

WTO (2006) *World Trade Report 2006*, Online. Available <www.wto.org/english/res_e/booksp_e/anrep_e/world_trade_report06_e.pdf> (accessed on 15 March 2007).

11 Industrial catch-up during transition and globalization

The case of the Chinese steel sector

Pei Sun

Introduction

The catch-up of the newly industrializing countries (NICs) during the last several decades has been a focus of fierce debates by social scientists in various fields. For some development studies scholars, the phenomenal industrial and corporate growth in the NICs, especially in the East Asian developmental states, serves to belie the validity of the orthodox neoclassical development paradigm. It instead highlights the central role of the state in general and strategic industrial policies in particular in facilitating economic transformation (e.g. Amsden, 1989, 2001; Wade, 1990). In the eyes of sociologists and political scientists, the considerably varying track records of industrial catch-up across the developing countries invite explorations of underlying institutional variables, such as state–society relations and state apparatuses, which can help interpret the performance variation (e.g. Evans, 1995; Huang, 2002).

This chapter, based on a longitudinal examination of the state-led restructuring of the Chinese steel industry, aims to shed fresh light on the policy and institutional perspectives of industrial catch-up noted above. Moreover, two critical contextual elements, namely transition and globalization, are organically integrated into the analysis. First, the unique transitional institutional environment of China adds a new dimension of the catch-up story. Although it is widely recognized that the Chinese government has since the mid-1980s carried out activist industrial policies explicitly modeled on Korea and Japan in the hope of nurturing globally competitive national champions in key strategic sectors, its actual implementation in China is by no means a simple replication of the Korean or Japanese experience (Perkins, 2001; Nolan, 2002). Instead, it is of particular interest to see how the institutional legacies from the central planning era, notably the state asset administration system and industrial policy enforcement mechanism, impact upon the intended industrial and corporate catch-up. In particular, the Chinese national champions face dual challenges of transforming themselves from fossilized state-owned enterprises (SOEs) into modern business corporations as well as the catch-up aspiration common to the other NICs. Thus, transition and late industrialization combine to influence the trajectory of catch-up in China.

Second, China's integration into the world economy, epitomized by its final accession to the World Trade Organization (WTO), has raised grave concerns for the competitiveness of large Chinese firms in the face of powerful global business giants. More generically, the advent of globalization, it is argued, has a profound and presumably adverse impact on the prospect of industrial catch-up in developing countries. On the one hand, after a detailed examination of the WTO agreements on intellectual property rights, investment, and trade in services, Wade (2003) concludes that the surge of international regulations makes illegal many of the industrial policy instruments once used by the successful East Asian NICs and is likely to lock in the appropriation of economic and technological rents enjoyed by the developed economies. On the other hand, Nolan (2002) has argued that the so-called global big business revolution and its associated global value chain "cascade effect,"[1] which during the last two decades or so gave rise to unprecedented concentration and dominance of business powers based in advanced economies, have rendered firms in current developing countries further disadvantaged to compete on the global playing field. Thus, it is an open question whether the supposedly unfavorable international environment in the post-WTO era functions to preclude the replay of the East Asian catch-up story in China.

Given this, the chapter attempts to contribute to the overall assessment of the catch-up capability of the NICs through a detailed study of a mid-technology sector in a unique transition environment and in the epoch of globalization. The transition parameter translates into the exploration of particular institutional determinants of the effective industrial policy implementation in China, while the globalization parameter highlights the external challenges for Chinese policy-makers and firms to achieve the catch-up.

Competitiveness and catch-up of the Chinese steel industry

Nowadays China has been a watchword in the international business press on the steel industry and trade thanks to its substantial weight in the global steel production and consumption system. As the largest steel maker and consumer around the world, China in 2005 produced 355.8 million tonnes of crude steel, accounting for 31.2 percent of the world output, and gobbled 327 million tonnes of finished steel, an equivalent of 31.6 percent of world consumption (IISI, 2005–6).

In a sense, the scenario portrayed above should not be so surprising, since historically successful NICs, such as Germany, Japan, and Korea, all had internationally competitive steel industries and firms in their heyday. Being aware of the strategic role of the steel sector in economic catch-up,[2] they employed various industrial policy instruments, including but not limited to subsidies, tax breaks, tariffs, and preferential loans via the centralized banking system, to overcome the initial investment barriers and they finally achieved their catch-up goals (e.g. D'Costa, 1999). The dark side of the catch-up account, however, is that, despite similar interventionist policies adopted, the state-led industrial transformation has not produced the intended results in a large number of developing countries. Institutional incapability on the part of the state, however defined in detail,[3] proves to be a crucial contributing factor to the limited capacity addition, technological inferiority and mediocre financial performance in their indigenous industrial sectors.

In the case of China, the explosive growth of output and consumption notwithstanding, the international competitiveness of the Chinese steel industry is not necessarily a mirror of the grand size it assumes in the global system. By gauging both the achievements and the gaps evident in the industry indicators, the following section presents a brief overview of the domestic sector competitiveness from the late 1980s to the early 2000s.

Achievements: output expansion and technical efficiency improvement

In China, rapid steel output growth has long been perceived as a symbol of successful industrialization since Mao's era. And the most significant achievement of the domestic sector in the reform era is the explosive capacity expansion unprecedented in the global steel industry development. As Figure 11.1 shows, in comparison with the EU, US, and Japan, the 1990s witnessed steady output growth in China, the speed of which is followed by a sharp rise in the early 2000s. The pace of expansion easily met the central planners' target ahead of schedule. For example, the 100 million tonnes threshold was surpassed in 1996, four years earlier than what was set by the Ministry of Metallurgical Industry (MMI) in 1993. Indeed, from the second half of the 1990s, the central government's concern was not so much the overall output expansion as the over-capacity of low-margin steel products.

The second, and more important, achievement of the steel industry lies in the significant improvement in the technical efficiency of steelmaking and in technological upgrading. Space prevents a thorough discussion of the iron and steelmaking process and its technological traits,[4] but, to understand the significance

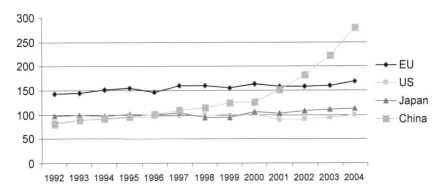

Figure 11.1   Crude steel output in China, EU, US, and Japan, 1992–2004 (million tonnes).
Source: International Iron and Steel Institute (IISI), *Steel Statistical Yearbook*, 2005.

of technical efficiency upon cost competitiveness in the sector, a brief introduction of the industry's technological features is quite in order.

The commercialization of the basic oxygen furnace (BOF) and the continuous casting (CC) process is widely considered the chief technological innovation in the 1950s and 1960s steel production. The BOF replaced the traditional open hearth furnace (OHF) by vastly speeding up the process of converting iron to raw/molten steel. The CC process allows steelmakers to bypass the costly process of pouring molten steel into ingots and the energy-intensive reheating of ingots for finishing. One of the consequences of the adoption of the BOF and CC is the decreasing energy consumption (EC) per tonne of crude steel produced which is a straightforward indicator of the input–output relation in steel production.[5]

Since the fast adoption of BOF and CC and the resulting significant increase in cost efficiency have proved the key contributing factors to the successful catch-up of the steel enterprises in the NICs, such as Japan and Korea (Yonekura, 1994; D'Costa, 1999), it is of particular interest to observe China's catch-up process in this aspect. From Table 11.1, we can easily see that the catch-up of the domestic sector has been generally quick. For instance, in 1988 the CC ratio was 93 percent in Japan, 88 percent in Korea, and 60 percent in the US, all well above the Chinese level – 14.7 percent. By 2004, however, China substantially closed the gap with the CC ratio climbing to 95.8 percent, as compared with 97.8 percent in Japan, 98.3 percent in Korea, and 97.1 percent in the US. Moreover, China performed

Table 11.1 Technical efficiency and upgrading in the Chinese steel industry, 1988–2004

Year	CC ratio (%)	OHF (%)	BOF (%)	EAF (%)	EC per tonne of crude steel produced (tonnes of equivalent coal)
1988	14.7	21.9	57.6	20.3	1.647
1989	16.3	21.3	57.8	20.7	1.636
1990	22.4	19.8	58.9	21.1	1.611
1991	26.5	18.4	60.3	21.1	1.601
1992	30.0	17.3	60.7	21.8	1.574
1993	34.0	16.1	60.6	23.2	1.545
1994	39.46	15.3	n/a	n/a	1.519
1995	46.48	13.7	66.7	19.0	n/a
1996	53.27	12.5	68.6	18.7	1.392
1997	60.65	8.9	73.3	17.6	n/a
1998	68.8	4.7	79.2	15.8	1.12
1999	77.38	1.5	82.7	15.7	1.08
2000	81.93	0.84	n/a	n/a	0.898
2001	87.51	0.55	83.5	15.9	0.876
2002	91.15	0.01	83.2	16.7	0.803
2003	93.52	0	82.4	17.6	0.792
2004	95.93	0	84.5	15.2	n/a

Source: *China Steel Yearbook* (1989–2005).

noticeably better than other developing/transition countries in this regard, the 2004 CC ratio being 92.7 percent in Brazil, 65.9 percent in India, and 54.3 percent in Russia (IISI, 2005). Consistent with the government directive, the OHF was largely phased out after 1999, and the gap in energy consumption narrowed given that the benchmark in the advanced economies is around 0.7 tonnes of equivalent coal.

Gaps: uncompetitive product mix and persistent industrial fragmentation

Although it is beyond dispute that output expansion and improvements in technical efficiency represent a laudable achievement of the government industrial policy, the implementation gaps between the central government's objectives and the policy outcomes tend to be substantial in a number of important areas that have a crucial bearing on the industry's long-term competitiveness.

First, the government has long been aware of the serious structural imbalance of product mix in the indigenous sector – a predominant share of undifferentiated long steel products such as structural shapes and wire rods used for construction works, in comparison with a significant shortage of flat products such as plates and sheets used in the manufacture of automobiles and household appliances. Consequently, marked foreign penetration in the higher-value-added steel segment, whose demand in the 1990s by the downstream sectors was burgeoning, leaves a vast majority of domestic firms in the lower position on the value chain. To redress the uncompetitive product mix in the indigenous industry, central government agencies throughout the 1990s repeatedly stressed those products the capacity for which should be given priority to expand, the target ratio of high-grade products to the total, the backward products and equipment that were to be phased out and the urgency of import substitution (*Chinese Steel Yearbook*, 1992–2002).

The results of the policies aimed at structural transformation and import substitution, however, have turned out to be rather disappointing. A rough proxy for the degree of value addition of finished steel products is the plate/pipe ratio which is, in turn, the output of plates and pipes divided by the total finished products (because plates, including "thin plates," e.g. sheets and coils, and pipes/tubes generally enjoy a much higher premium than commodity products, such as structural shapes and wire rods). Figure 11.2 presents the trend of the plate/pipe ratio in the domestic sector. Surprisingly, despite the government's repeated calls for structural change, there was no improvement at all in the overall segmental structure from 1989 to 2003. Moreover, the situation even deteriorated in the very early years of the new century. The ratio fluctuated in the range of 30–40 percent during most of the time[6] and slipped to 32.6 percent in 2003, lower even than the 1989 base level of 37.02 percent, let alone the original 45 percent target for the year 2000. Therefore, a disaggregation of the overall capacity expansion suggests that the output of low-end products grew at a higher speed than the high-margin ones.

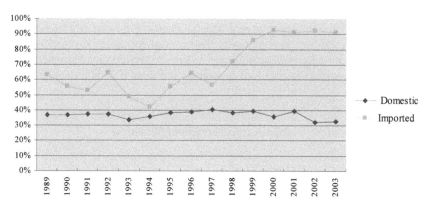

Figure 11.2   Plate/pipe ratios of imported and domestic finished steel products, 1989–2003.
Source: Author's calculation and straightforward citation of data reported
in *Chinese Steel Yearbook* (1990–2004). Note: Plate/pipe ratio means the
proportion of plates and pipes in the total finished products imported or
domestically made.

The other trend shown in Figure 11.2 is the composition of annual imported
steel products. Unlike the domestic counterpart, the plate/pipe ratio rose sharply
from 1997 toward more than 90 percent. On the positive side, this implies that,
unlike the first half of the 1990s, foreign entry into low-end segments is no longer
easy since the plates and pipes have accounted for the vast majority of imports.
The dark side of the story is the government's failure in import substitution in
the high-premium segments. A telling case is that in the late 1990s the center
attempted to contain the aggregate level of steel import by setting an import ceiling – 7 million tonnes in 1999 and 10 million tonnes in 2000. The goals later
proved self-defeating as the annual import of plates and pipes alone reached more
than 10 million tonnes in the two consecutive years. The inability of the domestic
steel firms to meet the sophisticated demands in the country's downstream sectors
rendered the import ceilings completely ineffective.

To further illustrate the implementation gap, Table 11.2 focuses on a selected
set of high-value-added products. Consistent with the previous discussion, while
the output growth of these products has been impressive since the early 1990s,
the foreign penetration in these segments has become entrenched as well. Aside
from the fact that the indigenous capacity expansion of high-end products lags
behind the surging demand in downstream sectors, there is a considerable *quality*
gap between domestic and imported products. For instance, the manufacture of
exterior bodies in some sedan cars requires highly sophisticated electro-galva-
nized sheets that none of the domestic firms can supply. Even for some varieties
of galvanized steels that the domestic makers *can* supply, they tend to suffer a
30 percent trade discount to imports due to the significant quality gap (Woetzel,
2001, p. 100).

Perhaps the most crucial element of the steel industrial policy goals since the

Table 11.2 Domestic output expansion and import penetration in selected high-premium steel segments, 1990–2003 (thousand tonnes)

Year	Cold-rolled sheet		Cold-rolled silicon sheet		Galvanised sheet		Tinplate		Colour-coated sheet	
	Output	Net import	Output	Net import	Output	Net import	Output	Net import	Output	Net import
1990			103		235	170	21	222		
1991					261	200	33	377		
1992					397	720	61	400		
1993			156		500	505	79	527		
1994	1,938		170		456	282	176	396		
1995	2,180	1,850	178	180	727	697	209	518	127	227
1996		3,093*	179	363	776	722	211	464	170	309
1997		2,880	238	407	618	776	363	421	156	413
1998	4,500	2,676	252	448	1,000	960	550	269	250	299
1999	5,800	4,458	352	626	1,490	1,626	854	215	320	521
2000	7,635	5,327	357	829	1,279	2,072	1,010	315	404	481
2001	9,278	5,226	867	816	2,195	2,088	1,100	168	826	715
2002	10,517	6,793	962	834	2,516	3,227	1,159	258	592	1,093
2003	11,702	9,451	1,042	1,485	2,759	5,310	1,266	346	1,334	1,086

Source: *China Steel Yearbook* (1991–2004) and author's calculation from data provided by the China Iron and Steel Association.
Notes: Net import is the difference between gross import and export. * The figure is the gross import.

late 1980s is the consolidation of the whole sector into a number of large and internationally competitive national champions. The rationale for the intended restructuring and rationalization lies in the intrinsic nature of the steel industry that the economies of scale (EOS) in steelmaking are too large to ignore. EOS refers to the reductions in the cost per unit of output that can be achieved as the scale of operations is increased. The scale at which the average cost curve reaches its lowest point is termed the minimum efficient scale (MES) of production, which acts as a straightforward indicator of the varying magnitudes of the EOS existing in different sectors. As the name suggests, plants or firms wishing to obtain the maximum cost efficiency must be at least of this size. According to a series of engineering estimates on the MES in the steel industry (Pratten, 1971, 1988; Cockerill, 1974), for individual integrated[7] steel plants the MES can be expected to be 8–10 million tonnes per annum, and there may be significant benefits to be gained by multiplant firms from an even larger scale, provided that effective use of financial, marketing, and procurement resources can be made.[8] Owing to the presence of significant EOS, a "rational" steel industry structure should be one characterized by intensive oligopolistic competition among a small number of giant firms.[9]

Mao's development strategy of regional self-sufficiency resulted in a highly fragmented steel sector (Wong, 1986), in which individual firms operated chronically below the MES and served their own regional demand. From the start of the 1990s, however, the state endeavoured to end the fragmentation. It is expected that, through organic growth and government-orchestrated mergers and acquisitions, several national steel giants that can compete in the global level playing field can arise from the industry consolidation process.

Nevertheless, the evolution of the industry structure since the late 1980s suggests an extremely skewed size distribution, as shown in Table 11.3. Whereas the last fifteen years have witnessed a proliferation of steel mills, only a tiny number of them managed to exceed the MES of the industry. By the year-end 2004, except for Baosteel, Angang, Wugang, Shougang, and Magang, all the other undersized producers were still plagued by cost inefficiencies to varying degrees.[10]

With regard to industry concentration, the four-firm concentration ratio (CR4) is used as a rough estimate of the degree of the concentration in a particular industry. It can be seen from the last column of the table that, in spite of the government's consolidation goals and efforts, the CR4 declined sharply from around 33 percent in 1988 to 18.5 percent in 2004. The government in 1998 set the CR4 target of the year 2000 at 40 percent, because it thought that the mergers and acquisitions it had mediated, such as that of Baosteel and Shanghai local firms, and its orders to eradicate backward capacities by setting an output ceiling in 1999 and 2000, would make the goal achievable. Nevertheless, the State Economic and Trade Commission (SETC) and the State Bureau of Metallurgical Industry (SBMI)[11] were later incensed by the fact that output ceilings and the CR4 target proved a complete policy failure at the turn of the century. Entering the twenty-first century, the SETC again set a grand target on increasing the concentration ratio such

Table 11.3 Size distribution of the Chinese steel industry, 1988–2004

Year	Total no. of steel firms	Of which: output > 8 million tonnes	CR4 (%)
1988	1478	1	33.23
1989	1550	0	32.35
1990	1589	0	31.16
1991	1637	0	31.02
1992	1744	1	31.70
1993	1667	1	31.00
1994	1669	2	31.27
1995	1639	3	31.23
1996	1495	1	29.22
1997	1516	3	28.43
1998	1078	2	33.27
1999	1042	2	31.26
2000	2997	3	32.09
2001	3176	3	28.53
2002	3333	3	24.84
2003	4119	4	20.98
2004	4992	5	18.52

Source: *China Steel Yearbook* (1989–2005) and author's calculation.
Note: CR4 means the concentration ratio of the top four steel firms measured by their combined output over the industry total.

that the top ten steelmakers should produce 80 percent of total crude steel in 2005, only to find that their output share had already dropped to 34.6 percent in 2004.

Summary

The preceding analysis of the Chinese steel sector reveals a mixed message on the performance of the Chinese state in improving industry-level competitiveness. Impressive progress has been made in the expansion of steelmaking capacity and the enhancement of technical efficiency. However, the capacity growth of higher-value-added products failed to keep pace with that of their undifferentiated, low-margin counterpart, and the central government's consolidation efforts have so far proved a failure.

Fragmented governance structure of the Chinese steel industry

The mixed catch-up experiences of the indigenous steel sector prompt us to examine the institutional determinants behind the industry's evolution. Accordingly, the following section outlines the key characteristics of the state asset administration system and industrial policymaking and implementation mechanisms in the domestic steel industry.

State asset administration in the domestic steel sector

Once situated at the commanding heights of China's central planning system, the indigenous steel sector was, until very recently, a predominantly state-owned one. And the governance of the steel SOEs was typical of the fragmented and decentralized state asset administration mechanism in China. Unlike the conventional Soviet model, in which the industrial SOEs were vertically organized into respective central line ministries with the local governments treated as "transmission belts" in the chain of command, the delegation of ownership and control rights to local governments at all levels has been a defining feature of the Chinese-style state asset administration since the late 1950s (Wong, 1986; Granick, 1990; Qian and Xu, 1993). That is, the Chinese state-owned industry tends to be fragmented into pieces under a *joint* control of vertical line ministries and horizontal local governments. Within the two types of competing agencies, there is a concept of "primary control" in respect of each given SOE. In a word, it is primarily controlled, however vague the meaning of "primarily," by either its proximate governments or the line ministry.

To the extent that the authority balance between branches and localities varies considerably across state-owned industries, the governance of the steel sector is clearly one that favors regional decentralization. During the 1980s and most of the 1990s, except for a couple of leading steelmakers including Baosteel, which were primarily managed by the Ministry of Metallurgical Industry (MMI),[12] all the other large and medium-sized steel SOEs fell into the "local primary control" category. To be precise, while they received professional guidance from the MMI, managerial appointment and operational control were lodged in the hands of local authorities. Additionally, as can be recognized from Table 11.3, there are more than 1,000 small steel mills that were largely outside the sphere of the MMI's administration. They are local small SOEs at the county level, or township and village enterprises (TVEs), or newly established private firms under the patronage of local governments. Thus, the MMI had a very limited ability to micro-manage the small mills.

With the deepening of the economic reform in China, most of the central line ministries were abolished in 1998 and the MMI was downgraded to a state bureau (SBMI) affiliated to the SETC with a cut of staff numbers from 300 to a mere eighty. The post-MMI period has witnessed a significant change in the governance structure of the steel industry, since the central government finally decided to "grasp the large and let go of the small." Only four large steel SOEs, namely Baosteel, Angang, Wugang, and Panzhihua Steel were cherry-picked to the "national team" under direct central administration, with the local influence being presumably diluted since 1998. Concretely speaking, they were chiefly affiliated with the CCP Enterprise Work Commission from 1998 to 2002 and with the State-owned Assets Supervision and Administration Commission (SASAC) since 2003. On the other hand, the operational control of the remaining large and medium-sized steel SOEs has been completely released to local governments, though certain authorities concerning investment project approval and asset disposal are still held by the center. The SBMI continued to regulate the whole industry until 2001, when its successor – the Iron and Steel Industry Association – started to play a non-administrative coordination role, such as the collection and dissemination of industry information.

Mechanisms of industrial policymaking and implementation

The term "industrial policy" first appeared on the Chinese official document, "The Seventh Five-Year Plan of the National Economic and Social Development (1986–1990)," released in 1986 (Jiang, 1996, p. 65). And the first document dedicated to the formulation and implementation of industrial policies came into being in March 1989, when the State Council issued "Decisions on the Key Points of the Current Industrial Policies" (*Guowu Yuan Guanyu Dangqian Chanye Zhengce Yaodian de Jueding*).[13] It was stipulated that the State Council – China's cabinet – was responsible for the formulation of the industrial policies whereas line ministries and provincial governments were required to work out detailed plans for implementation (*shishi banfa*). It was also requested that the State Planning Commission (SPC), state banks, tax and foreign exchange regulatory agencies, and regional governments coordinate in an effective fashion to enforce the industrial policies.

Consequently, the MMI in February 1990 released the first comprehensive version of the industry policy in the domestic iron and steel sector (MMI, 1990, available in *China Steel Yearbook*, 1991). The policy document specified a whole list of steel products and the associated steelmaking technology and equipment that were respectively to be encouraged, restricted, or forbidden to produce or adopt. To carry out the plan, the document provided that any project with an investment cost above RMB50 million must be approved by the SPC under the endorsement of the MMI *or* the concerning provincial government. For those with a cost under RMB50 million, approval from the MMI *or* the relevant provincial governments was compulsory; and the under-RMB50 million projects that were simply approved by the regional governments had to be reported to the MMI for recording. The annual fixed-asset investment plans of the large and medium SOEs had to be submitted to the MMI for examination. If any firm planned to make the products and use the equipment in the restriction catalogue, application had to be submitted to regional metallurgy bureaux and finally approved by the MMI.

A crucial point arising from the details of the regulation on investment quota and plans was that the MMI could not *unilaterally* enforce the industrial policies they desired. First, bypassing the MMI, steel firms could obtain investment approval via the channel of provincial governments regardless of the RMB50 million threshold.[14] Second, the MMI's leverage over large and medium SOEs' investment decision was limited, For instance, the word "examination" used in relation to the annual investment plans was rather vague: what if the MMI was not satisfied with the plan after its examination? This clearly implies the nature of the dual authority relationship discussed before.

Third, in the formal industrial policy statement, the MMI openly asked the relevant central and local agencies for cooperation. Foremost among them were central comprehensive commissions such as the SPC and the local governments. It was stated that the MMI and its local branches shall "report (*hui bao*) to them the situations and problems in enforcing steel industrial policy and seek (*zheng qu*) their support." Furthermore, the MMI stressed the need for help from state banks, tax and price administrators, the State Bureau of Industry and Commerce Administration (SBICA), and so on. In order to enforce the industrial policy rigorously, state banks were not to provide loans to projects that involved inferior products and outdated steelmaking equipment in the restriction and prohibition catalogues; the financial, tax and price administrators were to devise differential loan rates, tax rates, and guidance prices to promote the strong and constrain the weak; and the SBICA was to erect an effective entry barrier by not granting licenses to firms that violated the industrial policy requirements.

Finally, even the MMI itself admitted that its capacity to control the steel SOEs was rather limited. For example, it openly complained about its lack of authority over managerial appointment, material allocation, investment regulation, and its clash with the revenue-seeking local governments over policy priorities (*China Steel Yearbook*, 1992, pp. 399–401).

When China finally embraced the market economy in the 1990s, the 1989 version of the national industrial policies, with the legacy of central planning, needed to be revised in accordance with the rapid change of the Chinese industrial sector. After protracted negotiation and bargaining among central and local bureaucracies, the State Council finally in March 1994 managed to issue "The Guidelines on the 1990s National Industrial Policies" (*Jiushi niandai guojia chanye zhengce gangyao*).[15] Compared with the last version, the document no longer vaguely designated the State Council as the policy making body; rather it stated explicitly that the SPC was the coordination center of industrial policymaking and implementation. Line ministries were responsible for day-to-day implementation, whereas the SPC should play a key coordination role between other central agencies and line ministries to ensure policy efficacy. Reports on the progress of industrial policy enforcement written by the SPC needed be delivered to the State Council periodically. With regard to the specific policy tools, the instruction attached much importance to the regulation of the fixed-asset investment and various preferential policies such as preferential bank loans, priority of the domestic and international stock flotation, and the right of attracting foreign investment. Thus, the involvement of the banking system and the securities regulatory bodies in the industrial policy process was inevitable.

Although the document stated that the SPC should cooperate with other state agencies to formulate detailed industrial policies in individual sectors in the short term, only the comprehensive automotive industrial policy came out in an official manner during the rest of the 1990s. It is said that the drafts of industrial policies in some sectors were revised more than ten times but still could not satisfy all the central and local parties' concerns (Jiang, 1996, pp. 185–186). Consequently there has been no direct upgrade of the 1990 version of steel's industrial policy, though the general principle, including industrial consolidation, technical upgrading, and import substitution, remained the same and was reiterated in the Eighth (1991–1995) and Ninth (1996–2000) Five-Year Plans and annual speeches by ministers of the MMI.

The implementation of industrial policies was made more complicated by the revival of the SETC since 1993, which proved itself a significant counterbalance to the SPC's authority in the area of industrial policy. According to the author's interview with an official at the SPC, the Industrial Policy Bureau, the Planning and Investment Bureau, and the Technical Renovation Bureau established within the SETC all deeply engaged in the making of specific industrial policies and the distribution of the technical renovation fund, a key industrial policy tool in China. The Industrial Development Bureau in the SPC, on the other hand, was the formulator of the five-year and ten-year plans and a gatekeeper of large capital construction projects, a term indicating the greenfield expansion of capacity as compared with technical renovation projects.[16] The power of the SETC vis-à-vis the SPDC reached its zenith in the late 1990s after all the remaining line ministries were merged into it as state bureaux. Nonetheless, the situation did not last long, because in 2003 the SETC was cut into three parts which were in turn merged into the National Development and Reform Commission (NDRC, the successor of SPC), the SASAC, and the Ministry of Commerce. Fixed-asset investment has again been under the sole control of the NDRC while the SASAC has a large say in the restructuring of the state industrial sector.

Linking governance structure with industrial policy efficacy

As discussed above, the industrial policy process in China involves intensive bureaucratic bargaining and consensus building among the central and local government actors, which in turn have different incentive and payoff structures. Without their consent and support, industrial policies are at a high risk of failure, *especially for those involving the redistribution of economic resources and rents across firms and regions.* And students of the Japanese and Korean developmental states will immediately realize that the configuration of the Chinese bureaucracy represents a significant departure from the structural arrangements of Japanese/Korean-style industrial policymaking and implementation, in which "peak" or supra-ministerial agencies, such as MITI (Japan) and EPB (Korea), prevailed over other bureaucratic agencies in industrial planning and acted as the coordination centres at the implementation stage (Johnson, 1982; Onis, 1991; Evans, 1995; Weiss, 1998).

Bearing this in mind, it would not be difficult to understand the mixed policy outcomes identified in the last section. On the bright side, the massive output expansion can be largely attributed to the contribution of steel mills under the primary control of local governments: During 1988–99, the output of local major steelmakers more than tripled from 11.7 million tonnes to 37.7 million tonnes (*China Steel Yearbook*, 1989, 2000). This is consistent with the general picture of the local-government-led industrialization, or the so-called "local state corporatism" (Oi, 1992, 1999; Walder, 1995) during the reform period, when local governments took the lead in promoting business growth, which was in turn induced by the center's reform strategy of administrative and economic decentralization (Montinola *et al.*, 1995; Qian and Weingast, 1997).

However, the failure of the consolidation of the steel industry has been largely to do with the fragmented and decentralized governance system.[17] In particular, the objective incongruity between central policymakers and local implementers dictates the difficulty of achieving cross-regional mergers and acquisitions, which could have served as a potent vehicle for industrial consolidation and competitiveness enhancement. Large-scale mergers between steel SOEs were rare throughout the 1990s. And even when they happened, as in the case of Baosteel merging with local Shanghai firms, they were largely takeovers of weak firms by a stronger one, rather than a strong–strong combination that might pursue a potential synergy gain.

To understand this phenomenon, we need to keep in mind that cross-regional mergers are in the first instance the combination of two firms controlled by two different government agencies. Each of them may be both a convenient instrument by which local leaders could shore up the local economy *and* the power base from which officials and firm managers could derive substantial private benefits. Accordingly, a prospective merger/takeover involves a complicated redistribution between different bureaucratic organs of financial revenues, vested private rents, and policy burdens such as the labour welfare arrangements, such that the transaction cannot proceed through the open market. Rather, informal, behind-the-scenes negotiations orchestrated by a dedicated central authority are essential (if not sufficient) to make a delicate deal satisfying all the parties concerned.

Therefore, such kinds of state-brokered mergers, even if successful in the end, are bound to be slow and laborious especially when the center has to arrange a merger of two regional-level SOEs.[18] Another route of consolidation is the promotion of a merger between a centrally controlled national champion and a local state firm so that the number of bargaining parties can be reduced from three to two. No matter which route the central government may choose, the stylized fact in the domestic steel sector turns out to be that a state-orchestrated merger is feasible *only* when the proposed merger involves a strong–weak, rather than a strong–strong, combination. From the standpoint of local governments, the rationale is that only when a firm deteriorates into a financially distressed position beyond prop-up by local resources available would the local government be prepared to surrender its control to outsiders. In such a scenario the merger could move on precisely because the loss-making enterprise is no longer a valued asset but a liability to the local leaders. Self-evidently, however, the administrative strong–weak mergers cannot help lay a solid foundation for the fast build-up of the corporate competitiveness originally envisaged by the center.

Concluding remarks

Linking governance fragmentation and industrial policy enforcement, the preceding detailed analysis of industrial and corporate changes in the steel industry during transition and globalization reveals both achievements and setbacks on the part of the Chinese state in constructing an internationally competitive industrial sector. While the Chinese government has done an impressive job of developing essential manufacturing capabilities in the domestic steel sector, the speed of product upgrade has failed to meet the surging demand in the high-premium segment and the state-led restructuring of the fragmented industrial structure has proved an outright failure. This chapter argues that both the structural fragmentation of the state governance structure that prevents the concentration of the state-generated rents and the poor coordination within the bureaucracy that arises from the incentive incongruity between the central and local authorities constitute the most important institutional obstacles to effective industrial restructuring.

With respect to policy prescriptions, the past experience unequivocally suggests the imperativeness of ending the fragmented and crisscrossing administrative system. Although the formal dual leadership arrangement has been phased out since the late 1990s, the center needs to keep recentralizing the tax, banking, and land-use administrations that have previously been captured and abused by the local authorities to prop up inefficient local firms at the expense of national policy goals. The loopholes in the investment regulation system also need to be seriously addressed by the center to avoid the perverse effects observed in the last two decades. Moreover, the center should convince local officials that the achievement of industrial policy objectives accounts for a large weight in its whole preference set in order to change the expectation that their promotion or demotion prospects are chiefly determined, in an authoritarian manner, by short-term local GDP numbers and showcase construction projects.

All in all, the trajectory of industrial and corporate catch-up in the NICs has never been linear and the profoundly new elements of transition and globalization render the Chinese catch-up story even more open-ended.

Notes

1 According to Nolan and Rui (2004, p. 99), "a value chain is a systematically coordinated production and delivery process, comprising all the steps leading to an ultimate 'downstream' sale from the initial 'upstream' raw material processing . . . Giant or core companies, acting as 'systems integrators', penetrate the global value chains deeply both upstream and downstream." It is held that the global giants have created an explosive "cascade" effect that is rapidly resulting in concentration among the first- and even second- and third-tier suppliers, which makes the competition landscape even more challenging for developing country firms.
2 Steel is a typical intermediary good that serves as a critical input for further industrialization in a large number of downstream sectors, such as real estate, shipbuilding, automobiles, and petroleum, so the expansion of steelmaking capacity is always one of the primary goals of the NICs.
3 For instance, D'Costa (1999, p. 100) ascribes the less than successful development of the Brazilian and Indian steel industries to the lack of state autonomy. "Brazil and

India were beholden to various political forces and regional rivalries. The inefficiency of the Indian public sector steel company was partly a result of bureaucratic regulation that undermined coherent decision-making. Numerous government agencies worked at cross-purposes, slowing the investment momentum and creating a technologically deficient industry."

4 For more details, see Jones and Cockerill (1985, chapter 10) and Figueiredo (2001, chapter 4).

5 The electric arc furnace (EAF) differs from the above two used in the integrated steel mills in a fundamental sense: Scrap steel/metal is used as the chief raw material that can be converted into finished products directly in the EAF. Since the EAF units are much smaller than integrated steel plants owing to different steelmaking processes, they are also known as mini-mills. They became quite popular in industrialized countries during the 1980s, but on account of the scarcity of scrap and high cost of electricity their significance in late industrializing countries is rather limited.

6 The only time when it exceeded the 40 percent threshold was 1997, the plate–pipe ratio hit 40.16 percent.

7 "Integrated" here means that the making of steel involves processing iron ore right through to the finished products, and all these steps are undertaken within a single steel mill.

8 The author's interview with staff at the Shanghai Baosteel Group Corporation in April 2004 echoed the above estimation. They argued that, for an integrated steel company to be internationally competitive, 10 million tonnes of capacity is a must.

9 In theory, there is a positive correlation between market concentration and the MES. In other words, other things being equal, an industry with a higher MES can accommodate only a smaller number of incumbent firms to achieve production/operational efficiency (Martin, 1993; Cabral, 2000).

10 The extent of such inefficiencies is determined by the distance between firms' scales to the MES along their average cost curve. Of course the MES of minimills using the EAF technology is much smaller than the 8 million tonnes threshold, so the above discussion is confined to the integrated steelworks only.

11 It is the successor of the MMI, which was abolished in 1998.

12 It is worth noting that even in this case the influence from local governments cannot be ignored. For a case study of Baosteel in this aspect, see Sun (2005).

13 The Chinese version of the document is available in Appendix 2 of Jiang (1996).

14 Of course, the SPC and later on the SETC were both the central agencies for which they had to lobby in the case of above-RMB50 million projects.

15 The Chinese version of the document is available in Appendix 3 of Jiang (1996).

16 In practice there was at best a thin line between the two types of projects and, as mentioned in the last section, firms and local governments always exploited the ambiguous classification and the divided regulation structure.

17 OECD (2003, p. 166) points out that "China holds some unenviable world records when it comes to the fragmentation of its industrial structure." Huang (2002) documents the unsuccessful administrative consolidation attempts in the automotive sector from the mid-1980s to the late 1990s. Even in the very limited number of sectors, such as oil and petrochemicals, where the consolidation of the traditional "feudal" industry has been relatively successful, the centralization of the once decentralized powers and resources to national holding companies CNPC and Sinopec was replete with intensive bargaining and compromises with regional vested interests, and the integration of the subordinate business units into a real corporate whole is far from complete (Nolan, 2001, chapter 7). Therefore, the failure in the steel sector consolidation is representative of the whole picture of the Chinese industrial sector during transition.

18 The repeated failures of consolidating steelmaking capacity in the northern China area (*Huabei*) is directly related to the difficulty in brokering a merger between Shougang, a primarily Beijing-based firm, and those controlled by Hebei province. Since Shou-

gang is not a centrally controlled SOE, it has experienced a lot of obstacles to efficient cross-regional acquisitions when the dedicated central support was not put in place (e.g. Nolan, 2001, chapter 9).

References

Amsden, Alice H. (1989) *Asia's Next Giant: South Korea and Late Industrialization*, New York: Oxford University Press.

Amsden, Alice H. (2001) *The Rise of "the Rest": Challenges to the West from Late-Industrializing Economies*, New York: Oxford University Press.

Cabral, Luis M.B. (2000) *Introduction to Industrial Organization*, Cambridge, MA: MIT Press.

China Steel Yearbook, various volumes (1989–2005), Beijing: The Chinese Iron and Steel Association.

Cockerill, Anthony F. (1974) *The Steel Industry: International Comparisons of Industrial Structure and Performance*, Occasional Paper 42, University of Cambridge, Department of Applied Economics; republished London: Cambridge University Press.

D'Costa, Anthony P. (1999) *The Global Restructuring of the Steel Industry: Innovations, Institutions and Industrial Change*, London: Routledge.

Evans, Peter (1995) *Embedded Autonomy: States and Industrial Transformation*, Princeton, NJ: Princeton University Press.

Figueiredo, Paulo N. (2001) *Technological Learning and Comparative Performance*, Cheltenham: Edward Elgar.

Granick, David (1990) *Chinese State Enterprises: A Regional Property Rights Analysis*, Chicago: University of Chicago Press.

Huang, Yasheng (2002) 'Between Two Coordination Failures: Automotive Industrial Policy in China with a Comparison to Korea,' *Review of International Political Economy*, 9 (3), 538–573.

International Iron and Steel Institute (IISI) (2005) *World Steel in Figures*, Brussels: IISI.

International Iron and Steel Institute (IISI) (2005–6) *Steel Statistical Yearbook*, Brussels: IISI.

Jiang, Xiaojuan (1996) *Tizhi Zhuangui Zhong de Chanye Zhengce: Dui Zhongguo Jingyan de Shizheng Fenxi ji Qianjing Zhanwang* (Industrial policy in transition: an empirical analysis of the Chinese experience), Shanghai: Shanghai People's (Sanlian) Press.

Johnson, Chalmers (1982) *MITI and the Japanese Miracle: The Growth of Industrial Policy, 1925–1975*, Stanford, CA: Stanford University Press.

Jones, Trefor T. and Cockerill, T.A.J. (1985) *Structure and Performance of Industries*, New Delhi: Heritage Publishers.

Martin, Stephen (1993) *Industrial Economics: Economic Analysis and Public Policy*, Englewood Cliffs, NJ: Prentice Hall.

MMI (1990) '*Yejin gongye bu guanche guowuyuan "guanyu dangqian chanye zhence yaodian de jueding" de shishi banfa*' (The MMI implementation guidelines on "the decisions on the key points of the current industrial polices" made by the State Council), 16 February, Beijing: MMI.

Montinola, Gabriella, Qian, Yingyi, and Weingast, Barry R. (1995) 'Federalism, Chinese Style: The Political Basis for Economic Success in China,' *World Politics*, 48 (1), 50–81.

Nolan, Peter (2001) *China and the Global Business Revolution*, Basingstoke: Palgrave.

Nolan, Peter (2002) 'China and the Global Business Revolution,' *Cambridge Journal of Economics*, 26 (December), 119–137.

Nolan, Peter and Rui, Huaichuan (2004) 'Industrial Policy and Global Big Business Revolution: The Case of the Chinese Coal Industry,' *Journal of Chinese Economic and Business Studies*, 2 (2), 97–113.

Oi, Jean C. (1992) 'Fiscal Reform and the Economic Foundation of Local State Corporatism in China', *World Politics*, 45 (October), 99–126.

Oi, Jean C. (1999) *Rural China Takes Off: Institutional Foundations of Economic Reform*, Berkeley, CA: University of California Press.

Onis, Ziya (1991) 'The Logic of the Developmental State,' *Comparative Politics*, 24 (1), 109–126.

Organization for Economic Cooperation and Development (OECD) (2003) *China in the World Economy: An OECD Economic and Statistical Survey*, London: Kogan Page.

Perkins, Dwight H. (2001) 'Industrial and Financial Policy in China and Vietnam: A New Model or a Replay of the East Asian Experience?' in Joseph E. Stiglitz and Shahid Yusuf (eds). *Rethinking the East Asian Miracle*, New York: Oxford University Press

Pratten, Cliff F. (1971) *Economies of Scale in Manufacturing Industry*, Occasional Paper 28, University of Cambridge, Department of Applied Economics; republished Cambridge: Cambridge University Press.

Pratten, Cliff F. (1988) *A Survey of the Economies of Scale*, Economic Paper No. 67, Commission of the European Communities.

Qian, Yingyi and Xu, Chenggang (1993) 'Why China's Economic Reforms Differ: The M-form Hierarchy and Entry/Expansion of the Non-state Sector,' *Economics of Transition*, 1 (2), 135–170.

Qian, Yingyi and Barry R. Weingast (1997) 'Federalism as a Commitment to Preserving Market Incentives,' *Journal of Economic Perspectives*, 11 (4), 83–92.

Sun, Pei (2005) 'Industrial Policy, Corporate Governance, and the Competitiveness of China's National Champions: The Case of Shanghai Baosteel Group,' *Journal of Chinese Economic and Business Studies*, 3 (2),173–192.

Wade, Robert (1990) [2004], *Governing the Market: Economic Theory and the Role of Government in East Asian Industrialization*, Princeton, NJ: Princeton University Press.

Wade, Robert (2003) 'Creating Capitalisms: Introduction to the 2003 Paperback Edition,' in *Governing the Market: Economic Theory and the Role of Government in East Asian Industrialization*, Princeton, NJ: Princeton University Press.

Walder, Andrew G. (1995) 'Local Governments as Industrial Firms: An Organizational Analysis of China's Transitional Economy,' *American Journal of Sociology*, 101 (2), 263–301.

Weiss, Linda (1998) *The Myth of the Powerless State: Governing the Economy in a Global Era*, Cambridge: Polity Press.

Woetzel, Jonathan R. (2001) 'Remaking China's Giant Steel Industry,' *The McKinsey Quarterly*, 4, 93–102.

Wong, Christine P.W. (1986) 'Ownership and Control in Chinese Industry: The Maoist Legacy and Prospects for the 1980's,' in U.S. Congress Joint Economic Committee (ed.), *China's Economy Looks Toward the Year 2000*, Vol. 1, Washington, DC: U.S. Government Printing Office.

Yonekura, Seiichiro (1994) *The Japanese Iron and Steel Industry, 1850–1990: Continuity and Discontinuity*, Basingstoke: Macmillan.

12 The importance of ultra-high-speed railways for China in the twenty-first century

John Kidd and Marielle Stumm

Introduction

In opting for a transport system for the twenty-first century, this chapter proposes that China will need to consider broad economic and ecological arguments if it is to sustain its current growth patterns. As both European and US manufacturers and consumers, and now Chinese consumers, become more closely interdependent it is time to look closely at the balance of air, land and sea freight costs. Using a dedicated (traditional) railway train, the end-to-end delivery time of containers from China to Europe is currently about fifteen days, but maglev ultra-high-speed systems could reduce this to two days. In comparison, air freight is limited to about 100–140 tonnes per plane (fast, but expensive per tonne/km), and post-Panamax boats carrying over 10,000 containers take thirty-five days from Asia to Europe, or forty-five days if the ships have to round the Cape of Africa, if they are too big for the Suez canal. Of all systems, maglev has the lowest cost per kilometre, can deliver in volume and is very fast.

An additional advantage of the maglev system is its very low ecological impact. The track has a low environmental footprint and its motive power comes from the superconducting electromagnets' reaction against the fixed 'linear motors' in the guide track; it thus requires less power than conventional electrified rail systems. The maglev system has very few moving parts or components that touch or slide upon the other, so wear is minimal and air friction is low, as are the total running costs. It follows that the costs per tonne/km or passenger are also very low.

We suggest that regional infrastructure developments need to be considered in a global context when China looks to its transport system and how it will supply its own needs over the next two or three decades. Indeed, the governments of China and the countries of ASEAN, Central Asia and Europe must, in conjunction with the US, review their logistics implementations and operations costs broadly, paying due consideration both to time-to-market and to ecological impacts.

Early railway infrastructure

The Industrial Revolution, which began in the UK in the 1750s, has now had an impact on most parts of the globe. Its early focus was on introducing machine

power to augment human strength and this produced many new industries including the railways. The first UK commercial steam-engine railway was the Stockton
to Darlington track in 1825. At the time many stationary coal-fuelled steam gener-
ators were invented to run work stations such as lathes, weaving machines or water
mills (instead of inconsistent water power), and mobile steam engines quickly
powered the railways and ships promoting rapid transport of people and, more
importantly, goods, thereby accelerating the Industrial Revolution. The railways
also facilitated the development of the interior regions of many countries. The US
and Canada were joined coast-to-coast by rail in 1869 and 1885 respectively; and
Russia completed the world's longest railway (the Trans-Siberian Railway – TSR)
from Moscow to Vladivostok (9,300 kilometres) between 1891 and 1916. This
was the 'Age of Invention' (Dugan and Dugan, 2000; Standage, 1999).

China's railway network developed sporadically – its Eastern Railway was
built upon an accord with Russia in 1895, which laid a route through Inner Mongolia via Harbin to Vladivostok before the longer all-Russian route was built
north of Manchuria. By 1898, a 550-mile spur line linked Harbin through eastern
Manchuria via the Liaodong peninsula to the ice-free Port Arthur (modern-day
Lushan). There were severe logistics problems for these early eastern rail developments since they were far from European sources of rails and rolling stock – an
issue subsequently solved by imports from the USA, which continued well into
the 1930s.

All the coastal regional railways of China had a chequered history involving British, Japanese, Russian and Chinese ownership: they saw only sporadic
development, with subsequent destruction in times of war. But after 1949, following the inauguration of the People's Republic of China, railway development
was widespread across China, creating what is now, by kilometres installed, the
globe's third largest rail network. China also has a considerable road network,
currently growing very fast, as well as extensive inland waterway navigation and
a considerable volume of short-sea shipping to and from the major ports in Asia.

Current logistical pressures

China is not merely the world's premier low-cost assembler; currently there are
Chinese firms who are giants in their own right, feeding the huge internal Chinese
market as well as outlets across the globe. With its large supply of cheap labour
and rapid acquisition of technological prowess, China's recent industrial output
growth has allowed its share of the world's exported goods to triple between 1993
and 2005 (The Economist, 2007a). To move these vast volumes of goods the ports
of Asia are the biggest and busiest in the world, but even these ports may be confronted by new forms of logistics competition in the near future.

Although the UNDP and others are supporting Pan-Asian railway and highway
development, we suggest that the use of road-based freight is not cost-effective
over long-haul distances and that rail is the logical alternative. Air freight,
although rapidly increasing in tonnage moved (implied also by the numbers of
air-freighters on order from Boeing and Airbus) is a costly form of delivery. It

would seem that slow boats from China are the only mode of transport for bulk trade transfers. However, it is our argument that this is where rail offers an alternative (at least to Europe), and that, within this mode, ultra high-speed rail offers several advantages.

Steffen Schiottz-Christensen, managing director of Maersk Logistics (China) Ltd, forecast in 2006 that by 2008 China would account for more than 10 per cent of global trade. And, although China's logistics market was already the third largest worldwide in terms of spending, he argued that the country has inefficient goods distribution and transportation, especially compared with countries such as Singapore, Germany and France. In 2000 the logistics costs in China were 20 per cent of their GDP value, and by 2004 this had increased to 21.6 per cent, yet in the United States this cost hovers around 10 per cent. He went on to say:

> The distribution efficiency in China is relatively low, and there are a lot of opportunities to improve on this. Investments are now being made in additional infrastructure by the government which Maersk Logistics regards as very positive.
>
> Yet, the infrastructure for rail is insufficient. Commercial rail traffic in China is still in the development stage. The network of tracks is not sufficient and the trains are being used for other priorities: passengers, military, and bulk goods are being moved on rail – with containers getting the lowest priority.
>
> In a country of this size, containerized rail transportation offers a cheap, efficient and even an environmentally friendly way to move cargo. But a large part of China's long-distance cargo is moved by truck which requires a lot of fuel, has a high carbon footprint, and is costly.
>
> *Peoples Daily Online*, 19 December 2006

Figure 12.1 hints at the geophysical realities of Asia. There seems to be potential for laying rail track throughout Southeast Asia, but the north and northwest regions of China are guarded by mountains and deserts, so only three routes reach out from China to join to the Russian or the Central Asian tracks. The (re) development efforts are coordinated by UNDP, UNESCAP and the ADB. The main routes are (i) the Trans-Asian Railway (TAR) 1, which essentially provides feeders through eastern China and Mongolia to the Trans-Siberian Railway, but updated; (ii) TSR2, which is the route from Lianyungang through middle China to Rotterdam, often referred to as the 'Eurasian Landbridge', or somewhat colloquially as the 'New Silk Road'; and (iii) TSR3 might well link Singapore to Scotland via routes passing south of the Himalayas. The TSR3 link passes through several politically difficult countries with parts of the route having no planned track at present. It is assumed that this route will not come into existence, being perhaps superseded by the 'North–South route' from St Petersburg via the Caspian Sea to the Iranian port of Bandar Abbas and onwards by sea to East Asia, though this route too suffers from a clash of ideologies and leaders' aspirations. However, all is not lost as there are links being made from within Southeast Asia to China. As the *Railway Gazette International* reported on 1 January 2007:

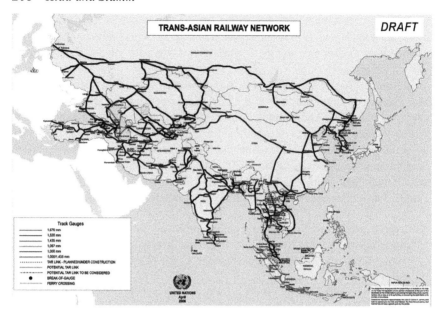

Figure 12.1   Eurasian railway route (re)developments. Source: UNDP/ADB development
papers.

Addressing the *28th Conference of Asean Railway CEOs* in Kuala Lumpur on
November 27th 2006, Malaysian transport minister Chan Kong Choy said the
US$1·8bn Singapore–Kunming rail link would be completed by 2015. Royal
Railways of Cambodia Director-General Sokhom Pheakavanmony said work
on the Poipet–Sisophon link between Thailand and Cambodia would be fin-
ished by the end of 2007 or early 2008 and that the Asian Development Bank
(ADB) has agreed to fund upgrading of the RCR network. China is fund-
ing studies for the 225 km link between Phnom Penh and Loc Ninh on the
Vietnamese border, with a view to starting construction of this line, and the
145 km Loc Ninh–Ho Chi Minh City route, in 2007.

A major issue facing coordinated Eurasian railway redevelopment is that of
track gauge. Originally in the UK it was determined that the gauge had to be 4 foot
8½ inches (1435 mm – the so-called 'standard gauge'), which China has adopted,
along with the rest of Europe and the US. However, better load carrying and
stability are realized with the wider gauge (1520 mm) deployed across Russia,
and there is an even wider track in India (1676 mm). Moving goods between these
gauges at borders is time-consuming and most often done by exchanging axle
units throughout the trains. The enforced six to eight hours' delay is a frustrating
issue for passengers, and it is a security issue, as tampering is easier when freight
is stationary, or when it is being officially inspected. Further, because of age,
long distances and poor management control (for both construction and operation) Asian rail tracks generally will not tolerate high speeds – it is only recently

that China has upgraded many of its major lines, and currently passenger trains travel at a maximum speed of 160 km per hour, with freight trains travelling more slowly. Recently, higher speeds of 200 km per hour have become possible on 6,003 km of renovated track, but this constitutes less than 10 per cent of China's 75,000 km of railway lines.

China needs to maintain its growth potential and in the near future it will have an awkward population mix with many older people living longer. It will be necessary for the Chinese government to look to the future and consider how the trade flux will change as more goods flow backwards and forwards to and from Europe and the US, with commercial pressures to make these flows faster than at present (Table 12.1). We should note that components for Chinese assemblies come from several sources. Many suppliers will be local, but other significant parts will originate in Europe or the US so the total manufacturing cycle time comprising two long sea journeys plus local deliveries might be well over 120 days. Manufacturers will not tolerate such long delays on goods shipped in massive container ships that pass round the Cape (of Africa) to European ports or take twenty days to cross the Pacific. Reducing the cash tied in as a result of the long production cycle will become increasingly important.

Maglev systems

The time is now right to propose an ultra high-speed rail track for China crossing Central Asia to Europe to facilitate trade, passenger flows, and tourism. The time is indeed opportune, as major upgrades or (re-)developments to the whole Asian rail system are either taking place or proposed for the near future. Maglev-2000 of Florida Corporation (www.maglev2000.com) and Transrapid (www.transrapid. de) present reasoned arguments for ultra high-speed maglev, which could apply directly to the TSR2 Eurasian Landbridge project, and to the (re)development of Central Asian railway systems. Their technology is similar to that already in place and operating on the Shanghai to Pudong international airport route.

There are two competing systems of (full size) maglev. One, called Transrapid, is the basis of the Shanghai system, which originated in Germany, and the other is Maglev-2000, proposed by the Maglev group of Florida, USA. They differ basically in the nature of their levitation units. Transrapid is both propelled and braked by means of a synchronous long-stator linear motor. Ferromagnetic stator packs and three-phase stator windings are mounted on both sides of the track along the underside of the guideway. The operation principle can be visualized best by imagining a conventional (rotating) electric motor whose stator is cut open

Table 12.1 Comparative Eurasian route times (days)

maglev	2
Block trains	11–15
Ship – Suez canal	30–35
Ship – around Africa	~ 45

and unwound along the underside of the guideway. Its rotor (excitation) function is taken by the onboard levitation ferromagnets. The vehicle is both lifted and propelled by an electromagnetic travelling field produced by the longstator linear motor. Electronic systems guarantee that the clearance between units and track remains constant (nominally 1 cm); therefore this ultra high-speed system demands exacting tolerances for track construction. Maglev-2000 also uses the principal of a linear synchronous motor. AC power is fed to a set of passive aluminium loops in the guideway, which propel the vehicle, and braking has a conserving regenerative effect, returning power into the electrical distribution system. The Maglev-2000 system uses a superconducting inductive magnetic repulsion system mounted in the vehicle. The superconducting Maglev-2000 system can easily operate with gaps of 6 inches (15 cm) between units and the track, substantially reducing the cost of constructing and operating the guideway. The superconducting magnets permit heavier loads and steeper grades than the Transrapid.

The superconducting magnets of Maglev-2000 are more powerful than the ferromagnets used by Transrapid and they have a stronger propulsive power. Once powered up through their zero resistance circuits they will retain their strong magnetic force indefinitely as long as they remain below their transition temperature. Modern superconductors are cooled adequately by liquid nitrogen. Nitrogen is abundant in the atmosphere, cheap to liquefy, and non-polluting.

As the maglev travels over the guideway the interactions between the linear coils and magnets instantaneously control speed, levitation and stability, preventing stray movements in five dimensions: vertical, lateral, roll, pitch and yaw. They will automatically counter any external force, such as wind gusts, curves or grades. The movement of the maglev is akin to a surfer sliding downhill on waves that also provide horizontal movement towards the shoreline. Further, the principle of synchronized propulsion makes collisions between vehicles virtually impossible: if two or more vehicles were ever placed simultaneously in the same guideway segment they would be forced by the 'motor' in the guideway to travel at the same speed in the same direction.

In addition to their 500 km/h (310 mph) speed capability, maglev systems offer significant performance advantages compared to steel-wheel systems. The technology allows for climbing and descending of grades up to 10 per cent, which is almost three times steeper than conventional rail systems. Maglev vehicles can round 50 per cent tighter curves (horizontal and vertical) at the same speeds as conventional high-speed rail and the guideway can be banked to 12 degrees, allowing vehicles to travel through tight-radius curves but still at high speeds. The banking eliminates uncomfortable sideward forces, ensuring ride comfort for passengers, and indeed better stability for freight. Further, as the units do not need to gather power from overhead wires (like the TGVs), tunnels will be smaller in diameter, so will be very much cheaper to construct than those for TGV tracks. By 'TGV' we mean the high-speed steel-wheels-on-track passenger train systems in France – the *train à grande vitesse*. We group also in this class the German (ACE), the Spanish (AVE) and the Japanese Shinkansen trains, which, though there are distinct differences between them, may be compared directly with maglev.

There are arguments against implementing the 'large' maglev systems such as that in use in Shanghai, or promoted by Maglev-2000 of Florida. The 'Magtube' system uses the same principal of magnetic levitation and propulsion as the Transrapid but restricts the size of freight units to accommodate only small volumes per propulsion unit so it is cheaper overall (Fiske, 2006). Fiske proposes maglev units running at high speed in buried low-pressure tubes, operating very much like pipeline systems so creating a very high capacity – upwards of 20,000 tonnes per hour. His preliminary estimates indicate a capital cost of less than US$3 million per kilometre for Magtube (US-based costs). Construction in urban areas will be more expensive than rural areas, and elevated construction costs will be more costly than underground construction. Although the Magtube system may be cheap, it is associated with large re-packaging costs within logistics systems, which have matured over the past fifty years using standard 20-foot or 40-foot containers.

Comparative costs of rail systems

Analysis shows that TGV systems offer high passenger capacity. For instance: signalling systems can usually handle a train approximately every four to five minutes, with up to 1,000 seats per train. On a double TGV Duplex unit, a French high-speed rail line can, in theory, carry the same number of passengers as a Boeing 737 every forty-five seconds, equivalent to three parallel motorways (CIT, 2005; Coffey, 1991; www.maglev2000.com). It has to be remembered that the TGV will carry passengers only, and generally will not allow slower trains (i.e. freight) on the same sectors as this quickly reduces the overall track capacity. Maglev (of Florida) state that their M-2000 units can operate individually or as multi-car 'train sets' so a two-way guideway with single vehicles can carry 12,000 passengers or 120 trailer trucks per hour. Thus, with 'train sets' at peak periods and single vehicles at off-peak, a two-way guideway could carry over 100,000 passengers plus several thousand freight containers daily.

Because of commercial secrecy, oddly disclosed accounting, national politics, the dynamics of project submissions – even corruption – it is difficult to obtain clear cost comparisons. Many lobbyists assert that maglev is hugely costly so favour the status quo of steel-wheels systems.

The cost of building high-speed rail tracks (TGV) over difficult terrain can be four to six times more expensive than over flat land. Their tracks are expensive because the rails have to be strong, built of costly high-quality steel, since the TGV systems exert severe forces at speed, and their anchoring in the ballast bedding has also to be built to exacting standards to prevent any movement or change of gauge as the temperature varies. Maglev, in contrast, uses a quite cheap but solid construction system of vertical columns which support concrete guide beams clad with cheap aluminium electrical conducting plates.

Maglev state that their systems can also be used for freight (containers or RoRo, dry bulk or fluids) and all would travel at the same ultra-high speed as passengers, which makes good economic sense. Initially we do not expect enough passenger volume along the full length of the Eurasian Landbridge to justify mag-lev, but the freight demand will certainly be high. Manufacturing components and finished goods will 'flow' quickly between China and Europe; and China has a huge demand for minerals, oil, gas and, soon, water, which would 'flow' from the reserves in Central Asia to consumers in China.

The average high-speed TGV rail track costs would seem to be a little over €30 million/km (Figure 12.2 – ignoring the Channel Tunnel) and there is the extra cost of investing in rolling stock. For maglev systems there are usually only estimated costs, except for the Shanghai line, whose true costs are a little shrouded (Table 12.2).

The passenger vehicles for maglev cost about €1.5 million each (US$2 million) whereas steel-wheeled passenger units cost between US$1.5 and 3.0 million, and their engines about US$5 million each. Maglev may seem costly, but it can deliver many passengers per unit of time – and when compared with aeroplanes (upwards of US$100 million each) maglev is seen to be inexpensive. Maglev freight units would be cheaper, but require strong internal anchor points, and maglev units for oil and gas need superlative safety features. Mixed ultra high-speed traffic is pos-sible with maglev, and the freight income might be expected to reduce passenger costs to near zero over time.

Maglev systems appear to be cheaper than TGV systems and comparable to the cost of (slow) standard railway systems. Maglev might even be 'cheaper' than deep-sea shipping, as one would factor in maglev's very short journey times, which would release money tied in during the long transit duration of stock hold-ings of components and finished goods.

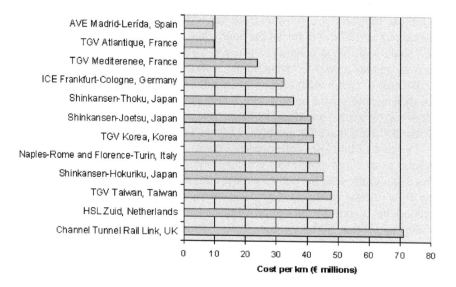

Figure 12.2 Comparative costs of high-speed rail track construction. Source: following CIT (2005).

Table 12.2 Costs of rail systems

System	Cost estimate (€ million/km)
Shanghai (track plus units and outbuildings)	15.0
Maglev-2000 (track)	5.0
Magtube (rural buried track: cheapest aspect)	1.5
High-speed TGV (average, track only)	30.0
'Ordinary' rail track (costs vary widely)	10.0

Sources: www.maglev2000.com; www.transrapid.de; www.magtube.com; www.railway-technical.com.

Issues affecting maglev take-up

We suggest that it may be opportune now to build an ultra high-speed rail link between the Chinese Pacific coast and Europe in order to promote trade, business passenger travel and tourism while also minimizing damage to the ecology (directly or though pollutants) and minimizing the depletion of limited stocks of fossil fuels. There are however several pros and cons – some factors relate to economic arguments, others to socio-political aspects as illustrated in Figure 12.3. We discuss these below.

	Economic factors	Socio-political factors	
Pros	Commerce and logistics providers Manufacturers of maglev and its systems	Wide grouping of NGOs such as UNESCAP, ADB, UNDP, TRACEA, CAREC, WTO…	Enablers
Cons	Traditional railway sector Investor fear of new systems Inertia	Social differences Politics Corruption External players such as Russia, US.	Detractors

Figure 12.3 Factors affecting maglev take-up.

Economic pros

Economic growth within Europe, particularly within the new members of the European Union to the east, is strong, partly thanks to investment by Taiwanese and mainland Chinese firms. According to Rocks (2007), over US$300 million has been invested in Central Europe recently by Asian firms to make electronics components (flat screen TV/monitors, computers and so on), with the investor firms stating that (a) they avoid tariff barriers by manufacturing in Europe, (b) there is a willing and educated workforce and (c) logistics are both shorter to market and well integrated throughout Europe. It makes sense to have a delivery to customer of only a few days compared to the extreme of forty-five days by boat from Asia to, say, Rotterdam and having then a further few days for final delivery.

We suggest that many commercial interests will be served better by ultra high-speed rail links and that these businesses will be strong consumers of the system as soon as the links are open. For instance, freight forwarders are always balancing costs and speed of delivery as well as looking to the security of the goods in transit. Manufacturers are always looking to the 'speed to market', which involves their final assembly being served with components 'just in time'. Even as China moves away from being an assembler to becoming more and more an originator of globally marketed goods it will not alter its reliance on components sourced from other parts of the globe, notably Europe and the US. This is the nature of globalization. Therefore we foresee the manufacturing lobby pressing the governments of Europe and China (and of India and Russia too) to seriously consider the economics of maglev systems as they offer very short route times.

The Industrial Revolution, the Information Revolution, and the Knowledge Revolution spawned many new firms that in turn created requisite intermediaries. It will be the same for maglev. There is much pent-up knowledge capital within Central Asia and a high capacity for innovation in China. Both regions will be able to compete in the development, building and operation of maglev systems, thereby driving down costs; in addition a wide set of related skills would develop in science and engineering.

Economic cons

The obvious opponents of maglev are the traditional railway and maritime sectors. There is a huge sunk investment in the railway system and in the shipping industry. New steel-wheel rail tracks are being laid and ports expanded. China plans to spend at least 2 trillion yuan (US$258 billion, at a rate of 100 billion yuan annually) to expand its rail network 35 per cent to 100,000 kilometres by 2020 (as stated in China's Eleventh Five-Year Plan). Vocal opponents have so far been strong enough to prevent even capitalist America developing wide-scale maglev evaluations notwithstanding their forecast benefits. High-speed trains like the TGV of France or the Shinkansen of Japan present obvious economic arguments upon their deployment and observed operational costs as well as arguments about the relocation of city workers to live in and commute to the countryside instead of crowding onto short in-city journeys. The maglev systems have to rely upon estimates – which are notoriously in error sometimes.

Policymakers in government are also afraid to commit to maglev because of the fear of other possible short-term drawbacks. In the short term there are the high costs of redeveloping existing rail links (in the case of China) or of developing new links where once none existed (as in much of Central Asia). Yet we have seen in Table 12.2 that maglev systems are not as costly as passenger-only high-speed railways. Of course there is the need to develop efficient transfer systems at the junctions of maglev systems and traditional railways (notwithstanding the present operational costs of axle-swapping at the intersections of gauge changes in the traditional systems). There will be a large human cost associated with the change from one technology to another, the learning curve will be steep, and many railway workers may be made redundant over time – a fact not desired by Chinese ministries. And, as with all new technologies, a nearly silent opposition comes from the fear of the unknown.

Socio-political enablers

It is likely that the business lobby will push for faster logistics, but there are other enablers who have been in the Asian region for a while. Amongst these are TRACEA with links to the European TEN-T programme, (UN)ESCAP, ADB and CAREC (ESCAP, 2003; EU, 2002; Sims, 2005).

The European TEN-T programme is running late, but it was designed to create an integrated network of high-speed rail and road highway systems crisscrossing the EU25 and linking into Russia and Central Asia. The roads link well enough, but the railways suffer from gauge incompatibilities at the borders of Europe with Russia, so freight has to be transhipped or trains have their axles swapped prior to the onward journey. The TRACEA programme coordinates the EU's promotion of its standards in the former Soviet republics and across Central Asia generally. The efforts of TRACEA and CAREC are explained well by Sims (2005), who also looks with hope to the initiation of a regional consensus similar to that which formed the European Union. We should note that CAREC reaches further geographically than the former Soviet 'stans' – incorporating Kazakhstan, parts of northern Iran and Afghanistan, the Xinjiang province of western China and the western part of Mongolia. It is similar in extent to the old 'Turkestan', which roughly represented the Turkic-speaking area of Central Asia.

CAREC notes all aspects of infrastructure development in Central Asia and how these have fallen into disarray after 1991. It proposes reforms, partly fostered by TRACEA, partly by the OECD (with respect to its anti-corruption initiatives) and partly by the *Human Development Report* (UNDP, 2006). All reforms are aimed at generating greater wealth for the local people through national and regional efforts in resource sharing and infrastructure development. The reforms embrace the oil, gas and mineral deposits in Central Asia, but also point to inequalities in supplies of (electrical) energy and water (needed for healthy living and for irrigation).

Socio-political detractors

As well as the 'fear of the unknown' or fear of being a 'first mover', a major detractor is the difficulty of working with more or less corrupt governments or their agents (Table 12.3).

It is not too hard to imagine that firms from China, India or Russia will find difficulties in working with each other, and will find it even more awkward if working with firms from nations with better anti-corruption reputations who have a duty to their own shareholders to report verifiable financial statements. The history of informers and collaborators in Central Asia during the Soviet era (even now perhaps) has made it culturally challenging to accept accounting systems which expressly allow for informers, especially anonymous informers, to be 'whistleblowers'. The Sarbanes–Oxley (SOX) Act of 2002 mandates informer hotlines, and US firms in particular have a duty to report openly according to SOX rules. It has long been known by the Asian Development Bank (ADB) that some 20–40 per cent of project finances in Asia are skimmed on receipt, making it impossible to achieve the target payback of projects. Furthermore, in order to appear on target, build quality is sacrificed and quality assessors are bribed to accept all faults, and money earmarked for maintenance is often used instead to complete the project, guaranteeing rapid performance degradation in operational use (Etienne, 2003). According to *The Economist* (2007b):

> It is said (with apparent sincerity) that some Chinese firms keep several sets of books—one for the government, one for company records, one for foreigners and one to report what is actually going on. By contrast, international accounting standards are built on foundations that China does not possess, such as truthful record-keeping and deep, clean, markets so that 'fair' valuations can be placed on financial instruments, property, or softer assets like brands and intellectual property.

Pravda (2003) noted that the reliability and timeliness of service along the TSR was poor, in part because of poor maintenance. But there is a simple-to-

Table 12.3 Indications of corruption and bribery

Country	Corruption perception (ranks 126 nations)	Bribery propensity (ranks 30 nations)
China	70	29
India	70	30
Russia	121	28
Czech Republic	46	–
Hungary	41	–
Poland	61	–

Source: Transparency International (2006).
Note: Lower ranks are better.

understand relationship between the Moscow HQ railway staff and the operations crews some 9,000 km away, who say 'we pretend to work, they pretend to pay us' (Kets de Vries, 2004). Furthermore, the TSR track and its more northerly branch, the BAM (Baikal Amur Mainline), were either constructed or extended using conscript labour from the Gulag (prison camps); the prisoners were not too concerned about construction quality.

There are large sociometric differences between the nations along the proposed Eurasia Landbridge route, and between the actors who wish to cooperate in building infrastructure and those who would use it later. Some of these aspects have been noted by Hofstede (1980, 1991), who says individual differences create organizational chaos if not managed transparently. We ask therefore, given the secretive nature of corrupt persons, how would transparency be promoted? Research indicates that both sides in a Russian and Chinese 'accord' look warily at each other, but for different reasons, and without open discussion their distrust may destroy the accord (Michailova and Worm, 2003; Hutchings and Michailova, 2004). There is therefore a real need to get staff in local, regional and international alliances to trust each other, but this is difficult to do, though not impossible (SOX, 2006).

Ecological impacts

There are many arguments within discussions on carbon trading and all depend upon different assumptions. Nevertheless the EU is determined to reduce its emissions overall and to address all transportation modes, which presently generate 24 per cent of its greenhouse gasses. This poses interesting questions as the emissions

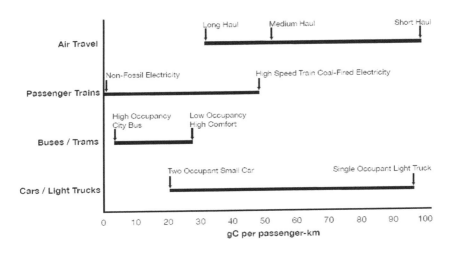

Figure 12.4   Relative carbon emissions. Source: following Feasta (2006).

in any one sector change as a passenger (or a tonne of freight) is moved singly or is 'consolidated'.

There are wide variations in the level of emissions from each of the various modes of transport. A small car with all seats occupied can release less emission than a half-empty bus, whereas a big car or a van with only one occupant can be worse than a long-haul flight per kilometre travelled. It therefore makes no sense to discriminate against one mode of travel by applying unique penalty licensing: the same rules should apply to all. Similar difficulties arise with freight transport. A light van can emit 1.6 kg of carbon dioxide to move a tonne a kilometre whereas a fully loaded 40-tonne heavy goods vehicle can move the same weight the same distance for only a tenth of the emissions. And sending a tonne of freight by sea in a big container vessel causes less than a hundredth of the CO_2 emissions from the van. Even sending the tonne by air can cause less emission than the van but the overall impact of the air journey would be worse if the full effects of the flight were taken into account (Feasta, 2006).

The Stern Report (Stern, 2007) has indicated that if we collectively do nothing the planet will be in grave danger, but for relatively little cost to our collective GDPs we can contribute to a better future. *The Stern Review* has shocked decisionmakers across the globe, and this chapter suggests that, on this point alone, decisionmakers ought to consider maglev as a way to address the problem. In addition the Intergovernmental Panel on Climate Change (IPCC) adopted the 'Summary for Policymakers' at their Paris meeting in February 2007. Their report, *Climate Change 2007: The Physical Science Basis*, assesses the current scientific knowledge about the natural and human drivers of climate change. It noted changes in climate and the ability of science to attribute changes to different causes, leading to projections for future climate change (IPCC, 2007). Its predictions are grave.

All aspects of the maglev are eco-friendly. The track has a low environmental footprint, being simply a concrete beam mounted on columns so animals and people are not inconvenienced by the raised track or its operation. The maglev technology is much quieter than other transportation systems as it does not produce any rolling, gearing or engine noise. The aerodynamic noise is low at speeds up to 250 km/h (155 mph), and is significantly less than TGV trains at high speeds. Electromagnetic fields produced by the maglev system are negligible and are roughly equivalent to the Earth's natural magnetic field, whereas the exposed sources of high voltage of a conventional electrified train or a subway system have about four to eight times the field strength of the maglev system. Maglev requires considerably less energy per passenger (50 per cent less, according to Transrapid) than conventional high-speed rail systems, and in addition there are no direct emissions from the moving vehicles to affect air quality. The electrical energy conversion at the track is very high for maglev, with some electricity being recycled while the trains are slowing down. Further, the up-front electricity cost can be minimized through the construction of new efficient power stations along the routes.

Maglev for automatic delivery systems

Maglev units can be modified to carry dry bulk products, gas or liquids. And, as they can be programmed with destination and return addresses (just like data blocks on the internet), they may be used to deliver minerals, fuels or water without the need for engine drivers or guards, having the empty units return automatically to be refilled.

CAREC studies have identified the need for China, Russia, India and the Central Asian states to move fuels and minerals across their borders for mutual regional benefits and for commercial sale to international markets. Of pressing concern, as noted in the *Human Development Report* (UNDP, 2006), is the need to have a reliable supply of clean water. The maglev bulk liquid units can transport all liquids quickly, reliably and cheaply in sufficient volumes to satisfy the varied needs of many customers.

Maglev for rural development and tourism

As the high-speed steel-wheel trains expanded their reach in Japan, France, Germany and elsewhere in Europe it became clear that workers preferred to abandon their previous crowded and slow city commutes in favour of living in the countryside. They are willing to pay more for a seat on the fast trains that would deliver them to their city centre workplace as quickly as the crowded commuter trains. There is no doubt that maglev systems would create the same benefits for commuters in China. At present journeys in major towns frequently take a long time, given the very crowded nature of urban road and underground systems (where they exist) at peak hours. A journey from the centre of Shanghai or Beijing to the residential outskirts may take one to two hours to complete in rush hour. In contrast, an hour's maglev trip could whisk commuters 200–300 km away, to tranquillity, clean air and a cheaper lifestyle.

The maglev routes would also contribute to eco-friendly tourism in several ways. First by offering non-polluting travel over long distances at high speed allowing intermediate stops in interesting regions. Of course aircraft can do this, but the tourist would have to connect to a mix of long-haul and short-haul flights often with incompatible schedules for individual tourists, and they generate heavy carbon emissions. Second, as the maglev becomes more commonplace it could offer pods of family size that might be removed from the maglev track to become road-based vehicles, like camper-vans, for local exploration. In this case the carbon impact could be minimized further as the rover vehicle could have a hybrid motor reducing its petrol demands. This would support tourism growth, bringing new money to remote communities.

Conclusions

Essentially we accept that globalization thrives on a global marketplace. It has been clear over the past few decades that a fast speed to market is demanded by consumers, be they end-users or intermediate assemblers waiting for subcomponents from suppliers across the globe. It is clear that the delay of forty-five days to send a container from Asia to Europe, or twenty days to the US, will not be tolerated for much longer. The total production cycle time is often actually much longer if China's assemblers rely on parts produced first in Europe or the US. Even now, Chinese and Taiwanese firms are setting up manufacturing plants in Eastern Europe to reduce their delivery times to European customers, and at the same time Europe is exporting more goods to Asia. As this flux of components and finished goods becomes more interdependent between firms in Europe, Asia and the US, the demand for the rapid delivery of components and finished goods will increase. However, there is a rapidly increasing awareness of the carbon cost of transport, and speed usually carries a high carbon cost.

Maglev systems, however, using the levitation and repulsive power of superconducting magnets, use very little power, most being used to overcome the air friction as the units travel at ultra-high speed (upwards of 300 km/h). The maglev track construction costs are low and, further, these units have few moving parts, or parts that roll or slide upon others, so their maintenance costs are low. This contributes to the very low predicted cost per passenger or tonne per kilometre. The maglev units are versatile, they can be constructed to carry passengers (in first class comfort), freight (in containers or RoRo), and also gas or liquids such as fuel oils or water (in fully automated units for round trips) and all units run at the same ultra-high speed. The total maglev system configuration can be designed to fulfil many needs at a total cost lower than the predicted costs of the current railway infrastructure expansion across Eurasia.

We suggest that the Eurasia Landbridge (from Lianyungang to Rotterdam) and other long-distance routes should be built (or rebuilt) using the maglev system as this would make very good economic and ecological sense. We also suggest it is important to link this rail development in China with the opening up and resurgence of Central Asia as a transport hub – both for the transit of freight across Central Asia as well as for Central Asia's exploitation of its own mineral wealth. We note that bodies like CAREC and UNESCO consider Central Asia to include Xinjiang as well as Mongolia. Therefore, in their committee deliberations, many major players are already represented, including the EU, Russia and China. The regional redevelopment of the Central Asian transport system stretches 6,000 km from the eastern border of Mongolia to Armenia and thus to the Black Sea (or to the Turkish/European rail network), and 3,000 km north to south (if we measure from the Russian border of Kazakhstan to the Gulf ports of Iran). From Mongolia, with a short(ish) extension to the east or southeast, the maglev track could reach the Pacific coast, reviving the Tumen River Development, and linking also to Beijing and its nearby ports. This plan, together with the development of the Eurasian Landbridge, also using maglev, would give China an enviable rapid eco-friendly transport system linking to the resources of Central Asia and to the markets of Europe.

Of course the initial construction costs of a maglev system will be very high, yet China indicates it is willing to spend billions (US$) on the expansion of its existing track. And, as Central Asia, Afghanistan, Iran and others need to upgrade their railways through renovation or new projects, it behoves these nations to reconsider their own potentially interdependent transport infrastructure (re)development projects. We suggest that all major development plans for steel-wheel railway projects be scrapped in favour of maglev systems, which could form an integrated system across Asia to the portals of Europe. Already the European TEN-T programme, and others in the EU's Seventh Framework, are considering using maglev to offer high-speed logistics for people, freight and liquids in line with the European Union views on increasing mobility and economic development coupled with reducing the effects of 'greenhouse gases'. In particular, it will be important to keep an eye on Russia. On 24 April 2007 the Russian government announced plans to 'bridge' the Bering Straits. Arkady Dvorkovich, presidential economic adviser, and the head of Russia's rail monopoly, Vladimir Yakunin, discussed 'Mega-projects of Russia's East' – an ambitious project to build a 6,000-kilometre (3,700-mile) transport corridor linking Russia with Alaska. This proposal has enormous significance to questions relating to the possible implementation of the Eurasian maglev.

References

Coffey, H.T. (1991) 'Maglev Design Considerations,' presented at Future Transport Technology Conference, Argonne National Laboratory, Portland, OR, 5–7 August.

Commission for Integrated Transport (CIT) (2005) *High-Speed Rail: International Comparisons*, Online. Available <www.cfit.gov.uk/docs/2004/hsr/research/pdf/chapter4.pdf> (accessed on 17 January 2007).

Dugan, S. and Dugan, D. (2000) *The Day the World Took Off: The Roots of the Industrial Revolution*, London: Macmillan.

The Economist (2007a) 'The Problem with Made in China,' 7 January.

The Economist (2007b) 'Cultural Revolution,' 11 January.

ESCAP (2003) *Foreign Direct Investment in Central Asian and Caucasian Economies: Policies and Issues*. Papers and proceedings presented at the Regional Round Table on Foreign Direct Investment for Central Asia, Dushanbe, 3 and 4 April

Etienne, G (2003) 'The Economy of Seepage and Leakage in Asia: The Most Dangerous Issue,' in J.B. Kidd and F.-J. Richter (eds) *Fighting Corruption in Asia: Causes, Effects and Remedies*, Singapore: World Scientific, 221–237.

EU (2002) *Central Asia Strategy Paper*, Online. Available <http://ec.europa.eu/comm/external_relations/ceeca/rsp2/02_06_en.pdf> (accessed on 17 January 2007).

Feasta (2006) *Background Briefing: Controlling Carbon Emission in the Transport Sector*, 20 December, Online. Available <www.feasta.org/energy.htm> (accessed on 17 January 2007).

Fiske, O.J. (2006) *The Magtube Low Cost Maglev Transportation System*, Online. Available <www.magtube.com/index.php/home>.

Hofstede, G. (1980) *Culture's Consequences: International Differences in Work-Related Values*, London: Sage Publications.

Hofstede, G. (1991) *Cultures and Organisations: Software of the Mind*, London: McGraw-Hill.

Hutchings, K. and Michailova, S. (2004) 'Facilitating Knowledge Sharing in Russian and

Chinese Subsidiaries: The Role of Personal Networks,' *Journal of Knowledge Management*, 8 (2), 84–94.

IPCC (2007) *Climate Change 2007: The Physical Science Basis. Fourth Assessment Report*, Online. Available <www.ipcc.ch> (accessed on 17 March 2007).

Kets de Vries, M.F.R., Shekshnia, S., Korotov, K. and Florent-Treacy, E. (2004) *New Russian Business Leaders*, Cheltenham: Edward Elgar.

Michailova, S. and Worm, V. (2003) 'Personal Networking in Russia and China: *Blat* and *Guanxi*,' *European Management Journal*, 21 (4), 509–519.

Pravda (2003) 'Russian Railways Look Confidently to the Future,' 5 September, Online. Available <http://newsfromrussia.com/main/2003/09/05/49812.html> (accessed on 20 January 2006).

Rocks, D. (2007) 'Made in China – er, Velkiko Turnovo,' *BusinessWeek*, 8 January, 43.

Sims, M. (2005) *Central Asia Regional Economic Cooperation (CAREC): Harmonization and Simplification of Transport Agreements, Cross Border Documents and Transport Regulations*, Manila: Asian Development Bank.

SOX (2006) <http://complianceandprivacy.com/News-CNIL-SOX-whistleblowers.asp> (accessed 10 December 2006).

Standage, T. (1999) *The Victorian Internet*, London: Orion Books.

Stern, N. (2007) *The Economics of Climate Change: The Stern Review*, Cambridge: Cambridge University Press.

Transparency International (2006) *Corruption Perception Index*, Berlin: Transparency International.

UNDP (2006) *Human Development Report. Beyond Scarcity: Power, Poverty and the Global Water Crisis*, New York: United Nations.

13 Managing the transition from administrative monopoly to regulated monopoly in China's strategic sectors

A case study of China's oil industry

Yang Chen and Richard Sanders

Introduction

The reform of China's 'strategic industrial sectors' (e.g. the utility sector, the heavy industries and the military and defence industries), which are still dominated by large-sized state-owned monopolies, has been on the agenda for further reform by the Chinese government since the end of 2003. The mainstream view within China (Zhang, 2005) is that the large-sized state-owned enterprises (SOEs) are less efficient than firms in the private sector and, as a result, will be less able to survive in the more open market provided by China's WTO entry. Therefore, in order to cope with the forthcoming challenges from international competitors, further liberalization, they argue, particularly in the area of competition policy, needs to be introduced within the strategic sectors. However, the question remains: under what circumstances will competition policy contribute to further successful reform of the strategic sectors?

In this final chapter we introduce as the background the ongoing debate concerning the encouragement of private business entry to the country's strategic sectors. We use the case study of China's petroleum industry to demonstrate that 'monopolistic regulation' is currently characteristic of the country's strategic sectors. This 'monopolistic regulation' has unfolded as the key institutional feature of the transition of China's oil industry from plan to market.

We accept that strong industry policy and strong competition policy are not *necessarily* in conflict. However, we argue that further reform of China's strategic sectors requires their proper sequencing and thus should focus on the construction of market-oriented institutions before the implementation of new competition policies. Without a functioning anti-trust law and independent industrial governing body, the introduction of competition policy would, on its own, merely lead to unregulated and destructive competition as exemplified in the former Soviet states. The transition of the current state-owned giants from monopolies with substantial regulating power to market-oriented regulated monopolies requires a process of institutional innovation, laying the foundation for the effective adoption of competition policies at a later date. This chapter aims to fill a critical gap in our understanding of the interaction between liberalization policy and regulatory policy in the context of China's post-reform transition.

Monopoly vs. competition: ongoing debate on the further reform of China's strategic sectors – new policy initiatives

In recent years, it has been widely accepted inside China that the 'non-public economy' has become an important driving force for the Chinese economy (Shi and Xie, 2002). The non-public economy has been growing at a rate several times higher than the average growth rate of the Chinese overall economy since the reforms began (Feltenstein and Iwata, 2005). Since 1997, the state has retreated from almost all competitive industrial sectors and small and medium-sized SOEs have been privatized following the policy 'keeping the big ones and letting the small ones go' (*zhada fangxiao*) (Ma, 2000). As a consequence, the state has retreated to the major strategic industrial sectors and currently directly owns and controls 177 large SOEs or 'national champions' in the industrial sectors that are classified as the backbone and pillars of the Chinese economy (SDRC, 2004). In these industries, the state holds substantial monopoly power.

Non-public businesses have not only excelled in light industries but also started exercising their muscles in capital- and technology-intensive industries such as the heavy chemical, infrastructure and utility sectors. Currently the share of non-public businesses exceeds 50 per cent in twenty-seven industrial sectors (CPEIR, 2006). In some industries the figure is as high as 70 per cent (ibid.). These non-public enterprises started as small and medium-sized businesses and their operation was mainly local and dispersed. In recent years, however, large non-public enterprise groups and specialized industrial blocs have been formed across regions. Nowadays, the average assets and sales revenue of the top 500 private enterprises in China has reached 1.29 billion yuan (approximately US$1,620 billion) and 1.41 billion yuan (approximately US$1,760 billion) respectively (ibid.).

In terms of location, the non-public businesses first developed in coastal regions but in recent years their growth in the central and western regions has accelerated. They no longer operate merely in the domestic market: since the government has progressively lifted controls on import and export policies, a growing number of non-public enterprises have engaged in exploring international markets (Naughton, 1995).

The development of the non-public economy, constituting more than one third of China's GDP, has entered a new phase of growth. The country's strategic industrial sectors, currently dominated by national champions, have become the targets of lobby groups for new private involvement. According to the lobbyists, large SOEs are less efficient than private companies and are therefore less competitive in world markets. In order to cope with international competition arising from WTO entry, further liberalization of the country's strategic sectors needs to take place.

As an echo of this intensive lobby, a new theoretical framework has been proposed (Bao *et al.*, 2005) and both party and government have passed new guidelines aimed at promoting the further reform of strategic industries by accelerating the development of the private sector (www.china.org.cn). Since the Sixteenth Party Congress in 2003, both the Chinese Communist Party Central Committee and the

State Council have proposed guidelines and policies to 'vigorously develop and guide the development of non-public economy' (ibid.). The core of these new liberalization policies lies in lifting barriers to market entry to non-public enterprises in those strategic industrial sectors which used to be exclusively occupied and monopolized by public enterprise.[1]

In 2004, the State Council issued 'Some Opinions of the State Council on Encouraging, Supporting and Guiding the Development of the Private and Other Non-Public Economic Sectors', in which the Council suggested measures to boost the non-public economy in seven aspects[2] and to lift market access barriers for non-public companies. The watershed came in the National People's Congress (NPC) and Chinese People Political Consultative Committee (CPPCC) sessions held in March 2005, in which the new liberalization policy guidelines were issued, involving thirty-six articles aimed at relaxing controls on market access for the non-public sector.

The fuzzy nature of the new policy initiatives

Although there is no specific mention of the term 'privatization' (*siyou hua*) in the new Party and government documents, the contents of the new policies clearly use the language of privatization and competition in the further restructuring of the strategic industrial, utility and financial services sectors in China.

Apart from encouraging non-public investment in the strategic sectors, the new policies focus on the further restructuring of China's huge SOEs – national champions in the pillar industries – since WTO accession. The implications of this restructuring are immense for China and the quest for appropriate mechanisms for the restructuring of these 'Red Chips' is critical if they are not to cause severe social and economic problems for China's further reform (Nolan and Zhang, 2003).

To date, most serious research on the restructuring of these industrial and commercial giants has addressed, at the micro level, the question of restructuring ownership and property rights and, at the macro level, the question of reducing government intervention and refining market mechanisms. A variety of methods of privatization, with an emphasis on management buyouts (MBO), have been tested and adopted in different SOEs depending upon varying central and local policy constraints over the past two years (Zhang Weiying, 2003). However, management misconduct in the process of MBOs has led to significant loss of state-owned assets and a rise in SOE layoffs that have caused both government and public great concern. The high-profile debate in autumn 2004 between Lang Xianping and Gu Chujun reflected that concern (Nanfang Weekly, 2004).

To the extent that public ownership involves a form of regulation, enterprise restructuring (including privatization) is considered to represent a fundamental change in the form of regulation. One of the major concerns of China's market-oriented reform has been the question of how to reform the governance structure inherited from the plan era. The official line regarding the objective of governance reform is the objective of building a mechanism characterized by 'small government, big market', in which the reduction of government intervention (*fangsong guanzhi*) becomes the essence of reform (Zhang Shuguang, 1999).

However, with regard to the role of regulation in the restructuring of national champions and the encouragement of non-public enterprises to enter the strategic sectors, governance mechanisms characterized by 'small government' do not necessarily entail policies of privatization and liberalization. Rather, regulatory reform needs to focus on the question of how to enable government intervention to work *with* market mechanisms, rather than working against them.

Our interpretation of the 'thirty-six articles' suggests areas that demand the development of innovative institutions to facilitate change and reform. The new policies grant domestic non-public capital the same rights as foreign capital in entering strategic industrial sectors and are more flexible with regard to the acquisition of shares of publicly-owned PLCs by the private sector but non-public enterprises are allowed to enter monopolistic sectors only with *the approval of the government* (our emphasis). Given the lack of anti-trust law at the state level and the void of competition authorities at the industrial level, it is difficult to clearly identify the governing body and define the boundary of its authority.

According to the first guideline, '*relevant* government authorities at both central and local level are *requested* to take actions *as quickly as possible* to modify and revise regulations, rules and policy stipulations that restrict the market entry of non-public enterprises'.[3] The use of 'requested' indicates that the application of guidelines will be facilitated not by law but by administrative orders/disciplines. The use of 'relevant' and 'as quickly as possible' reflects the flexibility of the guidelines.

The second guideline suggests that 'new policies aim at introducing market competition in the natural monopolistic industrial sectors such as energy generation, telecommunications, railways, civil aviation, oil and petroleum. On the premise of unified state plans, *except otherwise specified in separate stipulations of state laws and regulations*, the suggested market entry methods include (i) the acquisition of shares of public PLCs in these sectors, (ii) as a wholly-owned enterprise, as a joint venture, as cooperative enterprises for certain projects and (iii) through the acquisition by qualified non-public enterprises of rights of exploration and mining of mineral resources on an equal footing according to law' (ibid., our emphases).

The third condition argues for 'new policies to encourage non-public capital to invest in all the utility sectors for the supply of urban water, gas and heat supplies, public traffic services to sewage and waste operation and other public services. *On the premise of regulated acts of transfer*, new policies allow publicly owned utility companies to '*transfer*' [*zhuan rang*, equivalent to 'sell'] property rights and rights of operation to non-publicly owned enterprises' (ibid., our emphases).

The fourth condition states that 'in the financial services sector, new policies shall encourage the development of regional shareholding banks and cooperative financial institutions. *On the premise of strengthened legislation, regulated access, strict supervision and effective prevention of financial risk*, qualified non-public enterprises can initiate the establishment of financial intermediary services.

Non-public enterprises meeting *required conditions* are allowed to take part in the reform and restructuring of public banking, securities, insurance and other financial institutions' (ibid., our emphases).

The italicized discourses in the conditions above suggest that the lifting of barriers to market entry by private businesses to the country's strategic sectors remains subject to government 'regulations'. This leaves open the question of how to identify and define the role of the regulatory authorities. There are institutional voids in the new policy initiatives that lead, at the current stage of transition, to a conflict between the new policy initiatives that promote competition and those that favour the monopolistic status quo of the national champions in the country's strategic sectors.

The conflict between monopolistic national champions and competition policy

Those opposed to further liberalization argue that there is *always* an inherent tension between industrial policy and competition policy. In China, those who are sceptical of the new liberalization policies argue that the state's policy priority should be the creation of competitive capability amongst China's 'national champions' in its strategic sectors, particularly after WTO entry (Nolan, 2005). In a more open market, the competitiveness of Chinese national champions demands their ability to outperform international competitors, gaining market share and expanding profitably at their rivals' expense.

Currently, the national champions in China's strategic sectors are, by and large, national monopolies or oligopolies. On the one hand, these national champions tend to be uncomfortable with new liberalization policies. For the proponents of the national champions, competition policy designed to increase the level of competitiveness by promoting market structures populated with small firms who price at or near marginal cost may well lead to problems. On the other hand, for private businesses eager to enter the strategic industries, the extant monopoly by national champions is regarded as a dangerous form of meddling with markets leading to industrial inefficiency and incompetence.

Despite the government's issuing of guidelines with regard to competition policy, the tension between those favouring policies to nurture national champions and those favouring greater liberalization has not been relieved; indeed it has intensified in some industrial sectors. And, given the institutional drawbacks at the industrial level including the lack of anti-trust law and competition authorities, competition policies, such as they are, are likely to remain, in the foreseeable future, mere 'guidelines' with their application muddling through a 'grey area' in a case-by-case manner. In that light it is important to examine the ongoing dispute between the two factions in order to discover what innovative institutions need to be created to facilitate both forms of policy in the further reform of the strategic sectors.

The empirical evidence from countries with substantial anti-trust experiences indicates that there is no *inherent* conflict between industrial policy and competition policy. As Paul Geroski, the head of the UK Competition Commission, argues (2005a), the kind of 'competitiveness' that competition policy actually strives to create is virtually the only way a nation state can achieve the kind of 'competitiveness' to which industrial policy proponents aspire. Thus, new institutional innovations should ideally serve the purposes of both industry policy, by nurturing the 'ability' of 'national champions', and competition policy, by improving their 'incentives'. The innovative institutions should involve a balance between industry policy and competition policy, making them *complementary* to each other, rather than placing them in conflict.

A case of conflict between a national champion and a non-public newcomer in China's oil industry

In the heat of the launch of competition and privatization policies in China's strategic industries, the dispute between Maohua Shihua (referred as MS thereafter), a private PLC, and Maolian Gufeng (referred as MG thereafter), a branch of the publicly owned PLC China Petrol Engineering (Zhong Shihua) has not only raised broad social concerns but also attracted academic interest.

MS was a private PLC producing polypropylene whereas MG engaged in the petrol refining business. MG's mother company, China Petrol Engineering (Zhong Shihua), together with China Crude Oil (Zhong Shiyou) and China Aviation Petrol (Zhong Hangyou), dominates the extraction, processing and service of the oil industry in China. As a major supplier of MS, MG started providing liquid hyzrazinium, the raw material for the production of polypropylene, and a by-product of oil refining, to MS in 1998.

In October 2004, a dispute began between MG and MS over the price of liquid hyzrazinium. As the disagreement remained unsolved, MG stopped supplying it to MS, resulting in heavy disruption of MS's production and leading to substantial losses there.

MS was originally created and registered as a state-owned company in 1988. When it was founded, MS was a backyard (*sanchan*) company attached to Maoming Petrol Engineering Company and was a branch of China Petrol Engineering. MS went through shareholding restructuring in 1992 and floated on Shengzhen Stock Exchange in 1996. From its flotation to December 2002, the largest shareholder of MS was the Employee Mutual Support Association of Maoming Petrol Engineering Company (referred as EMSA thereafter). Maoming Petrol Engineering Company acted as the controller of MS while China Petrol Engineering was the ultimate owner of MS. When MS was floated, its annual production capacity was recorded as 14,000 tonnes of polypropylene and, after its listing on the stock exchange, MS was able to raise sufficient capital to invest in a series of new production lines. MS operated efficiently with a healthy cash flow and was listed every year as amongst the top fifty most sustainable and profitable PLCs in China by *New Fortune* magazine.

In December 2002, the privately owned property developer Beijing Taiyue Estate Ltd bought 29.5 per cent of MS's shares from EMSA and became its largest shareholder. Thereafter MS was classified as a privately owned PLC. Maoming Petrol Engineering Company became the second largest shareholder of MS by holding 17.8 per cent of the company shares. From December 2002 to December 2003, MS invested further to update the relevant technology and installed the most advanced production line in China. MS consequently increased the scale of its production significantly and doubled the level of profits in that year. At that time, MS purchased 80 per cent of its raw material, liquid hyzrazinium, from MG, who supplied it directly to MS through the tube linked from MG to MS's production line. Thus, MS found itself located at the lower end of the supply chain and MS's production by and large relied on supplies from MG.

The dispute over the price of liquid hyzrazinium can be traced back to May 2002. At that time, based on the examination of the business relationship between MG and MS, China Petrol Engineering regulated and defined the supply price per ton from MG to MS as:

price of liquid hyzrazinium to MS = non-planned liquid hyzrazinium price of the current month + 120 yuan.

In fact, this was the price framework that had been implemented since 1 January 2002. MS had no objection to this price framework; after all, when it was agreed, MS was still a branch company, with China Petrol Engineering as its ultimate owner. But even after MS was taken over by Beijing Taiyue Estate Ltd in December 2002 this price framework remained unchanged for several months. In September 2003, however, MG adjusted the price framework, leading to prices increasing by more than 500 yuan per ton. Although, at first, MS purchased the raw material from MG at the new higher price, MS bitterly complained about it and, in September 2004, finally refused to pay the extra charge. As a result, on 28 October 2004, MG stopped supplying MS with liquid hyzrazinium.[4]

According to MG, the original price framework between MS and MG was an internal market price negotiated between two branches of China Petrol Engineering. This internal market price was not the same as the normal market price. Once MS was taken over and no longer belonged to China Petrol Engineering, it was reasonable for MG to charge MS the normal market price. In 2004, the price of crude oil increased sharply in international markets, MG raised the price of its product to accommodate the change, and initially it was deemed by MS as rational market behaviour in that MS felt able to cope with the increase in production costs. As the price of crude oil continued to soar in late 2004, however, MS found it difficult to accept the higher prices and finally terminated its deal with MG.

MS regarded the adjusted price as unfair and hostile. In the process of negotiation, China Petrol Engineering offered to take over MS as a form of vertical integration but the private owner of MS refused the offer. Later China Petrol Engineering rejected offers of reconciliation from MS and decided to invest 400 million yuan in building its own polypropylene production facilities

Thereafter, MS decided to retreat from the oil and petrol industry. In January 2005, MS, with the endorsement of its assets in the oil and petrol industry, acquired

50 per cent of the shares of a utility company engaged principally in electricity generation and the supply of water for industrial production. MS invested further in the company acquiring 97 per cent of its shares, thereby entering into a new industrial sector.

On 28 February 2005, a conference was held in Beijing to discuss the case and its implications. Economists Zhang Weiying, Sheng Hong, Zhang Shuguan, Yang Shenming, CCP member Bao Yujun, and corporate lawyer Wang Xiaohua unanimously criticized the presence of 'administrative monopoly' in the oil and petrol industry, and MG's mother company China Petrol Engineering was blamed for abusing its monopolistic market power.

'Monopolistic regulation': the nature of China's oil and petroleum industry

Before analysing this case further, it is necessary to make a historical review of the relationship between MS and MG in the context of the development and transition of China's oil and petroleum industry. First we identify its structure and corporate governance. Second, we analyse the conflict between MS and MG in the context of the inherent puzzle between national champions and competition policies.

Industrial reform and the formation of duopoly

China's oil and petrochemical industry was developed from scratch in the late 1950s. The industry has always been classified as one of the country's strategic sectors and has consequently received the priority of state investment in accordance with 'the plan'. The oil industry was also a model industry indicative of China's new self-reliance. As indicated in Table 13.1, China's oil and petroleum industry contributed over a quarter of the country's energy production by the end of 1970s compared with 0.7 per cent in 1949.

Under central planning, the registered oil fields in China cover over 400 square kilometres and are exclusively owned and administrated by the state. The industry was directly governed by the Department of Oil Industry from 1955–1988.[5] Before the establishment of China Ocean Oil Corporation in 1982 and the launch of China Petrochemical Corporation (SINOPEC) in 1983, there was only one SOE operating in the oil and petroleum industry. SINOPEC engaged mainly in the oil refinery and it contributed 90–95 per cent of the country's refining capacity by the end of the 1990s. In 1988, as part of the restructuring of the State Council, the Department of Oil was replaced by the China Oil and Natural Gas Corporation (CONGC).

In the late 1990s, China's oil and petrochemical industry went through further restructuring. Beforehand, the two oil giants in China engaged in upstream and downstream production respectively. Production and marketing were separated, in that the production enterprises did not engage in the marketing of oil and petroleum products. In 1998, the National People's Congress passed the 'Plans for the Reform of State Councils', which involved decisions on the strategic restructuring of China's oil and petroleum industry.

Table 13.1 Percentage of total energy production (crude oil and natural gas), 1949–2003

Year	Total energy production (1,000,000 tons of SCE)	% of total energy production	
		Crude oil	Natural gas
1949	23.74	0.7	
1957	72.95	2.1	0.1
1965	188.24	8.6	0.8
1970	309.90	14.1	1.2
1978	627.70	23.7	2.9
1985	855.46	20.9	2.0
1991	1,048.44	19.2	2.0
1995	1,290.34	16.6	1.9
2000	1,069.88	21.8	3.4
2003	1,603.00	15.2	2.9

Source: China Statistical Yearbook 2004, p. 275.
SCE, standard coal equivalent.

As a result of the restructuring strategy, two large-scale integrated oil companies, China National Petroleum Corporation (CNPC) and SINOPEC – have been formed through administrative measures, with their business mainly divided by geographic location. SINOPEC operates to the north of the Yangtze whereas CNPC mainly carries out its operations to the south of the river. Both companies went through vertical integration and subsequently operated on a very large scale, from the upstream areas of oilfield exploration, extraction and refining to the downstream activities of petrochemical processing, petrol stations and the marketing of products. The 1998 restructuring established the duopoly in China's oil and petroleum industry. The aim of the restructuring was to cope with the sharp increase of oil consumption in the booming Chinese economy. As indicated in the following Figure 13.1 and Table 13.2, both petroleum production and consumption have increased significantly over the last decade and the trend will remain in the next decade. Since 1993 onwards, China has become a net importer of petroleum.

PetroChina Co. Ltd, set up from the core businesses of CNPC, was listed on the New York and Hong Kong Stock Exchanges in April 2004. The parent company, CNPC, held 90 percent of PetroChina's total equity and BP became one of PetrolChina's strategic investors. In October 2000, China Petroleum & Chemical Corporation, established from the core businesses of the SINOPEC Group, issued 16.78 billion H shares on the Hong Kong Stock Exchange. Within a year, the company issued 2.8 billion A shares on the Shanghai Stock Exchange. By 2001, the SINOPEC Group controlled 67.92 per cent of SINOPEC's equity. Exxon Mobile, BP, Shell and ABB Lummus became SINOPEC's strategic investors. Equity involvement by the global super majors was crucial to the successful listing of PetrolChina and SINOPEC (Nolan and Zhang, 2003). However, the Chinese government remains the largest shareholder. Reform over the past two decades,

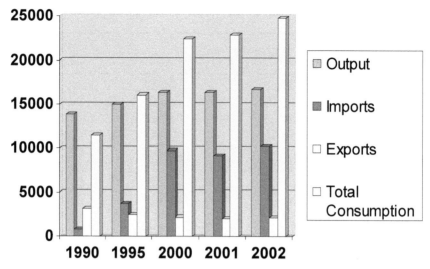

Figure 13.1 Total output, imports and exports of petroleum, 1990–2002 (10,000 tons).
Source: *Chinese Statistical Yearbook* (2004, p. 277).

particularly the shareholding restructuring, has transformed SINOPEC and CNPC from mere production units under the plan to corporations in international markets. Although they are publicly listed companies by structure, SINOPEC and CNPC inherited the legacy of the plan in terms of their governing mechanisms. This 'halfway house' mechanism employed by the two giants – as monopolies in the market while holding power as regulating authorities at the industrial level – is the institutional puzzle that has led to all sorts of problems that further reform needs to address.

Monopolistic regulation in the oil and petroleum industry

Owing to the legacy of the central planned economy, there is, currently, no integrated governing body for the oil and petroleum industry in China. Rather, various government divisions, including the State Development and Reform Commission, Ministry of Commerce, Ministry of Land and Resources, Ministry of Water Resources, State Electricity Regulatory Commission and State Environmental Protection Administration of China, exercise various forms of authority over the administration, R&D policies and other relevant industry policy issues related to the energy industry.

The Ministry of Commerce controls the import quota and entry to the domestic oil market and the State Development and Reform Commission holds the authority over the pricing of crude oil and other relevant products whereas the Ministry of Land and Resources is responsible for the strategic planning of the exploration and extraction of oil and natural gas. Given the lack of an integrated governing body at the industrial level, the administration of the oil industry in China is subsequently delegated to the two monopolies – CNPC and SINOPEC. Monopolistic

Table 13.2 International petroleum supply and consumption (million barrels per day)

	2002	2003	2004	2005	2006	2007	2008	2009	2020	2011	2012	2013	2014
Total production	78.18	79.37	81.91	83.77	85.42	86.90	88.42	89.95	91.35	93.09	94.82	96.54	98.33
Total consumption	78.10	79.60	82.25	84.26	85.72	87.20	88.72	90.25	91.65	93.39	95.12	96.83	98.63
US (50 states)	19.71	20.00	20.50	20.91	21.30	21.72	22.18	26.65	22.98	23.31	23.63	23.94	24.33
EU	13.81	14.22	14.58	14.73	14.73	14.72	14.72	14.72	14.72	14.79	14.89	14.94	15.01
Japan	5.03	5.58	5.38	5.45	5.50	5.55	6.60	5.65	5.70	5.71	5.71	5.71	5.72
China	5.16	5.54	6.54	6.98	7.11	7.24	7.34	7.50	7.63	7.94	8.26	8.57	8.88
India	2.18	2.19	2.22	2.25	2.36	2.47	2.58	2.68	2.79	2.93	3.07	3.21	3.34
All other countries	32.21	32.07	33.03	33.94	34.72	35.5	35.3	33.05	37.83	38.71	39.56	40.46	41.35

Source: adapted from IEA (2004).

regulation, in the context of China's oil and petroleum industry, typically means a situation in which monopolies are directly involved in the design and implementation of regulation including the industrial and competition policies of the industry.

In this monopolistic market, barriers to entry to the oil drilling industry are significant since only those enterprises that have been awarded a special certificate of exploration or drilling can be engaged in exploring and extracting the oil. Up to now, only the large monopolistic national champions – SINOPEC, CNPC and China National Offshore Oil Corporation (CNOOC) – have the exclusive rights of exploring and extracting the oil fields in China. Other state-owned or private enterprises with the capital and capability to engage in the business are not entitled to expand into the sector.

In 1994, the government loosened up barriers for non-public companies to enter into the wholesale market for oil and petroleum products. Before the formation of the duopoly in 1998, the structure of wholesaling and retailing markets in sections of oil refinery was in a state of monopolistic competition. The private oil enterprises, mainly engaged in businesses in the middle and downstream of the industry, were small in scale and deficient in the management of logistics, capital and information. Nonetheless, despite the problems they encountered, some private companies expanded rapidly and, as a result, the state-owned oil companies faced fierce domestic competition.

In May 1999, the General Office of the State Council issued the No. 38 (1999) document 'On the Liquidating and Restructuring of the Small Oil Refining Factories and Standardizing the Circulation Order of Crude Oil and Petroleum Products'. The document granted exclusive rights to SINOPEC Group and CNPC by stipulating that other extant enterprises were not allowed to engage in the wholesaling of petroleum products. Moreover, the No. 38 document granted SINOPEC and CNPC exclusive rights to take over other existing enterprises through merger and acquisition. Obviously, the objectives of the No. 38 document were to strengthen the ability and capability of the two 'national champions'.

As a new section of the business, market entry for retailing by petrol stations was easier in the end of 1990s, as the authority for licensing was delegated to local government. The free entry at regional level quickly led to rampant competition. In 2000, the State Commission of Economics and Trade delegated authority to SINOPEC and CNPC to issue 'The Urgent Notice Regarding the Restructuring of the Petrol Station Market', which allowed the two monopolies to engage in the restructuring of the petrol station market. The two giants engaged in fierce competition not only to build up their own new petrol station chains but also to take over existing petrol stations through merger and acquisition. After October 2001, newly built petrol stations throughout China were either solely financed or owned by SINOPEC Group and CNPC. There were 75,000 petrol stations in China, 50 per cent of them owned by the two giants, and the two firms' concentration ratio in the petrol stations market reached 60 per cent by the end of 2002 (Nolan and Zhang, 2003). In September 2001, the General Office of the State Council issued another document 'On the Further Restructuring and Standardizing of the Crude

Oil Market', which not only reinforced the duopoly's exclusive wholesale rights but also granted them exclusive retail rights.

As indicated in the above cases, the two monopolies have played 'dual roles' – being monopoly players in the market and regulators of the industry at the same time. Scholars (see, for example, Zhang Weiying, 2005) argue that the state-owned monopolies do not have incentives to increase efficiency and should be blamed for the slow progress of oil exploration and drilling and for the consequent shortage of oil supply in China. They argue that, although profits of large SOEs increased by 49 per cent in 2003, roughly 490 billion yuan (of which 33.6 per cent came from the oil and petrol industry), the SOEs should not be applauded for their achievements largely because these profits were generated under administrative monopoly. They also criticized the state-owned monopolies' abusing their market power, which was arguably one of the factors that led to the increasing price of fuel and power in the Chinese market. As indicated in Table 13.3 and Figure 13.2, our study shows that the purchasing price of upstream products has been higher than downstream products since 1998 onwards.

Institutional Analysis of the Formation of Monopolistic Regulation

Zhang Weiying (2005) suggests that competition policies should be introduced into the industry, including the lifting of barriers to market entry. But, if current institutional arrangements remain, will competition policy be effective in bringing about positive change in the industry? In order to address this question, it is

Table 13.3   Purchasing price indices of raw material, fuel and power (preceding year = 100)

Year	General index	Fuel and power	Raw chemical materials
1990	105.6	110.7	95.6
1991	109.1	112.9	99.8
1992	111.0	116.4	102.6
1993	135.1	136.7	114.3
1994	118.2	118.0	111.7
1995	115.3	108.7	127.2
1996	103.9	110.2	98.0
1997	101.3	109.3	97.1
1998	95.8	99.1	93.6
1999	96.7	100.9	97.6
2000	105.1	115.4	105.6
2001	99.8	100.2	98.4
2002	97.7	100.1	97.5
2003	104.8	107.4	102.9

Source: compiled by the authors from *Chinese Statistics Year Book* 2004, p. 275–280.

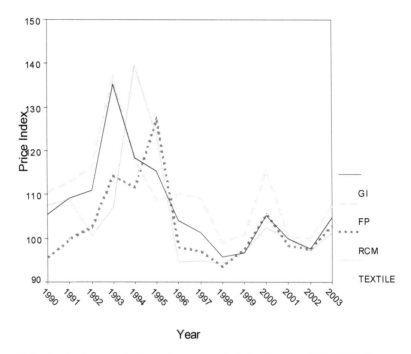

Figure 13.2   Purchasing price indices of raw material, fuel and power, 1990–2003. Source: compiled by the authors from *Chinese Statistical Year Book* (2004, pp. 275–280). GI, general index; FP, fuel and power; RCM, raw chemical material.

necessary to analyse the institutional arrangements that lead to the existence of 'monopolistic regulation' in China's oil industry.

Inherited from the centrally planned system, the governing mechanisms of the oil industry are still reliant on administrative management. As there is no independent industrial governing body, standards for market entry have not been unified. For example, given the lack of national industrial standards, SINOPEC and CNOP have developed their own corporate standards with regard to the safety codes of petrol stations, the basic standards concerning environmental issues and the equipment capacity in their operations and other companies have adopted the two giants' corporate standards as the industry benchmark. In terms of petrol retailing, local governments not only set up regional industrial standards, but are also the licensing authorities – and as such lay down the major barriers for market entry. The result has been that, without integrated national standards and industrial policy, quality assurance was very poor in the early development of petrol stations. Moreover, competition among local governments made it impossible to deal with a range of problems such as forgery and poor quality of equipment beyond the provincial boundaries. As a result, the central government had no choice but to intervene with administrative measures.

In the case of the management of exploration and extraction in the upstream of the industry, the rights of extraction are still distributed by administrative regions. On the one hand, CNPC, SINOPEC and two other large SOEs control the majority of the oil resources; on the other hand, under patronage of local governments, local companies exploit the limited resources with unsustainable extraction. The lack of independent governing mechanisms at the national industrial level leads to conflicts between a few large SOEs governed by the central government and a much larger number of local companies supervised by local government.

Reflected in the above two cases, co-occurrence between the segmented administrative monopoly over the upstream market and unregulated competition in downstream sectional markets is characteristic of the market structure of China's oil and petroleum industry. Apart from administrative segmentation of resources and markets (SINOPEC and CNPC control the domestic extraction and oil wholesale market, and three large SOEs have been allocated exclusive import licenses for oil products), the other main factor that has led to the co-occurrence market structure is the distorted non-market-oriented pricing mechanism.

So far, government has directly regulated prices of oil products and the market-oriented pricing mechanism has remained void. In the case of petrol stations, even now the 'government-directed price-floating system' that operates over crude oil under custom protection remains at the helm and, as a result, the domestic price of crude oil is higher than the international price and there have been significant profit margins in the downstream market for crude oil, attracting investments into such activities as petrol station retailing. At the upstream end, there are very high barriers to entry into the market for oil wholesale and oil import and the price of crude oil remains at a high level given the lack of competition. On the downstream end, as local government holds the authority over the issuing of licenses for petrol stations, the petrol station business is, by and large, a regional business with low quality assurance and unable to gain significant economies of scale. The regional trade blocks created by local governments make it almost impossible for large-scale competitive companies to operate nationwide.

As large SOEs, SINOPEC and CNPC have to shoulder heavy social responsibilities. Although the two giants have restructured as publicly listed companies, the state still holds over 90 per cent of their shares. Operational efficiency has to be compromised in the light of their political and social responsibilities such as the provision of employment. Therefore, the central government, as the owner and the largest stakeholder of the two giants, feels it has no choice but to grant monopolistic rights to them. In the case of petrol stations, given the lack of an independent industrial governing body and relevant market-oriented institutions to tackle the problems associated with unregulated competition, the central government has intervened by simply letting them enter into the market with exclusive rights. It has ended up with two giants competing in the merger and acquisition of small, local petrol chains. The competition between the two has raised the costs of merger and acquisition which, in turn, has led to the deterioration in the operational efficiency of the two companies.

Lessons from the liberalization of the Russian oil industry

Just like the Chinese oil industry, the Russian oil industry was hierarchically centralized and tightly administered under the Soviet Oil Ministry and all companies were state owned in the previous Soviet era. Compared with the gradual corporate reform in Chinese oil industry, the Russian oil industry adopted outright privatization to introduce market-oriented mechanisms and develop competition by breaking up the old hierarchies (Locatelli, 2006). In November 1992, all Russian state-owned oil enterprises were given independent legal (joint stock company) status and restructured into twelve vertically integrated oil companies of which the state's controlling shareholdings were quickly sold off to private owners within three years of establishment (McPherson, 1996). As the Russian government privatized the oil companies for the sake of covering its huge financial deficit, they sold the state shares to several key emerging private financial groups which subsequently became the new owners and governors of oil oligopolies and the status quo remains to date. The privatization programme subsequently produced the oligopolistic structure of the Russian oil industry

From the end of December 1991 to the end of December 1999, the privatization programme was accomplished with the establishment of ten (substantially eight) vertically-integrated oil oligopolies in the Russian oil industry. In 2003, the ten oil companies accounted for 90.4 per cent of the total crude oil production in Russia (Locatelli, 2004). The oil industry reform produced a new industrial structure based on new national private oligopolies which tied into a complex network of domination and were largely independent of the state and its overall political objectives. The Russian government did not have any means to directly control the vertically integrated oil oligopolies, although the government still controlled domestic crude oil and oil products pipelines and owned Rosneft, the fourth-largest oil company in the country.

As the nation's wealth ended up in the hands of the oligarchs and the price of oil soared from the end of the 1990s, the Russian oil companies had become 'cash rich'. Thus, they started exercising their muscles by lobbying the government to implement policies that were favourable to them (e.g. the amendment of the Production Sharing Act in June 2003).

The Russian economy is increasingly dependent on oil and natural gas exports; the World Bank estimated that Russia's oil and gas sector might account for up to 25 per cent of GDP in 2003 (World Bank, 2004). Given the fact that over 70 per cent of Russian crude oil production is exported directly, with the remaining 30 per cent refined locally, private oligopolies obviously have adopted a short-term strategy of seeking immediate liquidity by maximizing exports in order to rapidly increase the value of current assets. This strategy is known as *cash stripping* (Boussena and Locatelli, 2005).

Such short-term strategies of the private actors do not go well with a balanced long-term development of the industry or with the short-term aims of the Russian state. The state therefore finds itself confronted with a key question: what incentives should be introduced to direct the activities of oil companies towards long-term strategies instead of the current practices of asset stripping and cash stripping (Boussena and Locatelli, 2005)? Therefore, the state started to exhibit an inclination to take back the control of the oil industry to fulfil its economic and foreign policies.

It is argued today that the privatization process during the Boris Yeltsin era of 'bandit capitalism' was lacking in transparency and mostly seen as illegitimate (Black *et al.*, 2000). In the process of privatization, although it was finally accepted that a legal framework was essential to the restructure of the industry, the doubts concerning the form of legislation have never been resolved. As a result, despite the adoption of a legal framework based mainly on Western standards and practices, there has been serious uncertainty over rights of access to Russian resources as there was no single actor clearly defined and recognized as having power to allocate a legitimate and indisputable right of production and exploration to private companies (Boussena and Locatelli, 2005). This institutional void made it inevitable that the Russian state took back the control of oil industry through the old trick of administrative fiat and the lobbying of powerful contacts. As indicated in the following Table 13.4, Russian government recouped the state shares in leading oil oligopolies recently through aggressive merger and acquisition.

Privatization in an economy whose market institutions are embryonic has trapped the Russian oil industry on an institutional path that has so far undermined its long-term viability. Given these institutional restrictions, government monopolistic regulation was reintroduced, to some extent by fiat, to replace the dominant private interest groups as the manipulator of the industry to reconcile the short-term business interests and the state's long-term strategic objectives. The newly merged Rosnelt–Gazprom may exercise the state power and act as monopolistic regulator as Chinese state-owned monopolies CNPC and SINOPEC do in Chinese oil industry.

Table 13.4 Recent mergers and acquisitions in the Russian oil industry

Time	M&A programme	Consequence of M&A
2003	British Petroleum merged with Tyumen Oil	New company: TNK-BP 1) Russia's fourth-largest oil producer 2) Right to develop retail outlets in Russia and Ukraine
September 2004	Gazprom acquired Rosnelt	New company: Rosnelt–Gazprom 1) The state as the majority shareholder 2) Competing with Lukoil
September 2004	ConocoPhillips bought a 7.6% stake of OAO Lukoil	Form a strategic alliance
September 2004	The state reorganized OAO Yukos	

Source: compiled by the authors.

The need to manage the transformation from monopoly regulation to regulated monopoly

From the perspective of national champions, under the current institutional arrangements, SINOPEC and CNPC are trapped in a 'vicious circle' of being monopolies holding substantial regulatory power in the industry. They are getting bigger but they are not becoming more efficient. They are monopolistic regulators but they do not necessarily enjoy the benefits of the position they hold. As companies facing a growing level of competition from bigger and more efficient international firms, the two giants have to develop a path of growth in size *and* efficiency.

Recent developments in Britain and other developed countries provide Chinese reformers with both a theoretical framework and empirical evidence for the further restructuring of the strategic industrial sectors. As Geroski (2005b) indicates: 'It is now widely accepted that economic activities can be brought together geographically without necessarily bringing them under common ownership and control . . . These pockets of activities are often called "clusters". Creating a geographical cluster involving a number of rival firms in a particular sector, together with various up and down stream supporting activities, is, in a sense, creating a national champion, but it is a very different kind of champion than is usually envisaged. Championing a cluster is, in fact, championing the kind of intensively active market competition that makes participating firms competitive in the sense meant by industrial policy advocates.'

There has been a move towards a more competitive market structure in China's oil and petrol industry. On 1 January 2004, import quotas were replaced by automatic import licenses in the trade of petroleum products. In April 2004, the oil import market controlled by the state was gradually opened and ten crude oil import organizations were approved. Five organizations have become subordinate to SINOPEC Group and CNPC although the other five have independent trading powers. At the end of August 2004, fifteen non state-owned trading companies were allowed to import crude oil and petroleum products. As a result, private oil companies can now import crude oil and petroleum products directly.

However, national champions remain as monopolies with regulatory authority at the industry level. Given the status quo of the oil and petroleum industry, without national champions holding regulatory authority, there is a void of institutions at the industrial level determining industrial standards and quality assurance procedures. Therefore, an independent governing body with substantial governing authority should be created alongside further liberation of the industry. National champions should not be exempted from regulations.

From the perspective of private companies, they expect to be incorporated in the expansion of the industry as a constructive force and to be dealt with within a fair competitive environment. An independent governing body at the industrial level is more likely to protect private companies' property rights, raise the status of private entrepreneurs in society and coordinate business activities.

China's strategic industrial sectors are facing the same question of how to manage the interface of the public and private by making industry policy and competition policy complementary to each other. They are at the starting point of a long journey of institutional innovation.

Notes

1 Government guidance includes the following items. 1: 'Lift the relevant law, lessen the regulation and policies that restrict the development of non-public economy.' 2: 'According to the law, remove institutional obstacles, reduce the barriers of market entry and allow the non-public enterprises to enter industrial sectors, such as infrastructure sector, utility sectors and other sectors that used to be exclusive to the public enterprises.' 3: 'The non-public enterprises should be entitled to the same treatment as public enterprises in terms of the allocation of investment opportunities, tax policy, land and foreign trade policy.' 4: 'Create conditions for the development of the non-public economy, create a legal environment, policy environment and market environment characterized by fair competition and equal treatment.' (Translated from 'State Council Decisions Regarding the Encouragement and Guidance to the Development of Individual Economy and Other Non-Public Business,' State Council Document (3), 2005.)

2 1: To lift market entry barriers for non-public enterprises. In line with the principle of 'equal entry and fair treatment', non-public capital is allowed to enter any trades and industrial sectors that are not prohibited by law and regulations. Policy opinions on the orientation for reform are proposed with regard to non-public enterprises' market entry into monopolistic industrial sectors, such as utility sectors, infrastructure, social welfare, financial services, military and defence sector and the R&D sector. Non-public enterprises are encouraged to participate in the further reform and restructuring of state-owned enterprises.

  2: To increase financial support and tax relief to the non-public economic sector. New policy recommendations include: intensive credit support and increasing the proportion of loans to the non-public enterprises; expediting the development of multi-tiered capital markets and broadening direct fund-raising channels; encouraging innovations of financial services, developing tailored financial products and services for small and medium-sized non-public enterprises; establishing a reliable credit guarantee system and strengthening the supervision over credit guarantee institutions.

  3: To improve social support for the non-public economic sector. Policies aim at providing continuous professional training, encouraging R&D innovation and promotion in international market in non-public enterprises.

  4: To protect the legitimate rights and interests of non-publicly-owned enterprises and their employees. Major policies propose methods to establish a sound social security system for employees with non-public enterprises and to build up trade unions in these enterprises.

  5: To guide non-public enterprises in making progress. Non-public enterprises should conscientiously implement the nation's industrial policies and operate according to the law and regulations. New policies should encourage qualified non-public enterprises to grow bigger and stronger, increase the level of specialization and coordinate the collective development of industry.

  6: To enforce legitimate and effective government supervision over non-publicly-owned enterprises. New policies emphasize how to standardize administrative charges to non-public enterprises in order to reduce enterprise burdens.

  7: To strengthen guidance and policy co-ordination for the development of non-public economic sectors. The new policies suggest that media coverage should promote the development of non-public economic sectors.

(Source: Translated from 'State Council Decisions Regarding the Encouragement and Guidance to the Development of Individual Economy and Other Non-Public Business,' State Council Document (3), 2005.)

3 Translated from Chinese publication of the thirty-six articles: *Guowuyuan guyu guli zhichi he yingdao geti saying deng fei gongyouzhi jingji fazhang de ruogan yijian (guofa (2005), 3hao)* (State Council's Policy Recommendations Regarding the Encouragement, Support and Guidance for the Economic Development of Individual, Private and Non-public Business Sectors (State Council Document (2005), Issue 3)).

4 A 'dual-track' price mechanism operates within China's oil and petrol industry. There is an internal market price for relevant resources within the vertical supply chain of national champions, a price effectively determined from within 'the plan'. However, while these resources are traded within the planned 'track', there is another price for the same resources traded within the market 'track'. The latter is often higher than the former.

5 The Department was renamed several times between 1970 and 1978.

References

Bao, Sheng, *et al.* (2005) *'Yinggai ba guoyou jingji he siyoujingji hexie tongyi qilai'* (The state economy and private economy should be integrated), seminar speech, Tianze Economic Research Institute, Beijing, 27 February.

Black, Bernard, Kraakman, Reinier and Tarassova, Anna (2000) 'What Went Wrong With Russian Privatization,' *Stanford Law Review*, vol, pp.

Boussena, S. and Locatelli, C. (2005) 'Towards a More Coherent Oil Policy in Russia?,' *Opec Review*, 29 (2), 85–105.

China Statistical Yearbook (2004) Beijing: China Statistics Press

Chinese Private Enterprises Investigation Report (CPEIR) (*Zhongguo saying qiye diaocha baogao*) (2006) in *2006nian zhongguo di qici siyingqiye chouyang diaocha shuju fenxi zonghe baogao* (2006 statistical report of the seventh survey of Chinese private enterprises), Beijing: China Statistics Press.

Feltenstein, A. and Iwata, Shigeru (2005) 'Decentralization and Macroeconomic Performance in China: Regional Autonomy Has Its Costs,' *Journal of Development Economics*, 76, 481–501.

Geroski, P. (2005a) 'Profitability Analysis and Competition Policy,' *Competition Commission Working Papers, Essays in Competition Policy*, Online. Available <www.competitioncommission.org.uk/our_role/analysis_in_competition_policy_paul_geroski.pdf>.

Geroski, P. (2005b) 'Competition Policy and National Champions,' *Competition Commission Working Papers, Essays in Competition Policy*, Online. Available <www.competitioncommission.org.uk/our_role/analysis/essays_in_competition_policy_paul_geroski.pdf>.

IEA (International Energy Agency) (2004) *Analysis of the Impact of High Oil Prices in the Global Economy*, Paris: International Energy Agency.

Locatelli, C. (2006) 'The Russian Oil Industry between Public and Private Governance: Obstacles to International Oil Companies' Investment Strategies,' *Energy Policy*, 34, (9), 1075–1085.

Ma, J. (2000) *The Chinese Economy in the 1990s*, New York: Macmillan.

McPherson, C.P. (1996) 'Policy Reform in Russia's Oil Sector,' Online. Available <www.imf.org/external/pubs/ft/fandd/1996/06/pdf/mcpherso.pdf>.

Nanfang Weekly (2004) Available <www.nanfangdaily.com.cn/southnews/zt/2004zmnztk/2004zgrw/200412300049.asp>.

Naughton, B. (1995) *Growing Out of the Plan: Chinese Economic Reform 1978–1993*, Cambridge: Cambridge University Press.

Nolan, P. (2005) 'China at the Crossroads,' *Journal of Chinese Economic and Business Studies*, 3 (1), 1–22.

Nolan, P. and Zhang, J. (2003) 'Globalization Challenge for Large Firms from Developing Countries: China's Oil and Aerospace Industries,' *European Management Journal*, 21 (3), 285–299.

Shi Jinchuan and Xie Ruipin (2003) '*Zhidu bianqian yu jingji fazhang: zhejiang moshi*' (Institutional change and economic development: Zhejiang model), *Xueshu yuekan* (Academic Monthly), 5, 16–32.

State Development and Reform Commission (SDRC) (2004) *Annual Report*, Beijing: SDRC.

World Bank (2004) 'Russian Economic Report,' World Bank February (7), 4. Available <http://ns.worldbank.org.ru/files/rer/RER_7_eng.pdf>.

Zhang Shuguang (1999) *Zhongguo zhidu bianqian de anlie yanjiu* (Case studies of institutional change in China), vol. 2, Beijing: Zhongguo caizheng jingji chubanshe (China Fiscal and Economy Press).

Zhang Weiying (2003) *Qiye lilun yu zhongguo qiye gaige* (Enterprise theory and chinese corporate reform), Beijing: Beijing University Press.

Zhang Weiying (2005) '*Bixu wei feigong jingji jingru longduan hangye baojia huhang*' (The necessity of protecting non-public enterprise's entry to monopolistic sectors), seminar speech at Beijng University, 29 February.

Index

eBooks – at www.eBookstore.tandf.co.uk

A library at your fingertips!

eBooks are electronic versions of printed books. You can store them on your PC/laptop or browse them online.

They have advantages for anyone needing rapid access to a wide variety of published, copyright information.

eBooks can help your research by enabling you to bookmark chapters, annotate text and use instant searches to find specific words or phrases. Several eBook files would fit on even a small laptop or PDA.

NEW: Save money by eSubscribing: cheap, online access to any eBook for as long as you need it.

Annual subscription packages

We now offer special low-cost bulk subscriptions to packages of eBooks in certain subject areas. These are available to libraries or to individuals.

For more information please contact webmaster.ebooks@tandf.co.uk

We're continually developing the eBook concept, so keep up to date by visiting the website.

www.eBookstore.tandf.co.uk

For Product Safety Concerns and Information please contact our EU
representative GPSR@taylorandfrancis.com
Taylor & Francis Verlag GmbH, Kaufingerstraße 24, 80331 München, Germany

www.ingramcontent.com/pod-product-compliance
Ingram Content Group UK Ltd.
Pitfield, Milton Keynes, MK11 3LW, UK
UKHW021118180425
457613UK00005B/140